The
Overseas Homebuyer's
Handbook

The
Overseas Homebuyer's Handbook

A Complete, Practical Guide to
Choosing, Buying and Enjoying
a Property Abroad

Geoffrey Pilgrem

DAVID & CHARLES
Newton Abbot London

© Geoffrey Pilgrem 1991

British Library Cataloguing in Publication Data

Pilgrem, Geoffrey
  Overseas homebuyer's handbook: a complete, practical guide
  to choosing, buying and enjoying a property abroad.
  1. Europe. Residences. Purchase & sale
  I. Title
  333.338

  ISBN 0–7153–9864–4

Printed in Great Britain
by Billing & Son of Worcester
for David & Charles plc
Brunel House Newton Abbot Devon

CONTENTS

FOREWORD

Owning a home in another country is about fun – however you like to define it. This handbook is intended to help ease the way if you are considering, searching for, about to buy, living in (or are about to sell) a home in the European resort areas, countryside or easily accessible islands.

The help given is 'insiders' knowhow' based upon more than twenty years' experience of resort areas, major developments, individual properties and knowledge of thousands of existing and prospective owners of homes abroad. Most British buyers of foreign resort homes have bought their properties without the benefit of personal experience or knowhow. Most have stumbled into a rejuvenating new lifestyle with, literally, expanding horizons. And most will readily tell you that their lives have been dramatically changed for the better, that they feel fitter, that they have made new friends of various backgrounds and nationalities, that they have discovered new talents and interests or that they have rediscovered the pleasures of earlier interests which had been forgotten during the routine of everyday life. Some will tell you that they should have done it years earlier: others will say that they are glad that they are mature enough to appreciate the new opportunities in all their variety. But some have had their pleasure marred by lack of forethought. Some have had their ignorance or trusting innocence expensively exploited by the unscrupulous. Some have not had their fair share of fun. This handbook will ensure that you apply the required forethought, are well informed rather than ignorant and replace trusting innocence with questioning caution.

Clearly the first-time buyer of a resort home in another country does not have the cocoon of experienced and friendly family advice around him. Marriage, the arrival of children, career changes, family pressures, inherited windfalls, the departure of sons and daughters to set up their own homes and so on usually trigger off buying and selling a home here. The first-time buyer of a home abroad is therefore likely to be a very experienced buyer of property in

Britain. Does this experience translate? The answer is: not directly. The differences are explained in this handbook.

The whole process of owning a home in another country should be enjoyable, from the original thought to arranging the chairs in the living-room. Getting it right means moving from thought to well-informed action. Put simply, this handbook is intended to educate and inform, to enable the prospective owner of a home in another country to consider, choose, occupy and finally sell such a property with pleasure at every stage – and with profit.

The book begins with a historical perspective followed by the essential questions which you must answer and put to those whom you will deal with during your search, so that you can avoid the fundamental errors which could come between you and your intended aims. The most basic of these questions is: Why do you want a foreign home anyway? The techniques of agents and developers are examined, the different legalities are explained, some major resort areas and projects are assessed and described frankly. Chapters dealing with business buyers, the practicalities of conversion and renovation, the easy way to move furniture across borders, and how to look at a foreign home are included. Others contain specific advice on often overlooked aspects of foreign-home ownership.

The first part ends with advice on how to sell your resort home when the need arises, as it inevitably will, because nothing is forever. When you have finished the last page you should know enough to buy *and* sell wisely. Unless you live for the moment, buying wisely should include thinking ahead to the time when it makes good sense to sell.

It follows that education and information are good for you if you intend to buy a home in another country sometime in the future when commitments and capital permit, if you plan to buy soon, or if you have already bought (or have inherited) a resort home which you intend to sell. Ignorance is seldom bliss: in this context it is an invitation to select the wrong place and the wrong property at the wrong time. The learning process is also intended to be fun!

Introduction

Historical Development

You are not the first to have the urge to live somewhere more attractive however you define it. This urge is atavistic. Even primitive man was always on the look-out for a better sited cave. Traffic jams were reported at weekends on the roads out of Rome as those who were able headed for their porticoed villas on the Bay of Naples – in the second century BC. Nor are you the first to want to live in another country for fun, or work plus fun. Diodoro Siculo wrote glowingly about a place called Ebusos: it had, he said, attractive houses, good ports and was inhabited by *foreigners of all kinds*. He was writing about Ibiza over two thousand years ago.

Until the sixteenth century the motives for foreign travel – leading to settlement – were war, pillage, religion, diplomacy and trade. The latter of these motives is now becoming more and more important as British businessmen take the opportunities offered by 1992 and the European market.

By the seventeenth century young Englishmen were being sent to Europe for a year or two to broaden their minds and gain intelligence of things foreign. The Grand Tour established the concept of travel for fun. By the end of the eighteenth century there were an astonishing forty thousand or so young British men at large annually on the circuit of Paris – Northern Italy – Switzerland – Paris. Attracted by the edited highlights of their sons' visits, families began to travel – complete with servants! Winter sun drew them to the South of France and the then Italian town of Nice. When British aristocratic families created a winter season in Cannes in the early decades of the last century tourism begat resort development as we know it. The ebb and flow of tourists left a deposit of those who wanted to stay longer: villas, apartments, marinas and golf courses inevitably followed. Visitors became property-owners.

In the last decade of the twentieth century, millions of Europeans own homes in countries other than their own. Growth in demand is continuous but irregular. It is affected by interest and exchange rate fluctuations, the prevailing economic outlook, local and international politics and the perceived price advantages of one country or region against another at any given time. The timing of your own purchase is likely to be affected by these factors.

The growth in ownership of property in somebody else's country followed the creation of cheap travel by air in the late fifties. The transition from rental of an hotel room which began in the early days of Queen Victoria's reign to the purchase of a villa or an apartment was a progressive one. By the mid-sixties the first organised inspection visits by eager British buyers of homes on the Costa Blanca had taken place. Adventurous hunters of old bargains were exploring the Dordogne by car. Sir Richard Costain began offering homes on the now-famous Vale do Lobo estate on the Portugese Algarve. Port Grimaud began to rise attractively from unattractive sand-bars in the Bay of St Tropez. Stalagmite-like apartment blocks rose upwards on the costas and on the south coast of Mallorca. And an erstwhile builder of workers' homes around Madrid, Jose Banus, was supervising the tipping of rocks into the Mediterranean near Marbella to create the marina which would make his name known worldwide.

Until British Exchange Control Regulations were abolished in 1979 British buyers of homes in Europe were obliged, by law, to pay for them with an artificial currency: Investment Dollars or later, Property Dollars. Formal Bank of England permission was required to make the purchase and the currency was bought at a premium which fluctuated according to supply and demand from 16 per cent to 60 per cent at times. This was effectively a tax on the export of capital. It was a tax on money which had already been taxed. The regulations were resented and poorly policed. As a result many buyers evaded this iniquitous tax and omitted to ask the Bank of England for permission to export their cash. To further conceal their purchase of a foreign home from the British authorities, many deliberately failed to register their ownership with the local authorities. The Costa del Sol, in particular, attracted thousands of such freebooters. You don't need to cope with these problems now that we don't have restrictions on the export of capital unless you have a home bought in this way or have been left one. But you need to know about this period of history in case you are tempted by a quick 'bargain' for cash, no questions asked.

The Costa del Sol is notorious for many things: one is the

number of mature, well-sited villas with dodgy pedigrees; another is the quantity of anonymous East End company directors. The influx of such people to this sector of the Mediterranean coast during the early eighties reputedly gave owners of suspect villas a steady stream of suspect buyers who didn't want their ownership recorded either. However good the deal may seem resist the temptation to cut this corner unless living dangerously is your primary motive for owning a home in another country.

Why Buy a Home Abroad?

There are healthier motives for wanting a home in another country. You should ask yourself what is your motive or motives. Why do you want a property abroad anyway? If you attempt a one-sentence definition it will help clarify your thinking and you will be able to test any place and property you visit against this definition. Do you simply want to enjoy a better climate with three hundred days of sun a year guaranteed? Warm sea within a hop, skip and jump of your door? Clear invigorating air a few thousand feet above a spectacular view? Clean snow under a cloudless sky and swathes of wild flowers when spring arrives? Maybe it's the joy of living in a timeless stone village deep in unmechanised farmland? Or the challenge to your sailing skills offered by the five winds of the Mediterranean? It could be nothing more complicated than the opportunity to put your mind into neutral and your body in a hammock far from a phone, with a long, cool drink within easy reach.

I know a man who travelled, with difficulty, to a Mediterranean island with no airport in the sixties in order to spend six weeks without interruption writing a short book. He became diverted. The book has remained unfinished for three decades; but when asked why he is there he always replies that he is finishing a book. In the mean time he has owned a bar, lost it playing poker, owned other businesses and a now-priceless farmhouse, captained the local golf club, and has had a number of wives. What was his *real* motive for going to an island in the Med?

Many other people give what now seems an anachronistic reason for enjoying life outside Britain: to escape the remaining barriers of our class system. Those who give this reason usually learn the local language and make new friendships easily with expatriates and locals alike, to their obvious delight. The pressures of modern city life are often stated motives of those who retire early to other countries or who take frequent or extended holidays in their foreign homes: such people make a positive decision to do without a phone. Remaining healthy and living longer are often unstated reasons for choosing a benign climate and a more physically active lifestyle. But whatever your personal motives, you should wait for that very special feeling of well-being, that indefinable something which tells you: this is the place. Where you should buy is the key factor to your future enjoyment. It follows that you should avoid picking the wrong place for your temperament, personality and tastes. It helps to get the country right for a start: the chapters on countries and islands provide realistic information to enable you to make informed comparisons (or to enable you to make reappraisals if you already have a preference).

If you make the elementary mistake of getting the country and location wrong, you run the serious risk of enjoying less than your fair share of happiness. I know a few people who made this fundamental error through lack of care: they never admit that they got it wrong; they whinge incessantly to a dwindling audience about everything from the short life of a light bulb to the fact that the natives still don't understand English. Others, too idle to correct their mistakes, spend their time permanently bemused in British-owned bars. How do you avoid such a basic mistake? The simple answer is that you risk picking the wrong place for your personality unless you do your groundwork thoroughly. If mountains turn you on then you should take a good look at those accessible parts of France, Spain, Andorra, Italy (and even Switzerland and Austria, in spite of their restrictions on foreign-property ownership); then you will know which mountains appeal to you the most. The accessible seashore stretches from Calais through the Straits of Gibraltar down to Naples and beyond. The resort islands are scattered over the seabed from the Canaries to Cyprus: to visit only one or two makes no sense if you are an island person. Open country, if that's your thing, begins literally on the outskirts of Calais, Dieppe and Cherbourg; enough of it should be seen from a car window to enable you to make an informed judgement about what appeals to you.

What should you look for if living *and* working in another country is your intention? As national boundaries within the European Community fall in the face of liberalising legislation there is a trend, which will clearly increase, towards Europe as a practical alternative to the UK as an attractive environment for rural self-sufficiency or entrepreneurial dynamism. The background information and the practical advice in the following pages are, of course, directed primarily towards those who intend to live part or full time in another country for the pure and simple pleasure of doing so: for the great majority *escape* from work in all its usual forms is a positive motive. But if you actually want to work in Europe or its islands then you need an overview of conditions and considerations across the Channel (see Chapter 1).

When choosing a home in Britain your eventual choice is determined by a number of sometimes conflicting factors: the size and ages of your family and their individual needs; travel time to work or business; whether or not your work or business is likely to be relocated sooner or later – or radically changed; whether or not you entertain – for social or commercial reasons; how close you need to be to family or friends; whether or not a garden is important to you; city, town, village or country as a preferred environment; an old, mature or new home; a flat, a house, a cottage, a barn conversion, an estate or a mansion; future capital gain; whether or not an area is socially on the way up; and so on. Some of the essential criteria for choosing a home in Britain are beyond your control; others are compromises. The choice is not entirely voluntary. You will, however, have enough personal experience, after initiation as a 'first-time buyer' when young, to consider that buying a home here – in spite of the hassles – is no more than routine. Even your first home will have been bought with the benefit of second-hand experience from family and friends.

Buying a home in another country is a very different matter and the differences begin at Calais. Unless you are planning to set up a full working life for yourself abroad, and you are therefore younger than the typical buyer of a resort home, then the size and ages of your family are not so important: if you fit the statistics your children will have become independent. Travel time to work, possible job changes, or relocation of your business are factors which don't apply unless these are the actual reasons for your decision to live abroad. Redundancy would clearly be a factor for some. Proximity to family and friends would only be important if you wanted to be near *their* foreign homes. The question of entertaining or not would be influenced only by the life you intend to lead: if you want to enjoy visitors then you would have to accommodate them. City, town, village, country? Grouped houses? Old or new? These apply as basic questions wherever you plan to live. Capital appreciation must go on your list, difficult though it is for even experts to predict. And it's just as difficult to forecast which areas are likely to come up in the world. However, to repeat what has been mentioned already – and will be emphasised again – acceptable access to your home there from your home here is vital for easy enjoyment whenever the spirit moves you either way, unless a permanent move is planned.

Few people who buy homes abroad do so for solid, commonsense, practical reasons. They buy for pleasure, for a lifting of the spirits, to live longer, to relax in a beautiful environment in a predictable climate, to escape from or to something, to do things which are perceived to be more difficult in our own culture, to feel good with heightened senses. Basic human needs provide the motivation. This book is intended to help you to get what you want.

Part I

Choosing, Buying, Owning and Selling

1
WORKING AND LIVING ABROAD

You have the right to work in any country in the European Community. You, or your employer if you have one in Britain, can establish a business anywhere in the European Community. There are still some rough edges to be smoothed out in practice, but 1992 symbolises the realisation of the intentions of the Treaty of Rome that there should be free movement of goods, capital, businesses, skills and people within the Community.

There are, of course, still some formalities to be observed too. And there are some anomalies: newer members are permitted a transitional period during which the 'freedom rules' are bent somewhat to accommodate the awkward shape of their economies or their employment conditions for a few years following entry. Applications for membership from Malta, Turkey, Cyprus, Austria and others will undoubtedly mean transitional periods during which the full rules are not applied as they can all be expected to negotiate terms which give maximum initial benefits and minimum initial dis-benefits . . . assuming that they are granted entry to the community.

It is now easy to work or set up a business in most of the European Community and it's getting easier by the day in the others. But work of any kind requires a very different quality of contact with the locals than does a few holiday visits, semi-permanent living or retirement abroad. Apart from a mix of saleable skills, knowhow, expertise, adaptability, a spirit of adventure and some capital, if you intend to relocate your career to another country then you will need enough command of the language to avoid misunderstandings. It can be argued that the ability to speak, write and understand another language is sufficient qualification for immediate employment in general occupations in resort areas: in a normal everyday commercial or professional environment specific skills are, however, essential.

The Best Location

Whether you intend to work for a local employer in the foreign spot of your choice or plan to start a business of your own or are expecting to be moved by your British employer to manage an offshoot or an acquisition you, or your employer, will need to think long and hard about your living accommodation. If you are effectively being transferred by your company to foreign parts then your accommodation is likely to be an important part of your 'benefits package', agreed in advance and handled in the main by the company and its legal advisers. You may have much or little influence over the outcome depending upon your status with the company. If you are on your own then it is a very different matter. The location in general will have been chosen for commercial reasons. If work or business is the motive for your move where you live will be determined by more practical matters than those which apply elsewhere in this book. You are likely to be working or operating your business in a major population centre unless a rural or resort business is taking you abroad. You may be one of nature's commuters, unlike most continentals, in which case your choice of where to live will be wider than theirs normally is. Apartment living, within easy reach of the workplace, is the norm the other side of the Channel, with the apartment rented or leased rather than owned, and a weekend retreat owned within a comfortable drive of the everyday home.

Convenience of travel to and from the workplace must rank as a priority; convenient shopping is a must; conveniently located schools if you have school-age children (many questions need to be asked of your total lifestyle if you need to account for a family when relocation of your career is being first considered); hobbies, pastimes generally, socialising, how you intend to spend your weekends; do you intend to suffer the disadvantages of four rush hours each weekday for the advantages of a siesta where this civilised custom prevails?

The questions are personal, based upon your existing experience and future lifestyle. When you have made the inevitable lists of your requirements you will have to make one fundamental and inescapable decision: do you buy or rent a home in your chosen foreign place of business? As we have seen, renting a home in a continental city has traditionally been the norm and it has a number of simple advantages if you are unable or unwilling to make a long-term decision about how long your stay may be. It is clear that if you are a businessman in control of your own commercial life then you make the decisions and you live with them. One of those decisions must be to allow yourself an escape route at minimum cost if you change your mind for any of the commonsense reasons: your business fails; your business succeeds, bringing with it the need to expand in another location; you have picked the wrong place and therefore need to relocate quickly; you find other more attractive ventures elsewhere; you decide in the light of experience that you want to live in another area, and so on.

Using an Agent

How and where do you start looking for your permanent home in another country? British agents who offer foreign homes and foreign developers represented in Britain cannot help you: they are only concerned with resort property. The commercial attachés of foreign embassies in London will be helpful or not according to national characteristics, some able and willing to provide leads to agents in the cities and areas which interest you and others simply suggesting that you write to national or regional associations of agents in their countries for comprehensive lists of formally registered agents. A number of London-based chartered surveyors have branch offices in major European cities; but they do not normally concern themselves with residential properties. They will show interest if you want an office or a factory, and if you retain them to find your commercial property they would reasonably direct you towards someone to help your search for a suitable home.

Clearly, you can do little in Britain to find an appropriate home within your budget convenient to your foreign business. There is no substitute for pounding the pavements yourself, initially to investigate the areas which are convenient and attractive, then to visit a selection of local estate agents (and agents are sometimes very local indeed across the Channel), and then finally to inspect specific properties which the agents have recommended. You will know that this process is time-consuming and tiring when searching for a home in Britain: you can safely assume that it will be more so in a foreign country unless you have much prior experience of local areas, habits and customs.

Hidden Costs of Buying Abroad

Do you invest in a home as well as investing in a business? If minimising risk is part of your commercial philosophy there is one drawback to this otherwise reasonable proposition: the initial costs of buying a home the other side of the Channel are greater by far than they are here in Britain.

The British government has never seriously bitten the bullet of applying taxes to home ownership. Every year or so there is a press outcry about the unreasonable additional costs of buying a home. Estate agents' fees are considered unreasonably high for what they do. Stamp duty is considered an unreasonable imposition. But abroad estate agents' fees start at twice what we are used to. Notaries' fees are payable in addition to those of a counselling lawyer. Stamp duty applies. The local form of capital gains tax normally applies to all forms of property: the family home here is not subject to this tax. Governments in Europe and elsewhere also levy their equivalent of VAT on home-buying. This tax is easily and economically collected and it is increasingly difficult to overlook even in the Latin countries where lapses of memory in such matters have a long tradition.

Buying costs including VAT will make up from 10 per cent to 20 per cent of the total purchase price of the home. These costs are, of course, passed on upon the resale of the property but clearly short-term profit on the purchase of a home in continental Europe is not routine as it is from time to time here in Britain.

Some attractively planned and fast-selling new developments in and around the capital cities, if bought off plan, increase dramatically in value when completed. Cute speculators have been known to buy into such projects for short-term gain, using the private/public contract procedure (see p64) which applies generally to property transactions in Europe to their advantage, and 'rolling over' the property quickly at a profit. But local knowledge, the ability to pick a winner and capital to play with are all prerequisites of such a venture. This has nothing whatever to do with the down-to-earth practicalities of living conveniently close to your new business. If offered such a proposition by an enthusiastic agent or developer turn it down.

As you are, by definition, responsible for your own decisions, then buying a home or not at the outset of your foreign career is just one tough decision amongst many. Buying a home when you have become established is a different matter. You will know when you feel you want to live in your new country without a backward glance. The heavy buying costs will not then be so hard to swallow because getting out without loss or at a profit, short term, will no longer be an issue. But when your foreign working life is tentative the 'front-end loading', in financial services jargon, must be regarded as dead money – in any language.

Property Price Fluctuation

You will know broadly what factors affect property values in and around our cities and major towns. The same factors apply in Europe, given that apartment living is the norm and suburbs as we know them are a comparatively recent phenomena on the Continent. Increasing standards of living and income are common factors but in some European areas additional influences are at work on property values. Some segments of the housing market in Brussels are influenced by the numbers of highly paid European Community employees in the city. Barcelona prices have been forced upwards by Spanish standard of living increases generally, the future European market and the explosive impact of the city's selection as the venue for the 1992 Olympics. The inhabitants of Lyon and Lille are two French examples of people enjoying dramatic increases in local incomes and property values as the result of the authorities' activities in promoting their towns.

You can rely upon your commercial instinct to tell you whether to rent or buy early in your foreign business career. You can, in any event, be guided by local custom:it is seldom wrong.

2
WHY? WHERE? WHAT?

The Irish keep the British off the bottom of the European league of second-home owners. However, demand by the British for homes in Europe has grown spectacularly since the mid-sixties. Owning a home in another country is now a normal expectation although the line on the demand graph does not show a smooth upward climb – the trough caused by the Arabs quadrupling the oil price in 1973 was deep enough to wipe out UK sales of European resort property for a few years. However, more and more of us are planning to spend more and more time outside our own country. But, in spite of this dramatic growth, statistics prove that we own comparatively fewer second homes than the continentals. Why is this? And does it affect us anyway?

Europeans traditionally live in apartments in towns and cities: we traditionally live in houses with gardens in the open suburbs or in the country. So is their urge to escape noise, neighbours and noxious fumes more urgent than ours? If this negative argument ever carried weight it no longer does today as continental standards continue to overtake ours. Britain now has fewer cars per head than equivalent European nations and the USA. Nor is a better climate the simple answer to more Europeans than British people enjoying two homes. The Danes, with a similar climate to ours, are many times more likely than us to own a second home out of town. Without the best climate, however defined, the Swedes, along with the French, have the highest percentage of households in Europe with second homes. And France, the largest country in Western Europe, has every kind of climate within its frontiers except that of the desert.

There are more earthy explanations for the greater degree of second-home ownership amongst Europeans: widely held assumptions about what constitutes an attractive lifestyle; and the basic need to own property. Except in Italy, where the incidence of home ownership is as high as ours, continentals usually rent their everyday homes. This fundamental need to own a home applies even in Hungary, just behind what was the Iron Curtain, where the average income is 10 per cent of the average in the Western world. On Friday evenings, rented city-centre apartments empty, the roads out of Budapest jam with queues of Skodas and Ladas, and small, privately owned second homes on the Danube Bend and around Lake Balaton are unlocked a couple of hours later.

Le Weekend is not only considered essential for wealthy and fashionable Parisians but also for Monsieur et Madame Average. One-fifth of Parisians own a *maison secondaire* compared with only one-fiftieth of Londoners. But almost 70 per cent of London's homes are owner-occupied compared to only 20 per cent of those in Paris.

How does this affect you? Firstly, you should be reassured to know that you are amongst hundreds of thousands of British people who own second or retirement homes in Europe or on the accessible islands. Secondly, you should also be reassured that you are amongst millions of continentals who own second homes. And thirdly, you should be even more reassured to know that overall demand is growing nationally and internationally for resort property.

Resort Property

Resort property can be defined as homes for relaxation, recreation and recuperation from everyday life.

The French, and to a lesser extent the Germans, have big countries with big physical differences between regions; so most think first of second homes within their own countries. The rising living standards of the Italians and the Spanish are creating increasing numbers of potential buyers of local resort property within easy reach of the major population centres. Inevitably, the Portugese can be expected to make the same progress. The Dutch and the Belgians have been the most enthusiastic buyers of resort homes outside their own small and crowded countries. To place it in context, against increasing competition for old and new resort property from the local population and from every other European nationality, the rising demand from the British for second homes for the past quarter of a century has been satisfied in somebody else's country.

Actual retirement to another country by the British is also increasing as the growth in numbers and buying/spending power of our pensioners escalates. Retirement to choice parts of our own coast continues as the decline of our traditional seaside resorts frees hotels and boarding houses for conversion and redevelopment. The sheltered housing market thrives and withers according to market conditions and some specialist companies are exporting their knowhow to Europe. However, we have seen a couple of hundred years of expansion of resort towns like Brighton, for example, which grew from a small fishing village into something imposing for the upper classes when enterprising speculative builders created their renowned Regency terraces. Brighton grew faster, if less elegantly, with the arrival of the railway from London and the introduction of annual holidays. The best parts of our coasts are now either fully developed or fully protected. What transformed Brighton from fishing village to fashionable resort was comfortable access by the few; what made it grow was easy and cheap access for the masses.

Nice and Cannes went through a similar transformation at almost the same time as Brighton, attracting much the same carriage trade. And the Riveria was also permanently altered by the arrival of the railway from Paris (see p10). The opening of Nice Airport had less effect on the development of this coast.

Accessibility

It is possible to plot the broad history of resort development on the basis of ease of access, given the expectations of the times. Coaches and horses, pacquet boats and feluccas, dining-cars and sleepers, limousines and sportscars, private jets and charter aircraft and even tunnels have been the means of escape. In this half century, ease of access by air has quickly led to the best and worst possible speculative property being built within an hour or so of every airport either in the mountains, or on the southern coasts and islands of civilised Europe.

The Dordogne was transformed from a depressed and depopulated beautiful backwater into something of value by romantic British exploring by car: to a lesser extent, the same applies to Tuscany. But cheap flights, especially cheap charter flights from various regional airports, have provided the easy access which gave Brighton and the Côte d'Azur a second boost a century earlier. The plane now does what the train did.

Those developers of resort projects on the Mediterranean who ignored the need to place their developments where they could easily be reached by millions learned this lesson the hard way. La Manga

Campo de Golf went slowly but surely downhill, in spite of good public relations, because the original developer, American Greg Peters, sited it poorly at the end of an almost two-hour drive along a rough road south of Alicante. Later owners of the development only achieved sales by massive, expensive and professional marketing which inevitably greatly increased the sales prices of the properties. Sotogrande flopped when Franco closed the frontier with Gibraltar for twelve years, making a two-hour drive along the notoriously dangerous coast road from Málaga airport the only way in. Almerimar, another Spanish golf and marina complex, also suffered from too few visitors because of access difficulties, amongst other problems, causing property values to stagnate there for over a decade.

To get the maximum pleasure from your resort home you must be able to use it at will, whenever you get the urge. You must not be deterred from enjoying your foreign home because it's difficult to get to. You should specifically avoid buying in an inaccessible spot, however magical, unless you are prepared to live inconveniently with your almost certainly unsaleable asset. Privacy, tranquillity, big and empty skies, timeless landscape: these can be bought if they are what you want – without being remote and inaccessible. Empty seashores are more difficult to find if the Mediterranean climate is a necessary ingredient of your ideal property.

If you care to speculate about where new motorways and airports are likely to be built in Europe in the next decade you may conclude that no major projects are likely. Perhaps the days of such massive infrastructure investment are over as far as the resort areas of the civilised northern coasts of the Mediterranean are concerned. Certainly the future of transport and transport needs are difficult to predict. In the last century the planner of the city of Barcelona thought ahead and designed the city on a grid system, with all the corners of all the blocks cut off to make for easy turning by the form of transportation which he was quite certain would be used in the future: the traction engine. Henry Ford II got it spectacularly wrong too when he waited for the rush to buy his infamous Edsel car: almost nobody bought it. And Freddie Laker collected his knighthood for his innovative approach to running an airline and shortly afterwards climbed into somebody else's aircraft to make his getaway when his own planes were impounded. The *Périphérique* in Paris is choked at those times of the day for which it was planned. The M25 has become a term of abuse.

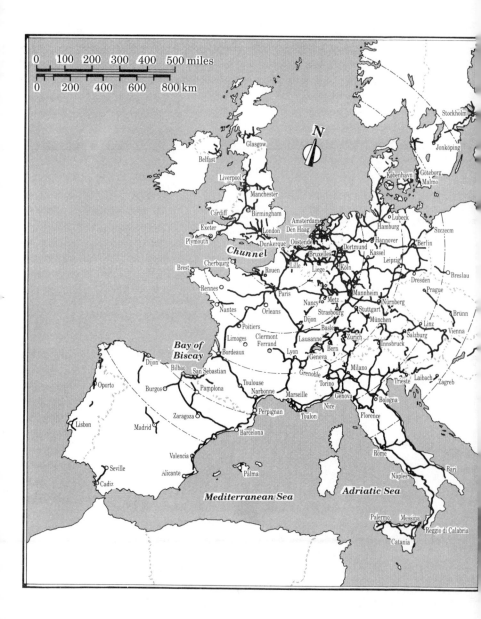

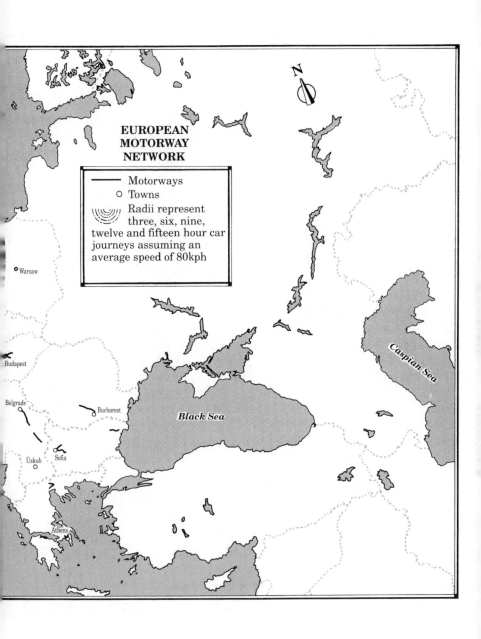

EUROPEAN MOTORWAY NETWORK

—— Motorways
○ Towns
)))))) Radii represent three, six, nine, twelve and fifteen hour car journeys assuming an average speed of 80kph

Warsaw

Budapest

Belgrade

Bucharest

Black Sea

Üskub Sofia

Athens

Caspian Sea

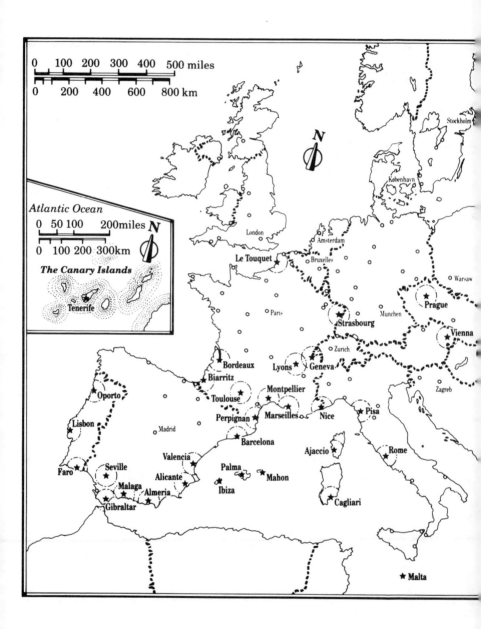

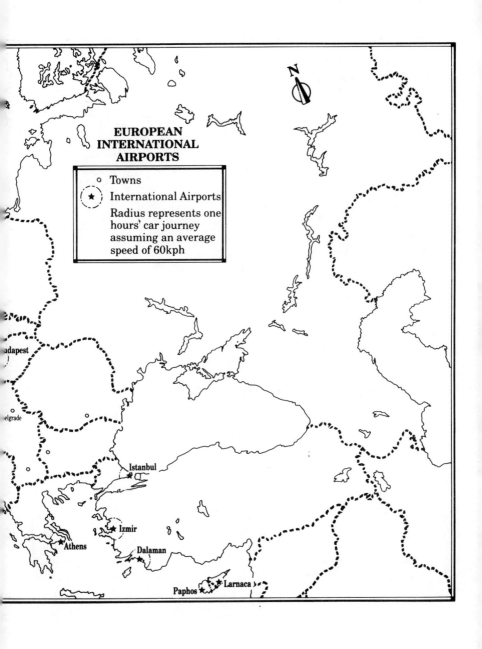

EUROPEAN INTERNATIONAL AIRPORTS

○ Towns

(★) International Airports

Radius represents one hours' car journey assuming an average speed of 60kph

N

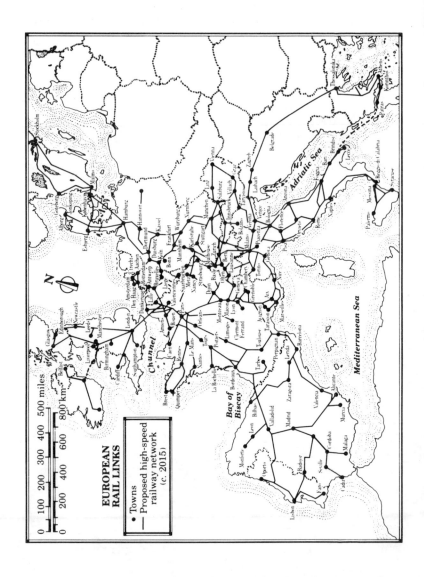

EUROPEAN
RAIL LINKS

• Towns
— Proposed high-speed
   railway network
   (c. 2015)

Clearly one basic factor in your list of things which you want must be easy access by road or air. It follows that if more and more people like you, and increasingly affluent locals, buy more and more resort property then the expansion of travel by air particularly will begin to clog existing airports if no provisions are made for greater traffic volumes. Roads cannot be expected to cope forever at peak times in resorts which are easily reachable by car. The way the *Périphérique* traffic jams transfer themselves to the South of France in August is a horrific example. You would be ill-advised to ignore these doom-laden thoughts: the problem will not go away.

It is prudent to take a pessimistic view of access. Physical expansion of some airports is possible but improved air traffic control and a new generation of aircraft are clearly also essential. If you were to make a list of new resort airports built in the eighties you would start and finish with Tenerife and that was a replacement, not an addition. You may not find it easy to predict the future of travel, tourism and the demand for resort homes; but for some major British companies, able to call upon the most professional advice, their judgement has been faulty in the extreme. Mistakes have been made on the grand scale.

Site Suitability

In the early seventies Sir Alfred McAlpine, one of our major contractors, began to market property to be built on their golf and marina complex near Almeria in the south of Spain. Gary Player participated in the golf course design. With this pedigree why was it a failure?

There were too many elementary defects in the project. The site was approached across half a dozen kilometres of moonscape. The natural beauty of the terrain was negligible. Although it was coastal, the site was flat and featureless, limiting the number of properties with sea views. The masterplan failed to integrate the golf course with the housing to maximise the quantity of homes with course views. The course was bisected by the estate's main road and the homes were without basic client appeal. However, the project's inexcusable defect was that the site was unsuitable for the complex. Golf, marinas and hundreds of villas, townhouses and apartments need people to make them profitable – a few thousand people, *all the time*. People can only get to Almeria in sufficient numbers by plane. Almeria airport is only a few kilometres from the site of this ambitious project but this multi-million-pound development by a British public company was placed near an airport which was *seasonal* with a poor service even at the height of summer. There was no competition amongst agents to secure the sale rights of the property on an exclusive basis and values on the estate stagnated for over a decade.

The following examples should ensure that you do not make the same fundamental access and other mistakes as some public companies have done.

Bernard Sunley located Isola 2000, a new ski resort, 100km (60 miles) or so behind Nice in an area previously unknown for the quality of its pistes. The starkly designed and hard-to-reach apartments did not attract queues of potential buyers when the project was launched in the sixties.

Scottish and Newcastle Breweries bought a million pounds' worth of land near Perpignan in France in the early seventies, when this was a lot of money. The site was no more than a few hundred metres from the Mediterranean but the land was so low lying that the sea was uphill. Sparse grass, scouring wind and no possibilities of sea views did not deter S & N from planning and building a golf and housing complex on the unsuitable land. Over the next few years the investment was written out of their figures.

Sir Richard Costain created Vale do Lobo on the Algarve in the mid-sixties in the confident belief that his personal friends would rush to buy homes around his Henry Cotton golf course, carefully isolated from any local community. They didn't. After twenty years of rows, resignations and finally revolutions, Costain's passed their remaining plots and problems to a Dutch entrepreneur at a very reasonable price.

Norwest-Holst in Portugal, Taylor Woodrow in Mallorca and Florida, Butlins in the Bahamas: these are some other well-respected British companies who discovered to their cost that resort property development in other countries is very different from providing homes on large estates around our cities and towns.

Marketing

Timeshare is not the subject of this book, but other major companies have resorted to near bully-boy methods to pressure the public into buying their units. Wimpeys and Barratts are two companies who have been criticised in the media for 'Press Gang' tactics in desperate attempts to sell their timeshare weeks.

Try to learn from the mistakes of large companies. As your own money is involved, it's more important that you don't make elementary errors of judgement. Being realistic, nobody personally suffers much from big company mistakes. There are traditional ways of minimising embarrassment within large organisations: losses are called something else; people are shifted around or out; heads occasionally roll, with golden handshakes as a painkiller; blame is apportioned according to the power and ambition of those able to exploit either; and culprits are often actually promoted.

If such mistakes are made by companies which are not big enough to sustain heavy losses then it can be serious for them and, in our context, for anyone who has bought property from them. Lawdon's were successful developers in the affluent south-east London suburbs. In the sixties its advisers persuaded the company that Menorca in general, and a specific site on the north coast of the island in particular, was the place of the future. Acting on that advice, it bought a large site, put in the basic infrastructure, and waited in vain for its advisers to introduce the hundreds of buyers needed for profitable trade. Lawdon's bled slowly to death over a decade and a half, eventually disappearing from the phonebook, along with the advisers in question. Fortunately, few members of the public were troubled by this mistaken investment. It simply didn't sell. This is one of a number of heartening examples of the public having instinctively, or otherwise, avoided buying badly sited, badly conceived and badly planned resort property.

Big and ambitious developments on hundreds of hectares of land should be viewed very cautiously, however well presented, because nowhere in Europe is there a comprehensive scheme of such a kind which has been wholly successful.

Lifetime Investment

World Health Organisation statistics assembled and assessed in late 1988 showed that Britain was almost bottom of the life-expectancy league, with only the Irish, the East Germans and the Poles having a quicker end. Sixty-five-year-old men can expect to live longer in twenty-one other countries, including Sri Lanka and Cuba; women of the same age will live longer in sixteen other countries. Greece, Spain, Portugal, Switzerland, France, Austria and Italy are all countries where life expectancy exceeds that in England, Wales, Scotland, Northern Ireland and Eire. It is beyond dispute that people live longer in the very areas which have developed in response to the demand from the British, and others, for second or retirement homes. Without the benefit of statistical knowledge buyers of resort homes have been getting it right. What you want is likely to be a more enjoyable lifestyle for as long as possible. What you can get is absolutely anything which you feel fits this basic requirement. Your resort home should be reachable without too much difficulty or expense unless you really do believe that Confucius was being serious when he said that it was better to travel than to arrive! And you can apply more solid commonsense to your choice than any number of large and otherwise successful companies have made in the past to their choices of area, location and specific site.

Aesthetic Attraction
The gut-reaction approach to buying a home in another country has already been referred to. Without a quickening of the pulse, a sharpening of the senses, a rejuvenating or even childlike lift of the spirit, and an eager anticipation of the new and adventurous you will not have the vital spark to cause the necessary internal combustion which will move you far enough. However hard you try you may not finally be able to answer the most basic question of all: Why do I really want an overseas home?

A German-born psychologist Dr Ernest Dichter invented something called Motivational Research, and became a millionaire by the application of his discovery to the American car industry and other suppliers of 'consumer durables'. In short, his theory, now generally accepted, is that deep-seated, unstated reasons motivate the purchase of cars and other non-essential products. A large and heavy conservative car is bought by a younger man seeking establishment entry. A Range Rover and matching wellies and Barbour coat tells you something about its owner when used primarily for the school-run. And we all know why a conventional man in his fifties decides to buy an open sports car after owning ordinary production models for all his motoring life. Man does not live by bread alone. He or she definitely does not *need* a Ferrari. Nobody, however valuable he or his corporate courtiers rate his time, actually *needs* an executive jet. Who on earth *needs* a mink coat?

It follows that nobody *needs* a home in another country any more than they need a Ferrari, a private plane or a mink. But you may *want* either or all of these things – for pure pleasure, for simple fun, for the hell of it.

Priorities

In my experience Dr Dichter's work is directly applicable to the whole business of buying and owning a resort property in another country. That is not to say that practical matters do not enter into the frame: on the contrary, they should be thought over early and lodged firmly in the front of your mind; then your subliminal motives can be founded on footings which will carry the weight of your choice. Ask yourself the following questions:

● How much are you prepared to spend on your resort home? Is it to be a moderate-priced property carefully chosen to sell easily, at a price ahead of inflation, when you are in a position to trade up later?
● Which area of which country do you prefer? Have you seen enough areas to know which attracts you? Can you live with the natives?
● Do you want a holiday home or one more suited to permanent living? Can you easily tell the difference between one and the other? Is it good sense to buy a holiday home now and then buy a more permanent home later, when you have satisfied yourself that your choice of country and area still suit you?
● Are you looking for seclusion or the convenience of nearby facilities and services? Is a compromise possible?
● What kind of lifestyle do you want to enjoy?
● What size of accommodation do you want as a minimum?
● Do you want to let your property when you are not using it? Would you feel comfortable about other people using your bed, chairs, crockery and so on? Would the extra income help you to buy a better property?
● Which seasons are you expecting to spend in your resort home? Do you want to encourage or discourage family and friends as house-guests?
● Should you buy now or later? What could you gain by either?

A recurring theme throughout this book is that nothing is forever. If you accept that resort property, like endowment policies, have 'front-end loaded costs' – commissions, legal expenses, taxes and so on – then you will not expect to sell within a year or two and recover your purchase price, in the same way that you will not expect the surrender value of a policy to benefit you in the early period of its existence. But you should keep in line with inflation or show a true profit after a couple of years, unless there are special circumstances, like new laws in France in the mid-eighties which cut second-home prices at a stroke, or economic disasters, like the quadrupling of the oil price by the Arabs in the early seventies, which wiped out the resort property business in Europe for a few years.

You can certainly buy what you can reasonably afford now with an expectation, but by no means guaranteed, that you would not lose if you wanted to sell after a stable economic period in national and international terms. But the risk is, of course, yours. Buying a resort property is a voluntary act: it is clear that selling your resort home should also be a voluntary act to be delayed, without financial embarrassment, if market conditions are not favourable.

3
WHO CAN YOU TRUST?

Developers, particularly if they do not live in the community in which they are building, need to be closely watched. In spite of some examples of outstanding speculative projects and others which are at worst unimaginative, the consensus is that developers wound, sometimes fatally, those communities which they choose to bless with their presence.

Estate agents in Britain are now usually subsidiaries of banks, insurance companies or building societies, chained to a range of in-house financial services; charges of 'conflict of interest' abound. Some have remained independent, either as one-man operations or as family-owned partnerships with or without branches throughout a locality. Some agents are members of trade bodies with codes of conduct, minimum standards and so on; others may also be qualified surveyors or valuers. But, in this country, to set up in business as an estate agent you need absolutely no qualifications, no licence, no experience; and there are no specific regulations which must be observed. All it takes is a telephone, headed paper and enough money for a classified advertisement in the local paper.

With around two-thirds of our houses owned rather than rented and a century and a half of building society funding to make buying easy most adults use estate agents, but only four or five times throughout their lives on average. So why all the ridicule? Estate agents vie with developers for bottom place in public esteem.

Overseas Developers

Can you reasonably expect a developer of resort property in another country to be different from his British counterpart? Certainly he can be expected to try harder. You are likely to be treated hospitably. Open-handed friendliness is the norm. Very professional salesmanship is often practised. Outright deception and lies are rare but not unknown. Patently, the interests of the developer's shareholders are paramount – as they are here – and these interests may be short or long term. You will be lucky if they chime with your own.

If the developer's interests are long term, if he is in the early stages of creating a large complex, for example, or has further sites in the locality for future development, then he may treat the buyer as king, to encourage personal recommendations from the satisfied buyer to friends – the sweetest and cheapest sales a developer can possibly make. To this end he will attempt to deliver on time according to specification and price. He may even listen to constructive criticism and improve his product as a result. He will arrange for things that go wrong to be fixed quickly with a smile. A real professional will anticipate the condition known in the trade as 'buyer's remorse' and will attempt to counteract its effects. He will be looking to increase his rate of sale by keeping his existing buyers happy. But it would be unrealistic to take such old-fashioned enlightened self-interest for granted.

The developer is in business to make profits from you. What else would you expect? Your approach to buying a property on a foreign shore or up a foreign mountain should be planned accordingly. The job of the developer and his staff is to get your signature on the dotted line. Their everyday routine is your new experience. They know how to open your heart and then your wallet. They are pros: you are amateurs. But you don't need to be ignorant amateurs. You're less likely to be persuaded to do something against your own best interests if you are well informed. You will be treated seriously if you ask accurate, intelligent and informed questions; greater confidence will demonstrate that you have done your homework.

We shall return to the subject of resort property developers later, to examine their competence, creativity and methods in some detail.

International Estate Agents

Are international estate agents any more deserving of respect than their domestic counterparts? We have seen how easy it is to become an estate agent for property here. How easy is it to become an agent for resort property overseas? What qualifications are needed? What experience? What licences are necessary? What regulations have to be observed? Well, one wet October day in 1968, it took me three hours followed by seven days' on-site training in the hot and dry

Bahamas to become a well-trained international estate agent; but the only reason it took me so long was because I'm a slow learner! I will say, however, that I was thoroughly grounded in the basics by true experts in resort development and marketing – and I've learned nothing more since. Absolutely no qualifications, experience, licences or the observance of any special regulations are necessary.

Open any heavy weekend paper at the overseas property page, call a few agents offering the very best resort property at the very best prices with expert advice and guidance included, and ask the essential questions listed at the end of this chapter. Listen carefully to the answers you receive: after reading this book you will know whether or not you are being dealt with by an expert, someone who is just one step ahead of your own knowhow, or a total ignoramus. Every weekend new, ignorant experts present themselves to new, ignorant amateurs. You will have no difficulty in deciding whether or not to trust the competence of the people answering your well-placed questions. Whether or not you can trust their candour is a more difficult judgement to make.

The first British estate agents began offering property in other countries in the early sixties. I would like to say that two and a half decades later professionalism is the norm, but alas, it is not so. With some glorious exceptions our finest continue to deserve their poor reputation. When it comes to hustling property in another country the average traditional British estate agent performs badly. There seems to be an almost wilful urge to do a sloppy job. Marketing skills have simply not developed. Some of the most blue-blooded agents are the worst. It is unwise to take their competence for granted simply because their name appears in every high street or on a prime West End corner. Whoever they are give them a quick but thorough going over with the 'Questions Test' (see p00) to establish whether or not you know more than they do.

What do you do if an incompetent agent just happens to have the selling rights to the exact property you want? In that case you may have to take the initiative to ensure that they don't accidentally sell it to someone else! And you can't gazump under the more honest European legal systems. The only defence you will have against agents who are unprofessional and downright sloppy is to be well informed; at the very least you must know enough to be able to get answers to the essential questions.

Local agents in the resort areas are not always efficient and dynamic. However, licensing of agents is the norm in Europe and entry to the profession is usually by examination. One-man bands are common. Outdated laws prohibit branches or chains of offices in Spain. Elsewhere a variety of chains or groups with branches exist. Do not be surprised around the Mediterranean if the local sign for 'Closed' remains on the door throughout the afternoon. It is not such a hard life.

How can you possibly know whether or not to trust an agent in a foreign country? If he or she is officially licensed or is a member of a recognised body, occupies a clean office with visible and audible signs of commercial activity and can make conversation then you can conclude that the agent is part of the local business community, with a reputation to lose and a door to knock on if something serious goes wrong. If he has been recommended to you by a reputable British agent, so much the better. You will in any event subject a local agent to the same quality of questioning you are being taught to apply to others, including notaries if they traditionally act for vendors as agents in your chosen locality.

Never decline a local agent's offer of a drink in a nearby bar or pavement café: you will want to see how he is received. However, as a simple rule *never* trust anyone you meet 'by chance' in a bar if they just happen to have a friend who wants to sell his excellent property cheaply and quickly. The resorts are full of very amiable people who supplement their pensions or make a living by hooking punters in bars 'accidentally'. Such a snip could prove painful. Such hustlers have low overheads – a few drinks a day – no offices, no licences and usually no right to work. Sometimes they are runners for one agent or developer: sometimes they are simply freelance, anxious to make a buck selling anything at all to anyone at all for a down payment in cash, naturally giving a generous discount 'because we're avoiding agent's fees'. These enterprising gents should be avoided like timeshare touts.

The enjoyment of friendly people in friendly bars and pavement cafés is an essential part of foreign living. From Dublin to Denia business is often done as routine in such convivial surroundings. And picking up local knowhow is carried out agreeably with your elbows on a counter and a glass in your hand. Pass the time of day with anyone who can help you learn about living in your chosen locality; but the moment they offer to help you find a property make your getaway. Some unscrupulous agents themselves use 'accidental' contacts in bars to drum up custom. Opposite each other in the main square of a small town on a Mediterranean island were two real estate agencies: one was an efficient German-owned enterprise; the other, equally efficient but dull, was Dutch owned. Encouraged by the German owner, one of his salesmen began stealing clients from across the square, following the prospects when they left the Dutchman's office, waiting until they stopped for the inevitable drink, and then 'accidentally' engaging them in conversation in whichever of his many languages was appropriate.

The Dutchman, who legitimately shared a licence with a local lawyer, had been in business solidly for ten years before the German came to town and opened across the square with much show but no licence. However, with the newcomer's personable multilingual salesman lifting the Dutchman's clients, one business prospered as the other declined. The Dutchman decided to retire early and sold his business just a few weeks before the German was arrested for taking liberties with his clients' money. Competition is good for business and the consumer. But theft is not the same as competition. If an agent or a developer's representative actually steals you from somebody else then you are taking a risk if you give him your money.

Hotel staff in resorts sometimes overhear guests discussing property purchase; telephone tip-offs to hustlers sometimes result in the 'accidental' encounters already mentioned. This situation has been known to happen regularly when prospective clients are relaxing over a drink, out of sight of agents who have brought them out from Britain on an inspection flight.

All is supposed to be fair in business but is it? Ethics are not what we thought they were anyway. But any prospective client who books an inspection visit through a British agent or developer's representative and then deals with an 'accidental' bar contact is behaving unethically – and deserves whatever he gets. In the same way, some prospective buyers have thought it streetwise to take an inspection trip organised by one agent to visit other agents in the locality. All organised visits of inspection are subsidised to some degree by those arranging them. Don't take such a trip if you intend to see anyone but those taking you out. It is always open season on unprincipled buyers; understandably, they are considered fair game at any time. If you wish to visit many agents and properties then take your time about it, do it thoroughly, and pay for it yourself.

Be Cautious

When it comes to deciding who can be trusted what criteria should you apply?

First, size is no recommendation at all. Small, in this context, is not beautiful; nor is big. Quality of knowhow, competence, service and what it finally costs comes in all sizes.

A new agent or developer isn't necessarily ignorant or likely to prove incompetent just because he's new. But you will, of course, attach value to the fact that an agent or developer has many years' experience in the specific area or type of property of interest to you. An agent with a large inventory, including all kinds of homes in all areas and countries, cannot be taken as proof of broad knowledge: it may be no more than an example of the 'shotgun approach'. Nor can a restricted list of available property be taken as evidence of selectivity and specialisation which is typical of the 'sniper's approach'.

You have been cautioned against dealing with agents or bar-touts abroad who have no offices. The same doesn't apply in Britain. Some of the most experienced and competent agents for resort property, usually specialists, combine their office with their home in various parts of the country. Others have impressive city offices – and skills to match. There are, of course, bandits in many guises, some operating from their back bedrooms, and others from panelled boardrooms.

An agent or developer specialising in 'exclusive' property is not by definition better than one offering a product at the bottom end of the resort-home market: each has chosen his segment of the market.

Trustworthy Qualities

A trustworthy agent or representative needs certain qualities. He or she (for ease of reading I will use the masculine form) will have an easy manner in writing, on the phone and in person. You will feel comfortable with him. He will be as good at listening as he is at talking. He will deal with your initial enquiry, the follow-up conversations, your tough list of questions, discussions about visiting a selection of homes, inspections, contract procedures and formalities generally in a professional and salesmanlike manner. He will welcome the comment that you wish to take up references on him, and he may offer you the name of a satisfied client if confidentiality is not important. He will not hesitate to introduce you to those who know him within the area or estate from which he makes his living.

He will not take you to the most expensive restaurants in the area in order to impress you: he will be more likely to take you to restaurants which are typical or special to the region. Politely but firmly he will assume command of your inspection visit to give you a thorough exposure to what he has to sell. He will not bow and scrape to you at any time and he will expect you to give him as much respect and consideration as he gives you.

I make no distinction here between an international estate agent and a sales agent for a developer because clearly one is no more or less trustworthy than the other. But they are different animals. The international estate agent may or may not specialise in an area; he will offer a range of property, some new and some resales; he is not tied to one or two developers. A sales agent is unlikely to offer a range of properties unless the developer to whom he is contracted has such a range on the site or sites which he currently has in his construction programme.

UK Developer-owned Sales Office

Another different animal is the developer-owned sales office in the UK. Developers are seldom certain what serves them best: dozens of small international estate agents covering every part of the British Isles; an exclusive deal with one international agent, with or without performance clauses, penalties and bonus payments; a non-exclusive deal with a sales agent who handles other products; an exclusive deal with a sales agent with or without incentives; or a selling organisation owned and run by the developer. Some large resort developments have gone down each of these routes if the sales life of the complex covers a number of years. Large developments with a long sales life never, in my experience, achieve the sales targets set by the development company's financial controllers. Therefore the pressures on sales staff are great enough from time to time to cause corners to be cut with clients. Caution is always recommended.

The Question Test

Once more we return to the essential question and the quality of the answers. What are these questions? The following list was prepared by the Federation of Overseas Property Developers, Agents and Consultants for inclusion in their acclaimed guides for potential buyers.

1(a) Is the property in which I am interested being offered by its owner, its developer or an agent acting on their behalf?

1(b) Does my British agent have an association with an agent in the locality of my choice who is legally licensed?

1(c) What are the risks in dealing with an unlicensed agent?

2 Is the property being offered with clear title? Is it free and unencumbered?

3(a) Are the costs of connecting water, electricity and drainage included in the selling price? If not, what are these costs likely to be?

3(b) What are the acquisition and conveyancing costs usually incurred by the purchaser under the traditions and regulations of the locality?

4(a) What are the formal stages of property purchase in the country in which the property is situated?

4(b) Is the purchase contract binding? Is it in a foreign language?

4(c) What essential points should be covered by the purchase contract to ensure that both parties are adequately protected?

5(a) Should I seek legal advice on the purchase of an overseas property?

5(b) Must I use a solicitor to draw up the conveyancing of my overseas property?

5(c) Can I sell my overseas property freely and transfer the proceeds abroad without difficulty?

6(a) What are the annual costs likely to be incurred by the owner of property in the country or area of my choice?

6(b) If the property is in a development complex, are there any charges for communal facilities?

6(c) What is a community of owners? Is membership obligatory? What are the benefits? What are the costs? Are the statutes in a foreign language?

7 Should I open a bank account locally? What are the advantages of having a local bank account?

8 Should I insure the property and its contents? What are the expected rates of premiums?

9 Can I let the property to friends? Can I make a formal agreement with a rental agency? What return can I expect? Will this restrict my own use of the property unduly? Is tax payable on my rental income?

10 Could the view of my property or its amenities be affected by unsightly future development? Is there a zoning plan for the surrounding area?

11 Are there any local regulations which affect the purchase of property by foreign nationals? If so, what are the formalities?

12(a) If I buy a plot of land on which to build in the future, are there any conditions of building permission? Are there time limits for such building? Are there height or size limitations?

12(b) Must I use an architect? Must I use a nominated architect? Must I use a nominated building contractor?

12(c) Are there any other formalities which I should observe if I build a home on a plot I have purchased?

13(a) Is furniture included in the price of the property or do I arrange to furnish it myself? What is the approximate cost of furnishing to a basic or a high standard?

13(b) If the property has a garden, is the cost of planting included in the sale price? If not what is the cost likely to be? Who maintains my garden in my absence? Could a garden be planned and built which would require little or no maintenance?

13(c) How much external maintenance is the property likely to need? Who is responsible for this maintenance? How much is it likely to cost?

13(d) Can a company be appointed locally who will manage the property in my absence and supervise cleaning etc for myself and my guests when we visit?

14 What is the most economical and reliable means of travel to my property? Are there privileges to be obtained for owners and their guests?

Commonsense dictates that not all of these questions apply all the time to all situations. You can select those which are applicable to what you are interested in. You will want to add some questions, in place of those you eliminate, if you are interested in an old property in a rural area, or if you are considering buying a resale home not on an estate. Questions about access and rights of way are pertinent in such cases; the supply of services should also be checked thoroughly.

An agent or a developer who is sound will welcome you asking these and other reasonable questions. They will be accepted as 'buying signals', evidence of serious intent. This, of course, assumes that the questions are put in a colloquial and cautious manner rather than one which is downright suspicious: you have no reason to expect anyone to respond well to that line of questioning.

4

PUBLIC RELATIONS, ADVERTISEMENTS AND PROMOTIONS

Developers of resort property often include public relations as an item in their promotional budgets. A PR campaign intended to promote awareness of a developer's product is, when well planned and well implemented, an efficient means of preparing the market so that advertising has greater impact. But unlike advertising, which is directly aimed at potential buyers, public relations campaigns depend upon the goodwill of the property correspondents of newspapers and magazines for success. Clearly, there is possible conflict of interest here. There is no doubt that some property correspondents and their editors have been unable to resolve this problem of where their duty rests – how to reasonably inform their readers of what is on offer – without giving a developer, whose hospitality they may have accepted, a blatant plug. Others have no difficulty in drawing the line in an acceptable place.

There is no doubt that PR is a valuable and legitimate means of getting media exposure for a new resort development. There are a few public relations specialists who are experienced in promoting foreign property projects and there are, of course, some clumsy amateurs. Absolutely no experience is necessary to set up in business as an international estate agent; nor are qualifications needed: the same point can be made about public relations consultants. But, frankly, there is no real need for specific experience of the resort property business in order to run a successful PR campaign for a developer.

The essential characteristics of a PR consultant are a sharp brain, an agreeable personality, an ability to absorb facts and marshal them into informative handouts, and organising talents, ideally accompanied with a degree of flair. With these basic talents PR companies can carry out their roles effectively, earning their fees from their clients to the satisfaction of both parties and the journalists upon whom they depend for exposure.

PR Strategy

The way in which a PR consultant earns his fees is straight-forward. He, or more often she, sells his abilities to a client, visits the development, acquires the facts in discussion with the developer's key staff, talks to those who have bought homes on the estate or within the complex being promoted, studies the locality for attractive features and points of interest, compares local prices for competitive property, and carries out further research on where the product fits into the marketplace internationally. Then the campaign is prepared. The usual routine involves a mix of press releases, press lunches or press conferences at which press kits (all the factual information, brochures, tourist office background etc) are distributed and presentations are made (often involving videos of the scheme, to the general indifference of the assembled journalists). The presentation reaches a high-point when the offer of a place on a press visit, more often known in the business as a facility visit, is made to the property writers and sometimes their partners or spouses. Dates are set, usually to ensure that the journalists, who are often known to each other anyway, travel in groups, enjoying a few days of hos-pitality in an attractive foreign spot, being shown the development and the local points of interest. The aim is that they write about the property in context when they return to their desks, preferably using a complimentary range of positive and colourful adjectives and adverbs. If the campaign is straightforward, with no hitches in the travel, accommodation, eating and weather, and if the development has credibility and the property seems reasonable value for money, then the result should be a number of favourable mentions in the columns of the publications for which the journalists write.

To some, this kind of PR activity is too cosy. However, our government and others, charities, multinational companies, banks and other institutions, pressure groups of all kinds, entertainers, manufacturers and so on use variations of the same methods to bring their policies, messages and products to the attention of the media and the public. This is acceptable in our society and there is no reason why developers of resort property should not employ public relations techniques to promote their estates, complexes, marinas and golf courses. But you should know when property is being properly brought to your attention as newsworthy rather than being blatantly plugged for whatever reason.

Balance or Bias?

The property columns of newspapers and magazines are produced weekly or monthly. Journalists rely upon receiving a flow of material for their articles. Press releases and other handouts provide them with news items. Facility visits provide them with first-hand knowledge of other countries, areas, developments and specific homes. All of this keeps them up to date and enables them to keep their readers informed. Most preserve a degree of professional detachment, preferring not to mention a development in which they have no confidence in spite of having enjoyed the hospitality of the developer through the efforts of a PR consultant.

However, there have been instances of a lack of judgement on the part of some property correspondents in the past. Free holidays given by developers to journalists should only be accepted if they are mentioned in any resulting articles about the properties involved. Discounts on the prices of resort homes offered to journalists should clearly be gracefully declined. Too lavish hospitality is a mistake for the giver and the receiver. Gifts of token value would raise no reasonable eyebrows but cases of vintage wine could be justifiably criticised as intended to carry implied obligations.

How do you decide what is and what is not an acceptable piece of journalism about resort property? Over-use of a developer's name, especially if he has a genuine or assumed title, can be a warning signal. More than one piece about the same developer or his development within a year in a regular column is also to be read with caution unless there is something particularly newsworthy to report. The inclusion of a developer's phone number in a piece about his property is also a sign of possible lack of judgement but a tailpiece, mentioning where details of property can be obtained is acceptable, especially if a statement is included to the effect that a facility visit was involved. Some publications consist primarily of handouts by advertisers reproduced, without attribution, to give the impression that they are editorial matter. Such material is produced usually without the intervention of PR agencies or journalists and is easy to spot.

You should not feel that a good, clean and professional PR job performed on behalf of a developer of resort homes poses any sort of threat from which you need protection. A fulsome mention of a development can easily be stripped of its opinion and reduced to basic facts: these basics will either attract you or not. You will either write to the developer for further information or not. You will, in any event, either believe what you read in the press or not according to your nature. Now, at least, you will know that a healthy degree of scepticism is called for.

Advertising

The same cautiously sceptical approach is normally applied to the reading of advertisements placed by estate agents generally. For twenty years or more the property advertisements of a well-remembered London estate agent called Roy Brooks attracted and amused by his use of a unique gimmick: his ads were honest to the point of hilarity. He created a successful business upon brutal but jokey frankness in his descriptions of property which he had on his books. Alas, his gimmick remained unique, disappearing with his death. The public customarily reads property ads with due allowance for exaggeration, which is one reason why agents attract such low esteem.

As readers usually make allowances for 'normal' exaggeration, complaints to the Advertising Standards Association about mis-leading advertisements are rare. Resort property advertisements generally offer a range or variety of properties rather than one property only (unless placed by an individual owner); so the question of misleading descriptions hardly applies. However, sharp agents and developers sometimes offer attractive-sounding homes which they know they cannot deliver: an attractive, low-priced ruin for conversion, with eye-catching photographs, which was actually sold months earlier; apparently bargain-priced apartments on the front line which have all gone long ago; or 'something ready to move into straight away' when what they really have are some half-built units on which they urgently need down payments to cover the cost of completion. There is a basic rule to be applied here: if you are caught by an advertisement for specific property agree to visit it only if you are convinced (a) that it exists, (b) that it has not been sold before you arrange your visit, and (c) the price has not gone up before you have had time to unpack.

Unsubstantiated Credentials

Misleading property descriptions in advertisements are not a common cause for concern in the trade. Wild, woolly and sometimes wilfully misleading claims about other fundamentals are a different matter. Some new and inexperienced but very ambitious agents try hard to give the impression that they are long established and very, very experienced. One troubling case, which caused insiders to laugh apprehensively, was the claim that: 'We are Europe's largest international property agency'. This claim appeared in the company's very first advertisement.

The records of the Federation of Overseas Property Developers, Agents and Consultants show that a few new agents have even made the claim that they are members of this body when they are not: a swift solicitor's letter from FOPDAC to the offending agent has often been the prelude to their disappearance from the property pages. There are, however, no credible explanations from the agents involved of their original lies about membership. A more creative approach has sometimes been used by agents anxious to gain credibility when they have claimed, truthfully, to be members of a trade body of which they were the only members. It is quite reasonable for you politely to ask for proof of membership of any organisation mentioned in an agent's or developer's ads: genuine members will take your request as proof of your seriousness; and you will be saved from possible trouble if you fail to get a conclusive answer.

One company, known for some years for their somewhat 'Sloane Ranger' attitudes, announced suddenly that they had ceased to be mere agents; they were now developers – not any old developers, but 'Europe's largest developer of resort property'. Their chairman's title, which was 'inherited from a continental relative', began to appear frequently in the property columns, being more mentionable than his more mundane family name. The company paid the few thousand pounds needed to acquire PLC status. Insiders waited for the inevitable and sure enough the company went into decline and was taken over amidst public acrimony and much private grief on the part of buyers who had unresolved problems with the title and management of their properties.

Until they went out of business in the eighties a handful of agents with common experience in London's rag trade regularly advertised that, besides offering the best resort property money could buy, they also provided legal advice. The competence with which they later used the insolvency laws suggested that they did, in fact, know something about the law but not in the way intended to be conveyed by their advertisements.

Sharp agents and developers sometimes advertise spurious guarantees as 'unique benefits'. When an American-backed company operating on the Costa del Sol led their property ads with offers of 'Buy-Back Guarantees' on the homes they were about to build insiders once again waited for reports of unanswered phone calls and letters. If you are offered such a guarantee proceed with extreme caution. Attractive rental returns are sometimes offered in advertisements for attractive property in resort areas. These are usually honest possibilities honestly expressed. But if you are offered *guarantees of rental* which are higher than normal for the locality and the standard of property concerned then you should look carefully at the long-term support for such guarantees when the developer moves on, having sold his last unit.

Given sensible caution and the examples of misleading or questionable claims you should be able to read advertisements for overseas properties with the same confidence with which you can read ads for properties here. Claims which exceed expectations should be easily spotted.

Marketing

A certain amount of normal exaggeration can also be expected from promotional material received after you have responded to an advertisement. Brochure material varies in quality and content from the amateurish to the very professional, from the informative to the bland, and from the honest to the dishonest. Having responded to the advertisement by asking for information on the property, you can be clear that the purpose of the brochure is to encourage a further response from you in one of three ways: to meet the agent or developer's representative to discuss your requirements in some detail; to book an inspection visit to the property without further discussion; or to arrange a meeting on site by appointment during an imminent visit to the locality which you have arranged for yourself.

Some brochure material is no more than photocopied sheets of property details, with or without Miniprints, a description of the delights of the area, and a covering letter. Other material can resemble a well-produced magazine, with layout, copy and colour photographs of the highest standards, costing as much as a round of drinks for four to produce. Whether or not the material has been put together economically or expensively has no bearing at all on the value to you of what is being offered. The words are what matter, the facts, not the physical appearance of the form in which the information arrives on your doormat. Photos gummed to photocopies on the one hand and glossy, moody shots of spectacular scenery, with copywriting to match, are more likely to be reflections of marketing attitudes, skills and budgets than pound-for-pound values of the properties being featured.

Amongst professionals engaged in marketing resort homes there have traditionally been two distinct approaches to the subject. There are those who say that a brochure should tell all, in order to encourage a potential buyer to book a visit immediately without further input, and those who regard a brochure as an aperitif, intended to sharpen the reader's appetite for a hearty discussion in person, so that a salesman can pre-sell the property and his own personality to the potential buyer, leading to a well-prepared inspection visit. Both views are valid.

There are some fundamentals to be considered when judging brochures and other supporting material. There should be a full run-down on the locality in which the development or individual property is set. The property itself should be fully described. Claims about the early provision of services and facilities should be examined for hyperbole. It takes two years of unbroken devotion to produce a playable golf course, for example. A marina of any consequence requires a couple of years or so of carefully programmed construction to reach the point of fully serviced berths coming into use rather than a few months. Hand-on-heart predictions about capital appreciation in photocopied or glossy prose should be dismissed without further thought; so should over-optimistic forecasts of rental returns. Promotional material which gives you a solid amount of information on the developer or agent generates more confidence than that which gives few clues about the people you are expected to deal with.

Sloppily written copy, unsophisticated layout, helpful and well-intentioned but ignorant attitudes and poor standards of material generally cannot be defended. Misunderstandings, some misery and irritation of greater or lesser degree can result. Deliberately misleading information is altogether different: it is coldly intended to take your money under false pretences. Good businessmen often cover themselves sensibly by printing disclaimers under the Misrepresentation Act on their promotional blurb. Some sharp operators do likewise. Some do not. Clearly a certain amount of healthy scepticism is also called for on this subject.

Exhibitions

Some thousands of intending buyers of homes in other countries attend one or more of the exhibitions which are staged in London and other cities each year to provide an opportunity for agents and developers to present their offerings to members of the public eyeball to eyeball. A few more thousand prospective owners of foreign property visit exhibitions which are held in smaller towns by individual agents or developers. This means of meeting possible buyers is considered useful and economical to many of the most experienced people in the business; some newcomers find the idea of an exhibition irresistible; other long-established agents take the view that shows are exhausting, time-consuming and inhabited by curious time-wasters. Few members of the public who attend exhibitions leave without getting the maximum benefit from a series of free consultations, whether or not they are interested in buying a home in the country or area being presented to them. Many would-be owners of foreign homes regard such shows as educational, enabling them to get a feel for places they do not know, and eliminating locations and kinds of property which do not suit their personalities and pockets.

Clearly exhibitions serve a useful purpose for both exhibitors and visitors. But there is seldom time to explore either your needs or the exhibitors' properties on offer. Reasonably, exhibitors will happily spend time imparting the selling points of their properties. Reasonably, you will spend time listening to all the information directed at you. But then the time will come for the exhibitor to ask if the property or the project interests you. If it does, say yes, give him your name and address and expect a follow-up call or letter. If you have no interest say so and save your time and his time and money.

A general principle can be applied to the whole business of promoting the sale of resort property. Agents and developers are spending time and money bringing their wares to the notice of the public. When they overstep the mark of acceptable promotion they deserve to be told so bluntly by anyone who knows what he is talking about. However, nobody obliges you to respond to an advertisement or a piece in a property column; nor are you obliged to talk to an exhibitor at a show about his property. But when you do respond to advertisements or otherwise show interest in property on offer then you must expect the recipients of your interest to follow up your enquiry. Some prospective buyers of homes abroad seem to resent this. They have the simplest of solutions: they can be as honest as they would expect the agents or developers to be. It is easy to say: 'I am interested in your property. Please tell me more.' And it is also easy to say: 'I am not interested in your property. I am looking for something different. But thanks for your attention.'

5

LOOKING FOR YOUR OVERSEAS HOME

Once you have chosen your preferred country and area, either with the help of Part II or from personal experience, your choice of precise property and its location are likely to be taken together: the property cannot be separated from its site and setting. For many the setting is more important than the home itself. Others are likely to be completely taken by an old property regardless of its surroundings. However, there are some general rules which you would be wise to follow – or ignore if the precise property or its views, environs or site characteristics move you emotionally.

You are unlikely to inspect property in another country on your own. It is common for sloppy estate agents in Britain to hand prospective buyers of homes in our cities and towns a set of keys and a map, suggesting that there are more important things than showing the properties they have been instructed to sell and would the prospect please return the keys when they have seen the place. You will be taken to see the properties offered overseas whether you are visiting independently or are taking advantage of an organised inspection trip. It is also common for sloppy UK agents to suggest that you see property which is quite outside your stated price range or size: foreign agents are sometimes tempted to offer too wide a spectrum of property for inspection. You can either accept this position as part of your education or you can make it clear that everyone's time is being wasted as you are quite clear about what you want to see.

The Immediate Surroundings

You are wise to scout the surrounding area within say a radius of 1km (½ mile) by car to satisfy yourself that nothing noxious lurks: ugly or malodorous industry or industrialised farming; major earthmoving which portends further disruption and a character change in the vicinity; new roadworks; run-down fifties' and sixties' estates or monolithic building; polluted rivers and neglected farmland. Any of these sights should be explained to you by the agent showing you around. You should also be on the look-out for positive attractions including the practical benefits of nearby daily shopping and other necessary facilities within a short walk of the property.

Local Climatic Variations

In some areas, including most islands, prevailing winds are an important factor. The Mediterranean has five winds: the Mistral, the Tramontane, the Scirocco, the Levanter and the Poniente; these are welcome or unwelcome according to taste and they do not only affect golfers or sailors. An offshore breeze at one point is sometimes an onshore gale just a few kilometres away. Trees or shrubs which do not grow vertically suggest that the prevailing wind is not a zephyr. Windbreak planting along field boundaries also indicates that farmers locally need to protect their crops at least for part of the year: farmers are not notorious for spending time or money unnecessarily. Windmills and windpumps, whether in use or not, also tell you something worth knowing. Barren areas on clifftops indicate that saltspray reaches that point during the blowing seasons. Screens of reinforced glass or similar material added around terraces or balconies by individual owners rather than the architect are easy to spot: usually, but not invariably, such additions will have been made for obvious and very practical reasons. When looking for your resort home you should decide whether or not wind is likely to be a problem and your choice of property should account for this decision. Anyone who subsequently grumbles about the fact that wind spoils his enjoyment has nobody to blame except himself.

Sun or Shade?

The question of sun and shade is of vital importance to many. Developers cannot necessarily be assumed to know much about resort development. Those who do know what they are doing seldom pay good money for land on a north-facing slope. But there are plenty of serviced plots available in seemingly prime locations of Europe's major resort areas, some overlooking justly famous golf courses or spectacular views; and many of these plots have been on the market since the sixties and seventies. Developers should know by now that buyers of resort homes generally travel from Northern Europe to the south towards the midday sun: when they arrive they do not want to sit on a north-facing terrace looking back in the direction they have come from, in the deep shade. If you are tempted to accept a cut-price offer of a plot on a north-facing slope overlooking a golf course or a stunning view you should consider how long it has had to wait for a buyer. Some substantial developments have failed because they were poorly planned on poorly selected terrain which included too much north-facing slope in its housing zones. You should not make the same elementary mistake of buying such land.

Some caution is needed with property which is on east or west slopes. Smart developers or agents sometimes ensure that their potential buyers from other countries are shown east-facing homes or land only in the mornings, when the sun is a delight, and west-facing property in the afternoons or when the sun is beginning to set over mountains or sea. The ambience at these times may be all that you need to fulfil your ambitions; but you should insist upon visiting the property at the other end of the day because it may then be in deep shadow.

Most apartments built today in the resort areas are designed so that all enjoy a view. This has not always been the case. A number of developers have bankrupted themselves during boom times by creating waterfront, marina-side or course-fronting buildings which were so poorly conceived that more than 50 per cent of the units could not see the sea, the boats or the golf course. The developers, in these cases, made elementary mistakes. You should not buy apartments which have been as poorly planned as these unless you are happy to live in a property which is likely to be difficult to resell. No positive case can be made for buying a villa, a house in a group or in a town or village, or an old home in the country, or a ski property which has a poor view or no view at all. But some people buy such property. You should do so only if you find the specific home irresistible.

Standards of Workmanship and Maintenance Charges

Some resort homes should be firmly resisted. Many properties were built in the fifties and sixties when skills and expectations were lower than they are now, and when local labour was cheap.

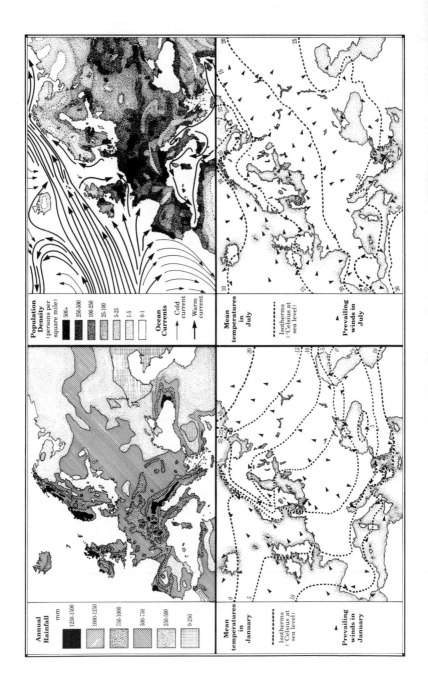

Annual Rainfall

mm

- 1250-1500
- 1000-1250
- 750-1000
- 500-750
- 250-500
- 0-250

Population Density
(persons per square mile)

- 500+
- 250-500
- 100-250
- 25-100
- 5-25
- 1-5
- 0-1

Ocean Currents

→ Cold current

→ Warm current

Mean temperatures in January

- - - - Isotherms (Celsius at sea level)

Prevailing winds in January

Mean temperatures in July

- - - - Isotherms (Celsius at sea level)

Prevailing winds in July

Skills, expectations and labour costs have all moved upwards since then. Future maintenance charges are now one factor included in all enlightened architectural briefs. A careful look at the exteriors of resale Mediterranean apartments will reveal sun-bleached woodwork, rust-streaked façades beneath cracked balconies, blown rendering and dirty and flaked paintwork on many early and some later buildings. The owners of apartments in such buildings have, by the visual evidence, decided to allow the appearance to deteriorate rather than to pay for the necessary maintenance. This should be a warning to you. Maintenance charges never get cheaper. Maintenance of a resort home, as with housing generally, affects saleability as well as day-to-day impressions and overall value. Look for the creative use of trouble-free materials and finishes. Grass is expensive to maintain in Mediterranean areas; groundcover and other self-sufficient, weed-choking plants are preferable. Be very cautious before buying a home which annually costs more and more to look after unless you consider that, on the evidence which you can see, money is being wisely spent to keep up an attractive face on a well-loved building.

You should sensibly apply the same cautious approach to grouped housing complexes. As with apartment buildings, continental custom or law ensures that owners are obliged to become members of democratically organised 'owners associations' responsible for looking after the property and the collective interests and responsibilities of the owners. You need to read the rules or statutes of any such organisation before committing yourself to buying a home in a complex or apartment building but, in any case, you would be able to see how effective they were simply by looking intelligently around the place at every common area.

Low-maintenance Materials

It follows that if you are considering buying an apartment or linked house under construction then you should look for the use of maintenance-free materials and finishes. Alternatively you should examine a copy of the specification to satisfy yourself on this vital aspect.

Villas or other individual detached homes anywhere present fewer problems. Those which were built during less sophisticated and demanding times are often poorly constructed, but many are in positions which are not readily available to today's developers.

Those built in localities where flat roofs are normal need special scrutiny: some movement between parapet and roof is normal but ceilings should be examined for tell-tale signs of damp penetration. Some owners in areas subject to wind and rain have traditionally tolerated leaking roofs. 'Arab' tiles laid to a low pitch sometimes let in the rain when it's driven horizontally by strong winds. Older property on the island of Menorca is prone to this condition: when asked why they make few attempts to counteract this problem locals will tell you that it is simpler and more agreeable to go to a bar and have a few drinks with your friends until drier conditions return. A sound roof is, however, likely to be the most fundamental requirement which you should look for on older properties: reroofing is not cheap anywhere and often involves insulation under current regulations.

Mains Services

Water and sewerage supplies and connections are basic requirements. Most European and island locations have better water than we enjoy in Britain. Some country properties have their own wells or deposits. Sewerage is either by mains collection or, outside towns, by individual or collective septic tank. If you can smell sewage then the arrangements do not work effectively and you should either adjust the asking price to allow for a replacement tank or buy something other than the property in question. Do not buy a resort home on a coastline polluted with raw sewage.

Property Dimensions

Floorspace is only important if you underestimate your own needs. Many are made miserable by choosing a resort home which proves cramped in practice. Newer French property is generally the smallest in Europe; some is ludicrously inadequate by the standards of any other nationals. Nobody would reasonably object that property of any age on the Maltese islands is too small – not even the Dutch or the Belgians have so much living space as standard. Judging the actual living space off plan or while a property is under construction is difficult. The British, in any event, do not know how much living space they have expressed in square feet or square metres: other European nationals always know how many square metres of usable floor area they have in their homes. To give an idea to you, the common or garden 'semi' in Britain has a floor area of around 75 sq m or 800 sq ft. Our normal 'semi' has a small hall, a kitchen, a living-/dining-room, one bathroom/lavatory, two adequately sized bedrooms and one small bedroom and an upper-hall or passage on two floors. A reasonable size for an apartment with two bedrooms in most resort areas is 75 sq m (800 sq ft) except in France where such a size is considered in the luxury category. Balconies or terraces should be added to this floor area; but you should be warned that some developers and agents include the total area of terrace/balcony in their overall floor area figures in their published or printed material. Because you will not be able to judge sizes easily you should ask for clear information on this point.

For holiday use for two people a one-bedroomed apartment of around 60 sq m (650 sq ft) plus outdoor sitting area is adequate. Studio apartments, popular with developers years ago, are not often included in the mix of new apartments on offer today; but resale studios are frequently available, in good positions at relatively low prices because they have limited appeal. Some studios are large enough to be usable by couples who simply need somewhere to sleep when not on the beach or on the golf course. Studios in ski resorts are best left to French buyers. Studio sizes vary widely: those less than 35 sq m (375 sq ft) in area are likely to be claustrophobic for British buyers.

Villa or detached home sizes vary widely. Plots of a smaller area than 1,000 sq m (about ¼ acre) should only be considered adequate if they are exceptionally attractive. Plot size is hardly important if you are actually fronting a fairway, a marina or the ocean; nor is land area material to enjoyment of a spectacular mountain view; nevertheless, a plot less than 1,000 sq m (¼ acre) in area is unlikely to give the privacy which we associate with a detached house. Large gardens are a real responsibility wherever they are: a few thousand kilometres away they could cause sleepless nights. You will know the frequency of your visits to your resort home and you will know the length of your usual stay. Your garden and planting generally should take account of these factors: to buy a property with a demanding garden would create problems unless gardening is your hobby and frequent visits or visits of long duration are planned. Careful garden design and planting or redesign and replanting can ensure the absolute minimum of maintenance if this is required.

Estate Property

If you intend to buy on an estate, either under construction
or in existence, then you will need to use your eyes, ears and
powers of deduction as well as your ability to ask direct questions.
The most obvious aspect of an estate is whether or not it looks well
maintained at the point of entry. A new estate under construction
is likely to present itself well because the developer wants to sell
his product. Some years after the last property has been sold by the
developer, when the residents (the individual owners) manage the
estate, design and planning defects are likely to show if they exist.
It either looks good and well loved or it looks bad and unloved. Do
not buy on an estate which seems run down judged by its common
areas. How does the appearance of the shops and facilities strike
you at first glance? You should be looking for signs of reasonable
prosperity. Go into an estate shop and buy something, anything,
to check on the quality of the merchandise, display and service: the
prices should be compared with those which generally apply in the
area. If the areas around the estate shops and facilities – car parks,
planted or paved areas, loading zones, rubbish collection sites etc –
are reasonably tidy and workmanlike then a certain civilised attitude
can be assumed. If it looks unattractive, as if nobody cares, you
should buy somewhere else.

Noise

On islands anywhere, and in the popular tourist areas, aircraft noise
is a factor which could limit or eliminate enjoyment of your resort
home. Property within a kilometre or so of a busy flightpath is best
left to those hard of hearing: at peak periods planes taking off in the
early hours can cause a condition akin to a nightmare.

Late-night noise from bars and discos from customers on short
holidays can seriously disturb the peace of those living a slower
paced, more regular life. Do not buy a resort home where this is
a danger unless you intend to let your property profitably to such
people during the holiday seasons.

Old property of character or picturesque ruins in country areas
require a different set of criteria. If you have not lived in a country
area before then you may have an unreasonably romantic idea of
the noises and smells which are normal. This should be weighed

during your preliminary thinking. Animals naturally smell and are sometimes noisy. Chemicals used in farming smell; the means of spreading or spraying them are sometimes noisy. A tractor pulling a harrow in the distance, with a flock of birds following is not at all the same as tractors ticking over outside your terrace, stinking of diesel. Harvest time or the *vendange* are traditionally the periods of work and celebration, positive rather than negative benefits for owning a home in somebody else's countryside.

Isolated Property

Isolated property in the countryside, anywhere, carries a worry factor. If you are attracted to isolation and the implied peace which goes with it then you can either dismiss the possible anxieties which could occur when you are absent or not. Some break-ins have been reported behind the immediate coastal strip of the Costa del Sol and in other similar areas where drug addicts are sometimes tempted to burgle for easily sold items to buy their next fix. One of the benefits of living in a foreign rural community is that you would intend to become part of it: those who do so generally have no difficulty in informally or formally arranging for neighbours to keep a friendly eye open; some tell the local police when they are leaving their home and when they expect to return.

The final piece of advice about looking for your resort home is that you should not compromise unless you feel completely comfortable about doing so. Your family home in Britain is a compromise: your home in another country is for your own simple pleasure.

6
LEGAL PROCEEDINGS

You are likely to have bought and sold a number of properties in the UK and therefore you will be familiar with the basic routines. But our legalities, formalities and conventions are out of step with those in the rest of Europe and elsewhere.

There are more similarities between European real estate legal systems than differences: Roman Law and the obsessions of Napoleon are the underlying reasons for these similarities and they will become apparent as you read on. Except in Scotland, where real estate law is not the same as in the rest of Britain, there is one basic difference between continental habits and our own when it comes to buying property: the preliminary contract to buy is a firm and binding private agreement with financial penalties if it is not honoured by either party. Gazumping or the reverse is not generally a cheap option as it is here. The Deed of Transfer is a public document.

This chapter is intended to give you a layman's guide to procedures in the major resort countries of Europe. It is background not a do-it-yourself course. There is no substitute for retaining an experienced lawyer for your specific purchase. Without expert legal advice you risk losing time, money and the home on which much future happiness depends. Even if local habit does not ordinarily require the intervention of a lawyer in property purchase you should still use one. Even if the agent handling your purchase is pleasant, personable, professional and has the credibility of a primate you should still retain a lawyer to act for you.

The pace of change in Europe is quickening. Attempts are constantly being made to standardise practices within the European Community. Real estate laws can be expected to change and the various buying costs will surely alter as governments tinker with ways and means of raising taxes. However, this set of examples will give you a broad understanding of the routines: your lawyer will know the current position in detail at the time of your purchase.

I am indebted to the Committee of the Federation of Overseas Property Developers, Agents and Consultants and their legal adviser, Keith Baker of John Venn & Sons, for permission to use their renowned Legal Notes.

This book, and therefore this chapter, is directed at individual buyers of residential property which is self-contained and freehold as we understand the term. The purchase of land for development, agricultural property, purchase with local mortgage finance (see p242), and any type of company purchase is outside the scope of this chapter. Taxes, as they relate to the ownership of real estate throughout Europe, have hitherto been subject to a certain amount of traditional flexibility, often with the connivance of some authorities in some localities. However, membership of the European Community and democratic government are not cheap institutions and real estate and other taxes are now more and more collectable. You would therefore be wise to accept the rules and conventions as they are now rather than as they were in the past.

Specialist Foreign-property Lawyers

It is clear that your own family lawyer is not necessarily the best person to deal with your overseas purchase. Unless he or one of his partners has the expertise he will find it necessary to pass on your business to a lawyer who has the appropriate knowhow. You will therefore need to decide whether or not to retain a specialist through a lawyer whom you know personally, or whether you go directly to someone with all the necessary expertise. Some foreign legal practices have been set up in the UK to service British clients; some British practices have opened offices in Europe for a similar reason; others have arrangements with foreign legal practices to provide advice to their British clients; some lawyers in the area in which you intend to buy or sell a property may have English-speaking staff and may be qualified to offer a full service to you. Clearly there is an argument in favour of retaining a UK-based practice simply for the convenience factor.

Spain

Lawyers and Legal Advice

The *abogado* (barrister) is the counselling lawyer and the *notario* (notary) is the conveyancing lawyer. The intervention of the notary is indispensable but advice should be obtained from a barrister. It is not recommended that you sign documents until you have taken legal advice, nor that you use the same barrister as the vendor.

Exchange Control

There are no restrictions on purchase imposed by UK regulations but in order to obtain the enforceable right to repatriate funds from Spain on resale it is necessary to import the funds into Spain through an authorised Spanish bank which must issue a Certificate of Importation. This certificate must be produced to the notary who prepares and witnesses the conveyance. The conveyancing stage by or to a Spanish resident, including a developer, must take place in Spain, but resale involving the payment of the price outside Spain is legitimate provided the conveyance is prepared by and executed before a Spanish Consul. However, the effect of such a sale is to restrict the right of repatriation of funds out of Spain in the event of a future resale within Spain. This is not considered to be a serious disadvantage in practice. In any event, this question of exchange control and its effects are likely to be modified as further standardisation under EC regulations comes into force.

Procedural Stages

From decision to buy to legal commitment

Some developers (but not usually individual vendors) like buyers to sign an option or contract of reservation, usually against the payment of a nominal deposit. It is considered safe to sign such a document before making title and planning searches but verify whether or not the deposit is returnable if you do not proceed.

At this stage you, or your legal adviser, should make enquiries at the local Land Registry and Municipal Authority to verify that:

(a) The vendor has registered title to the property. If title is unregistered follow strictly the advice of your legal adviser as there is some risk associated with purchase from an unregistered owner.
(b) There are no mortgages or other charges registered on the property. If the property is not *libra de cargas* (free of charges) then it is almost certainly unsafe to buy.
(c) Planning consents have been obtained and complied with and building regulations have also been observed. General enquiries as

to plans for further and future development can usefully be coupled with these enquiries.

(d) The vendor is up to date with payments of municipal and wealth taxes.

You or your legal adviser must also calculate the liability for the municipal tax known as *Plus Valia*, if any, and negotiate which party is to be liable for its payment.

Structural surveys are not common but now is the moment to have one carried out if at all.

If the property is part of an estate or a block of flats you should obtain:

(a) A copy of the co-ownership rules.

(b) A copy of the latest accounts of the community of owners.

(c) A statement from the community of owners of the vendor's balance of account with the organisation.

Next you will sign a *contrato privado* (private contract) which is the stage equivalent to exchange of contracts in England. The intervention of the notary is not yet required but the private contract is a legally binding contract to buy on the terms stated in that document. Private contracts are not lengthy documents but will contain the names and description of the parties, a description of the property, the price, the method of payment and any special conditions negotiated by the parties. Not less than 10 per cent of the price will be payable on signing, and a higher figure is frequently sought by developers. Where stage payments are to be made before legal title is given, particularly in the case of developments in the course of construction, rigorous enquiries should be made that the developer is solvent and that his programme is adequately funded. Verify also at this point whether the costs of connecting services are included in the price if not already supplied, and whether contents are included in the case of a resale.

From legal commitment to legal title

Completion of the purchase is likely to be a date and/or an event (completion of construction of a new property, for example) as stipulated in the private contract. You are at risk until a formal document (the *Escritura Publica de Compraventas* commonly known as the *Escritura*) transferring ownership from vendor to buyer has been prepared and witnessed, a function of the notary, and then entered in the Land Registry. So do not delay at this stage.

The *Escritura*, a certified copy of which is known as the *Primera Copia* (First Copy) will be your Title Deed. It is a fuller document than the private contract, and will state the names and descriptions of the parties, a full description of the property referring to rights of way and use, boundaries, unit location within the development if applicable, size and make-up of the unit, the title of the vendor (with Land Registry reference number), the price, method of payment or receipt of the price and any special conditions agreed. In addition the *Escritura* should also state that:

(a) The vendor is the legal owner of the property.
(b) The property is sold with vacant possession.
(c) The property is not subject to any charges.

Buyers are strongly recommended to have their First Copy entered in the relevant Land Registry. The notary will do this but only if expressly instructed to do so. The time taken for registration can be as long as eighteen months: chasing up is advised every three months or so.

Incidental costs
These are traditionally payable by the buyer and usually amount to about 8 per cent of the price of the property. They include the following:

(a) Value Added Tax known as IVA, payable to the developer at the rate of 6 per cent in the case of new properties and 0.5 per cent payable to the local tax office; and Transfer Tax, payable to the local tax office but often collected by the notary at the rate of 6 per cent in the case of resale property. The previous practice of grossly underdeclaring the price in the *Escritura* is not recommended.
(b) Notarial fees.
(c) Land Registry fees.
(d) The costs of completing Form TE–7 for funds imported into Spain and the filing of that form with the Foreign Investment Registry: this is usually done by the notary if specifically instructed to do so, or your own lawyers.

(e) Your own lawyer's fees will be additional to the above costs.

Ownership Obligations

If your property is in a building or complex, condominium rules will apply. During the time of your ownership you will have to pay for the upkeep of common areas, management and any other benefits which are enjoyed by owners collectively, as defined in the statutes of the owners association.

You will also have to budget for maintenance and repairs as and when necessary, either as a personal obligation if your home is not part of a complex or according to owners association rules if applicable: gas, water, electricity and telephone charges as they apply, municipal taxes (rates), income tax (if you let your property), and wealth tax. It is advisable to open a bank account locally to be able to pay these charges promptly, and in your absence by instructing your bank to settle bills submitted to them directly.

Resale

If you use a local agent to act for you make certain that he is properly licensed. If repatriation of funds from Spain is of importance to you your buyer must abide by the procedures outlined in 'Exchange Control' (see p66); you will need at that point your original Form TE-7 and a stamped copy of your buyer's Form TE-7. You as seller are liable for the Municipal Tax known as *Plus Valia* unless you agree otherwise with the buyer. Most incidental costs are payable by the buyer as explained earlier.

Your capital profit on sale may be subject to UK Capital Gains Tax and/or the Spanish equivalent. However, this too is an area for expert advice rather than do-it-yourself accountancy or tax law and you are recommended to take expert professional advice as to your liability if any. Indexation of gains operates in Spain and in the UK.

France

There are important differences between the laws relating to the purchase of new and resale property in France. This section is concerned with the procedures which apply to new property.

Lawyers and Legal Advice

All aspects of conveyancing are carried out by a *notaire* (notary). The same notary commonly acts for both parties but buyers can insist upon appointing their own notary which will not increase the total fees payable. Relatively few notaries can be expected to speak English.

Exchange Control

There are no restrictions on purchase imposed by UK regulations but in order to obtain the enforceable right to repatriate funds from France on resale it is recommended to import the funds into France through an authorised bank and to request a Certificate of Importation. The Deed of Conveyance must be executed before a notary in France.

Procedural Stages

General

All stages will involve understanding or signing documents in French. Ask for and obtain written translations as needed, particularly before signing any papers. Sales of unfinished developments (*ventes en l'état futur d'achèvement*) are the subject of rigorous legislative provisions for the protection of purchasers. Only your own independent legal adviser is likely to be able to ensure that a developer is complying with the detailed regulations. All payments must be made to a notary or guarantor. Development will usually be carried out by a company specific to the development in question (usually a *société civil immobilière*). Stage payments, supported by one of the various forms of guarantee, are normally involved: a 1979 law protects, *inter alia*, buyers of real property.

Every buyer must state whether or not he requires finance. If not he must waive his statutory protection by a handwritten statement. If he does need finance he must identify the sum needed and the lender. The loan application must be submitted within ten days of the date of the reservation contract. A resulting offer of advance from a French lender cannot be accepted prior to ten days of receipt and should be accepted within forty-five days of the date of the reservation contract. A copy of the loan application and the accepted offer must be sent to the vendor. Rejection of the application for finance entitles the purchaser to withdraw from the contract and obtain the refund of his deposit.

From decision to buy to legal commitment
Reservation Developers require buyers to sign a reservation contract against payment of a deposit of 2 or 5 per cent depending upon the timescale to completion. This deposit is returnable under certain restricted conditions but a reservation contract should be perceived as a legally binding commitment to buy.

Legal completion (acte de vente) At any time after the foundations of the property have been laid the developer can seek payment of up to 30 per cent of the total purchase price. The demand for payment will come from the notary. It will be accompanied by the following: a draft of the *acte de vente* (Deed of Sale); a copy of the *règlement de copropriété* (co-ownership regulations); plans and an abridged specification; and a request for payment of the notary's fees and costs. This stage payment must be made within thirty days of receipt of the demand and the documents. The co-ownership regulations set out the legal basis of the development as a whole: they cannot be modified except by a decision passed by a three-quarters majority of the owners. The Deed of Sale details the precise terms on which you are buying and recites, *inter alia*, the three essential guarantees: for completion, patent defects and latent defects. Buyers must have their official copy entered in the Land Registry to be able to resell: the notary will normally do this as routine; this can take between one and six months.

Physical completion The penultimate stage payment is always practical completion, as certified by the supervising architect. You are strongly recommended to make a personal inspection to satisfy yourself that the villa or apartment has been built and finished according to the specification. Patent defects must be notified to the developer in writing within six months of such a visit or from deemed handover if you do not visit but merely make the final payment. You are not legally entitled to withhold any funds to cover patent or latent defects, although it is lawful to lodge funds with a third party in this case.

Incidental costs
These are traditionally payable wholly by the buyer and can amount to 2–3 per cent of the purchase price. They include: VAT, which is usually included in the price of new property and involves exemption from *droits d'enregistrement* (stamp duty); notarial fees; and Land Registry fees. Translations of documents may involve further costs.

Ownership

You are legally bound by any condominium rules applicable to your property as set out in the *règlement de copropriété* (apartments) or *cahier des charges* (villa estate). As owner you will have to pay for the following:

(a) Maintenance and repairs as and when they arise, and in the case of an apartment, service charges.

(b) All or some of gas, water, electricity and telephone charges and domestic insurance.

(c) Municipal taxes (rates) and income tax if you let your property.

Open a local bank account to enable these bills to be met promptly.

Resale

If you use a French agent to find a buyer ensure that he is properly licensed. He is only allowed to act if he holds written authority. If repatriation of funds is important to you your buyer must abide by the following procedure. You should provide evidence of the original importation of funds, preferably by production of the bank Certificate of Importation. If you resell a property originally purchased before physical completion within five years of its first occupation you will suffer a deduction of 18.6 per cent VAT from the gross proceeds of sale.

Most incidental costs are payable by the buyer, but a resale may give rise to French Capital Gains Tax (*Taxe de Plus-value*). The sale is only tax free after twenty-two years of ownership. This complex tax formula reduces to allow for inflation and duration of ownership. Before the proceeds of sale can be repatriated a tax representative must be appointed to be responsible personally for the *Taxe de Plus-value*. If you are a UK resident your ultimate net capital profit on resale will also be liable for UK Capital Gains Tax; but a double tax treaty exists to ensure that you are not taxed twice on the same gain.

Portugal

Lawyers and Legal Advice

The *advogado* (barrister) is the counselling lawyer and the *notario* (notary) is the conveyancing lawyer. The intervention of a notary is indispensable but advice should be obtained from a barrister. It is not recommended that you sign documents until you have taken independent legal advice; nor should you use the same barrister as the vendor.

Exchange Control

There are no restrictions on purchase imposed by UK regulations but in order to obtain the enforceable right to repatriate funds from Portugal on resale it is necessary to obtain Bank of Portugal consent to import the purchase price and incidental costs. Funds must not be remitted to Portugal until the consent is issued but can then be transferred from a bank outside Portugal to an authorised Portugese bank. The import licence, or BAICP, must be produced to the notary who prepares and witnesses the conveyance. Resales involving the payment of the property purchase price outside Portugal are of uncertain legal status.

Procedural Stages

General

All stages will involve understanding or signing documents in Portugese. Ask for or obtain written translations, particularly before signing any document.

From decision to buy to legal commitment

Some developers, but not usually individual vendors, like buyers to sign an option or contract of reservation, usually against the payment of a nominal deposit. It is considered safe to sign such a document before making title and planning searches, but verify whether the deposit is refundable if you do not proceed.

At this stage you, or your legal adviser, should make enquiries at the relevant Land Registry and Local Authority to verify that:

(a) The vendor has legal title to the property. If title is unregistered follow strictly the advice of your legal adviser as there is some risk associated with purchase from an unregistered owner.

(b) There are no mortgages or other charges registered on the property. If the property is not *livre de onus* (free of charges) it is almost certainly unsafe to buy.

(c) Planning consents have been obtained and complied with and building regulations have also been observed. General enquiries as to plans for future development can usefully be coupled with these enquiries.

(d) The vendor is up to date with payment of munipical taxes.

Structural surveys are not common but now is the time to have it done if at all.

If the property is part of an estate or block of apartments you should obtain the following:

(a) A copy of the co-ownership rules.
(b) A copy of the latest accounts of the community of owners.
(c) A statement from the community of owners of the vendor's balance of account.

Next you will sign a *contrato promessa de compra e venda* (promissory contract) which is the stage equivalent to exchange of contracts in England. The intervention of a notary is not yet obligatory but the promissory contract is a legally binding commitment to buy on the terms stated in the document. However, a notarial authentication of the parties' signatures is quite common. In the case of uncompleted units such authentication is strongly recommended in order to secure the benefits of protective legislation for property investors. Promissory contracts are not lengthy documents but will contain the names and descriptions of the parties, a description of the property, the price and method of payment and any general or specific conditions negotiated by the parties. Not less than 10 per cent of the price will be payable on the signing of the promissory contract and a higher figure is usually sought by developers. Where stage payments are to be made before legal title is given, particularly in the case of developments under construction, make rigorous enquiries to satisfy yourself that the building programme is adequately funded and that the vendor is solvent. Verify also whether the contents and the costs of connecting water, gas, electricity and telephones are included in the price (if not already supplied).

Vendors can renege on their contract, but only by paying the buyer double the deposit.

From legal commitment to legal title
Completion of the purchase is likely to be a date and/or an event (eg completion of construction of a new dwelling) stipulated in the promissory contract. You are at risk until a formal document

(*Escritura Publica de Compra e Venda*) colloquially known as the *Escritura*, transferring ownership from the vendor to the buyer has been signed and witnessed, a function necessarily performed by the notary; so do not delay at this stage. The *Escritura*, a certified copy of which will be your Title Deed, is a fuller document than the promissory contract. It will state the names and descriptions of the parties; a full description of the property, referring to rights of way and use, boundaries, unit location within a development if applicable, size and make-up of the unit; title of the vendor, with Land Registry reference; the price; the method of payment, or receipt of the price as the case may be; and any other agreed conditions. In additon, the *Escritura* should also contain a statement (warranty) that:

(a) The vendor is the owner of the property.
(b) The property is sold with vacant possession.
(c) The property is free of all charges.

Buyers are required to have their Title Deed registered at the relevant registry: the notary will do this, but only if expressly instructed to do so. The time taken to complete registration is lengthy – from four to twelve months – and chasing up every two months or so is advised.

Incidental costs
These are traditionally payable wholly by the buyer and usually amount to 12–15 per cent of the purchase price of the property. They include the following:

(a) Transfer Tax (*Sisa*) calculated at varying rates above a base price for new construction and on all secondhand property at whatever price. Underdeclaration of the price in the *Escritura*, in order to incur a lower amount of Transfer Tax is not recommended: the Bank of Portugal obtains a valuation from the local tax office before issuing each licence for the importation of funds.
(b) Notarial fees.
(c) Land Registry fees.
(d) VAT may be payable on some building contracts. Incidental costs can be expected to be increased by the costs of your own legal advice and/or translations of documents.

Ownership

You are legally bound by any condominium rules which apply to your property.
Apart from such costs, as applicable, during your ownership you will
have to pay for the following:

(a) Maintenance and repairs as and when necessary in the case of
an individual home and service charges in addition in the case of
an apartment.

(b) All or some of gas, electricity, water and telephone charges and
domestic insurance premiums.

(c) Municipal taxes (rates) and income tax if you let your property.

You are urged to open a bank account locally in order to be able to
settle such bills promptly.

Resale

If you use a local agent to find a buyer make certain that he is
properly licensed. To obtain repatriation of funds from Portugal you
will need to produce your original import licence (BAICP). Most
incidental costs are payable by the purchaser. Your profits on sale
will be liable to UK Capital Gains Tax if you are a UK resident:
no Portugese Capital Gains Taxes apply to the type of property
described here.

Italy

Lawyers and Legal Advice

The *avvocato* (barrister) is the counselling lawyer and the *notaio*
(notary) is the conveyancing lawyer. The intervention of the notary
is for practical purposes indispensable but advice should be obtained
from a barrister. It is not recommended that you sign documents
until you have taken legal advice; nor should you use the same
barrister as the vendor.

Exchange Control

There are no restrictions on purchase imposed by UK regulations
but in order to obtain the enforceable right to repatriate funds from
Italy on resale it is recommended that you obtain official documentation of importation of the official purchase price and the incidental
costs. Funds can be transferred in any legitimate form and in any

currency: upon importation they should be deposited in an authorised Italian bank. It is, however, usual and most straightforward to transfer them via a UK bank. Resales which involve payment of the price outside Italy are permissible between non-residents; and in such an event the benefits of rights to repatriate the original funds on a further resale should be expressly assigned to the purchaser in the Deed of Conveyance. It is an offence for an Italian to receive or pay funds outside Italy and the offer or acceptance of such a proposition should be avoided until the restrictions are lifted, as expected, to conform to the EC intentions on free movement of capital between member states.

Procedural Stages

General

All stages will involve understanding or signing documents in Italian although this may be overcome by appointing a fully trusted person who is conversant with the language to act on your behalf under a Power of Attorney. You should, however, ask for and obtain written translations particularly before signing documents. For the execution of the Deed of Conveyance, and for other reasons later, it will be necessary for you to have a *codice fiscale* (a personalised tax code): this should be applied for in good time at the local tax office.

From decision to buy to legal commitment

Upon making the decision to purchase a property you, or your own legal adviser, should immediately make enquiries of the *Registro Immobiliare* or RRII (Land Registry) and the *commune* (municipal authority) to verify the following:

(a) The vendor has registered title to the property and that the chain of title is unbroken. If title is not registered, or if the chain of title is broken, follow strictly the advice of your lawyer as there is risk in both cases.
(b) There are no mortgages or other charges on the property. If the property is not free of charges it is almost certainly unsafe to buy.
(c) Planning consents have been obtained and complied with and that building regulations have been observed where applicable. It is practical to couple with these enquiries those about possible future developments in the area.
(d) The vendor is up to date with payment of municipal taxes.

(e) The property is not the subject of pre-emptive rights of adjoining owners in the case of some agricultural land.

It is, however, more usual for these enquiries to be carried out after the signing of the preliminary contract (see below). It is not customary to have a structural survey, but this is the time to do so if at all. Next you will sign a *Contratto Preliminaire di Vendita or Compromesso di Vendita* (preliminary contract) which is the stage equivalent to exchange of contracts in England. The intervention of a notary is not yet indispensable, but the preliminary contract is a legally binding commitment to purchase on the terms stated in that document. However, notarial authentication of the parties' signatures is quite common. Preliminary contracts are not usually long documents; but they will contain the following: the names and descriptions of the parties; a description of the property; the price; the method of payment; a guarantee by the vendor that he has full, unencumbered title to the property, and any general or specific conditions negotiated by the parties. Either 10 per cent or 30 per cent of the price will be payable as deposit (*caparra*) on signing the preliminary contract: it is important that the deposit be described as *caparra penitenziale* rather than *caparra confirmatoria* as in the first case, if the buyer does not perform the contract he merely loses the deposit, whereas in the second case the vendor may apply to a court for specific performance of the contract. Similarly, where there is a *caparra penitenziale* and the vendor is in breach of contract, he must pay to the purchaser double the amount of the deposit received, whereas if the deposit was *confirmatoria* the purchaser can also apply for specific performance.

Where stage payments are to be made before legal title is given, particularly in the case of developments in course of construction, make rigorous enquiries (including a search at the local Company Registry where the vendor is a company) to satisfy yourself that the vendor is solvent and that his building programme is adequately funded. Verify also at this point whether contents, if applicable, and/or the costs of connecting gas, water, electricity and telephone are included in the price (this is not usually the case).

From legal commitment to legal title
Completion of the purchase is likely to be a date and/or an event (eg the completion of construction of a new dwelling) as stated in

the preliminary contract. You are at risk until a formal conveyance transferring ownership from vendor to buyer has been signed, witnessed and entered in the Land Registry (either a *Scritura Privata* witnessed by a notary or an *Atto di Compravendita* known colloquially as *Rogito* and drawn up as well as witnessed by a notary). Do not delay at this stage. It is, however, not unusual for developers to delay execution of the conveyance until some time after having received the price and having handed over the property; this is sometimes for technical reasons and sometimes so that all conveyances can be made at one time, when all the units in a development have been sold. This is an undesirable situation from the legal viewpoint, but provided you are satisfied as to the developer's solvency it should not cause too much panic.

The conveyance, a fuller document than the Preliminary Contract, will state the names and descriptions of the parties, a full description of the property with reference to maps filed in the *Catasto* abbreviated commonly to NCT or NCEU (Cadastral Registry), boundaries, unit location within a development (if applicable), size and make-up of unit, title of vendor with Cadastral number, the price, method of payment or receipt of price as applies, details of rights of way and use, and any special conditions agreed between the parties. The maps, as registered, should be carefully checked and a drawing, accurately and clearly outlining the property sold, should be attached to the conveyance document and should form part of it.

The conveyance should also contain a statement (warranty) as follows:

(a) The vendor is the legal owner of the property.
(b) The property is sold with vacant possession.
(c) The property is not subject to any charges. Where the property is part of a condominium, its rules – *regolamento del condominio* – should be attached having previously been read and understood.

It is the duty of the notary who has witnessed the conveyance to file it at the Land Registry after having first registered it at the *Ufficio del Registro* (Stamp Duty Office) for tax purposes. Registration at the Land Registry constitutes conclusive evidence that the legal title vests in the purchaser, as against third parties, and the notary will give you a further copy of the conveyance bearing all the references. The timescale varies greatly from place to place; but after two months or so the matter should be chased up with the notary as it is important that registration be carried out as quickly as possible, to avoid subsequent charges having priority by being registered first.

Incidental costs
(a) Wide variations in buying costs apply, depending upon whether the vendor is a private individual, a limited company whose primary business is the buying and selling of real estate, a limited company not in the real-estate business or a co-operative. Stamp Duty, *Imposta di Registro*, or VAT, 'IVA', or a combination of the two forms of taxation may apply. The basis for either or both taxes is not the actual price paid but a notional value determined by local official tax tables.
(b) Notarial fees.
(c) Land and Cadastral Registry fees (usually about 2 per cent).

Incidental costs will be increased by those of your own legal adviser and/or translations commissioned by you.

Ownership
Before moving into a new property you should check that a *certificato di abitabilita* (habitation certificate) has been issued by the local authority. You are legally bound by any condominium rules applicable to your property.

During your ownership you will have to pay for the following:

(a) Maintenance and repairs as the need arises in the case of an individual property. In addition, in the case of any property forming part of a condominium, service charges will be payable; repairs and maintenance of external parts of the building and the areas owned in common with others, like staircases and lifts etc, will normally be included in the condominium charges.
(b) All or some of the gas, water, electricity and telephone costs, and domestic insurance premiums.
(c) Local tax (ILOR) and income tax (IRPEF) if you let the property. Ownership of property in Italy carries a duty to file an annual tax return regardless of whether or not the property produces income. ILOR, *Imposta Locales sui Redditi*, is payable in any event, calculated on the basis of the size and nature of the property as filed in the Cadastral Registry. IRPEF, *Imposta sui Reddito delle Persone Fisiche*, and ILOR are both covered by the double taxation agreement between Italy and the UK; but for property primarily

for holiday use the amounts are usually small enough to make the use of this tax treaty unnecessary. The tax return, Modulo 74Q, is relatively complex and should be completed, at least for the first time, with the assistance of a *commercialista* (legal or commercial adviser). It should be filed each year by 31 May for the preceding year: mistakes and delays can involve penalties.

(d) Municipal taxes (rates) for refuse collection etc. These are normally nominal only.

Where the property forms part of a condominium a general meeting of owners must take place at least once a year. At such a meeting an administrator is appointed to manage the day-to-day administration of the commonly owned parts of the building; and expenditure for service charges etc is approved. It is prudent to attend these meetings as owner, either personally or by proxy.

It is the duty of the vendor and/or the purchaser to notify the *questura* (police) of any transfer of ownership.

Resale

To obtain repatriation of funds out of Italy (which must be done through an authorised Italian bank) you should have your proof of importation available. Your profit on the sale will be subject to Italian Capital Gains Tax, INVIM. This is calculated on a sliding scale according to the amount of the gain and the number of years over which it has been made. The notary who witnesses the Deed of Sale collects this tax on behalf of the authorities.

If you use a local agent to find a buyer make sure that he is licensed.

Malta

Lawyers and Legal Advice

The advocate is the counselling lawyer and the notary public is responsible for the conveyancing. The intervention of a notary is indispensable but advice should be obtained from an advocate. It is not recommended that you sign documents until you have taken legal advice, or use the same advocate as the vendor although it is common for both parties to use the same notary public. FOPDAC or one of its members may be able to recommend a Maltese advocate experienced in conveyancing matters.

Exchange Control

There are no restrictions on purchase imposed by UK regulations but in order to obtain the enforceable right to repatriate funds from Malta on resale it is necessary to import the funds into Malta through an authorised Maltese bank which must issue a Certificate of Importation. In addition all purchases by foreigners must be approved through a procedure set out in the Acquisition of Immovable Property Act 1974 (AIP) as amended. The certificate of Importation of Funds and the AIP approval must be produced to the notary who prepares and witnesses the conveyance. The conveyancing stage must always take place in Malta. However, in the case of a resale between a non-resident purchaser and a non-resident vendor the price can in certain circumstances be paid outside Malta.

Procedural Stages

General

All contractual and conveyancing documents should be in the English language.

From decision to buy to legal commitment

In the first stage you will sign a preliminary agreement which is the stage equivalent to exchange of contracts in England. The notary usually prepares the preliminary agreement which is a legally binding commitment to buy on the terms stated in that document. Preliminary agreements are not lengthy documents but will contain the names and descriptions of the parties, a description of the property, the price, the method of payment and any general or special conditions negotiated by the parties. Not less than 10 per cent of the purchase price will be payable on signing the preliminary agreement and this amount will be kept by the notary as stakeholder or 'in escrow'. The making of stage payments is not normal prior to the signing of the final Title Deed. However, some development properties do have a system of ground rents, the amount of which should be clearly identified. Verify also at this point whether contents and/or the cost of connecting water, electricity and telephone (if not already connected) are included in the price.

Structural surveys are not common but now is the moment to have it done if at all.

After signing the preliminary agreement you must make an AIP application and during this period the notary will make enquiries at the relevant Land Registry and in notarial archives and the Works Department to verify that:

(a) The vendor has Registered Title of the property.
(b) There are no mortgages or other charges registered on the property.
(c) Planning consents have been obtained and complied with and building regulations have also been complied with.

If you require information on possible further developments in adjacent areas you must specifically ask the notary to make such enquiries.

If the property is part of an estate or block of flats you should also examine:

(a) A copy of the co-ownership rules.
(b) A copy of the latest accounts of the community of owners.
(c) A statement from the managers of the community of owners of the vendor's balance of account.

From legal commitment to legal title
Completion of the purchase is likely to be a date and/or an event (eg completion of construction of a new dwelling or a time period following the grant of the AIP approval) stipulated in the preliminary agreement.

The completion document is called a Public Deed of Sale which will be your Title Deed. It is a fuller document than the preliminary agreement and will state the names and description of the parties, a full description of the property, with a certified plan attached, referring to rights of way and use, boundaries, unit location within the development (if applicable), size and make-up of unit, the title of the vendor (with Land Registry references) the price, method of payment or receipt of the price, as the case may be, and any special conditions. In addition it should contain a statement (warranty) that:

(a) The vendor is the legal owner of the property.
(b) The property is sold with vacant possession.
(c) The property is not subject to any charges.

The notary must file the Public Deed of Sale at the relevant Land

Registry. He will also effect payment of Stamp Duty and lodge a summary of the Public Deed of Sale at the Land Registry for their retention.

Incidental Costs

These are traditionally payable wholly by the buyer and usually amount to about 5 per cent of the purchase price of the property. They include:

(a) 3.5 per cent Stamp Duty, there are penalties for under-declaration of price.
(b) Approximately £165 for the AIP approval.
(c) 1 per cent for the notary.

Incidental costs will be higher if you obtain independent legal advice from an advocate.

Ownership

You are legally bound by any condominium rules applicable to your property.

During your ownership you will have to pay for:

(a) Maintenance and repairs as and when they arise in the case of an individual property and in addition, in the case of a flat, service charges.
(b) All or some of water, electricity and telephone charges, domestic insurance premium.
(c) Local income tax (if a resident of Malta) and income tax (if you let your property).

Open a local bank account to be able to meet these payments promptly.

Resale

If you use a local agent to find a buyer make sure he is properly licensed. If repatriation of funds out of Malta is important to you, your buyer must abide by the procedure described in 'Exchange Control' (see p82) and you will need evidence of the original importation of your own purchase funds.

All incidental expenses are payable by the buyer. Your capital profit on sale may be subject to UK Capital Gains Tax but there is no Capital Gains Tax in Malta.

Switzerland

Lawyers and Legal Advice

The *rechtsanwalt* or *advocat* (barrister) is the counselling lawyer and the *notar* or *notaire* (notary) the conveyancing lawyer. The intervention of a notary is indispensable but advice should also be obtained from a barrister. It is not recommended that you sign documents until you have taken legal advice or that you use the same barrister as the vendor. FOPDAC or one of its members may be able to recommend a Swiss barrister or one of the small number of UK lawyers with experience in this field.

Foreign Investment and Exchange Control

There are currently no exchange control restrictions applicable either in the UK or Switzerland. However, Switzerland has quota restrictions on the purchase of Swiss real estate by foreigners, limited in 1985 and reducing each year to 2,000 consents with individual allocations for each canton. Common conditions attached to consents are a bar (save in exceptional circumstances) on resale within five years, an obligation to reside personally in the property for a minimum of 3–6 weeks per year and a bar on granting long leases. The grant of a consent does not imply that a foreigner will be permitted to buy the property upon resale.

Procedural Stages

General

All stages will involve understanding or signing documents in French, German or Italian, depending on location. Ask for and obtain written translations before signing any document.

From decision to buy to legal commitment

Some developers (but not usually individual vendors) like buyers to sign an option or contract of reservation, usually against the payment of a nominal deposit. It is considered safe to sign such a document before making title and planning searches but verify whether the deposit is returnable if you do not proceed. At this stage you, or your legal adviser, should make enquiries at the relevant Land Registry and Municipal Authority to verify that:

(a) The vendor has Registered Title of the property. If title is unregistered follow strictly the advice of your legal adviser as there

is some risk associated with purchase from an unregistered owner.
(b) There are no mortgages or other charges registered on the property. If the property is not free of charges it is almost certainly unsafe to buy.
(c) Planning consents have been obtained and complied with and building regulations have also been complied with. General enquiries as to plans for future development can be usefully coupled with these enquiries.
(d) The vendor is up to date with the payments of municipal taxes.

Structural surveys are not common but now is the moment to have it done if at all.

If the property is part of an estate or block of flats you should obtain:

(a) A copy of the co-ownership rules.
(b) A copy of the latest accounts of the community of owners.
(c) A statement from the managers of the community of owners of the vendor's balance of account.

Next you will sign a purchase agreement which is the equivalent to exchange of contracts in England. The intervention of a notary is not yet obligatory but the purchase agreement is a legally binding commitment to buy on the terms stated in that document. Purchase agreements are not lengthy documents but will contain the names and description of the parties, a description of the property, the price, the method of payment and any general or special conditions negotiated by the parties. Not less than 10 per cent of the purchase price will be payable on signing the purchase agreement and a higher figure is frequently sought by developers. Where stage payments are to be made before Legal Title is given, particularly in the case of developments in the course of construction, make rigorous enquiries to satisfy yourself that the vendor is solvent and that his building programme is adequately funded or bonded. Verify also at this point whether contents and/or the cost of connecting water, gas and electricity (if not already supplied) are included in the price.

From legal commitment to legal title
Completion of the purchase is likely to be a date and/or an event (eg completion of construction of a new dwelling) stipulated in the purchase agreement. You may be at risk until a formal

document transferring ownership from the vendor to the buyer has been prepared and witnessed, a function necessarily performed by a notary, and then registered in the Land Registry. So do not delay at this stage.

The Sale Deed is a fuller document than the purchase agreement and will state the names and description of the parties, a full description of the property referring to rights of way and use, boundaries, unit location within a development (if applicable), size and make-up of unit, the title of the vendor (with Land Registry references), the price, method of payment or receipt of the price, as the case may be, and any special conditions. In addition it should contain a statement (warranty) that:

(a) The vendor is the legal owner of the property.
(b) The property is sold with vacant possession.
(c) The property is not subject to any charges.

Buyers must have their Title Deed registered at the relevant Land Registry. A notary will carry this out if so instructed. The registration procedure takes 2–4 days.

Incidental costs
These are traditionally payable wholly by the buyer and usually amount to about 3–5 per cent of the purchase price of the property depending on the canton. They include:

(a) Transfer Tax (*Sisa*).
(b) Notarial fees.
(c) Land Registry fees.

Incidental costs will be higher if you obtain independent legal advice and/or your own translations.

Ownership
You are legally bound by any condominium rules applicable to your property. During your ownership you will have to pay for:

(a) Maintenance and repairs as and when they arise in the case of an individual property and in addition, in the case of a flat, service charges.
(b) All or some of gas, water, electricity and telephone charges, domestic insurance premium.

(c) National, cantonal and/or communal taxes on income and net wealth.

Open a local bank account to be able to meet these payments promptly.

Resale

If you use a local agent to find a buyer make sure he is properly licensed. Note the potential difficulties of sale to a non-Swiss referred to in Foreign Investment and Exchange Control (see p85). Most incidental expenses are payable by the buyer and your profit on sale will be liable for UK Capital Gains Tax if you are a UK resident.

7
GOLF COMPLEXES AND MARINAS

The Minister of Tourism for one of Spain's Autonomous Governments pointed at a 2cm thick dossier on the desk in front of him and said that they had just commissioned a study to point the way to the upgrading of their future tourism and resort development. The study cost many tens of thousands of pounds and used many thousands of words to say: build golf courses and marinas. This was an expensive statement of the obvious.

Golf Courses

Early Development
Pau, in the foothills of the Pyrenees in south-western France, was the first of the world's resort courses. Some of Wellington's officers, pausing from chasing Napoleon's troops out of Spain and Portugal at the end of the Peninsular War, enjoyed the atmosphere, climate, scenery, cuisine and people of this attractive town. They vowed to return with their wives and families to settle there after the battles were over. They did come back, to spend their time hunting, shooting, fishing, playing rugger, which they also introduced to the locals, and, inevitably, looked for suitable terrain for a golf course. They found the land and began to design and build a course, which opened for play in the mid-fifties of the last century. More villas and hotels were built and the colony and the local community prospered.

Since then there have been many periods of boom in the building of resort courses, but none comparable with today's situation. By the end of the nineteenth century courses were constructed in Oporto, Las Palmas in the Canaries, on the Riviera and elsewhere for the enjoyment of the British on holiday or living abroad. The first of the USA's courses had also been built by then, designed by men with Scottish names: Reid, Macdonald, Ross and Mackenzie.

Further booms occurred in the twenties and thirties, with resort courses being created in Estoril, a twelve-hole course in Sitges, harking back to the early days in Scotland before the eighteen-hole layout became standard; more in the South of France, across the Channel in Le Touquet, Deauville and Biarritz, and across the Atlantic, where golf and resort development began to synergise in Florida in something like its present form. Such growth ceased in Europe at the end of the thirties for obvious reasons.

Resort golf pre-war had been targetted upon the titled, the gentry and the newly rich. South of the Scottish border it was hardly a democratic sport in any case. Post-war it became gradually more democratic in Britain and the process was accelerated when the now famous courses on the Algarve and the Spanish costas were built to attract buyers of villas and apartments on what had until then been valueless tracts of coastal land in poverty-stricken regions of generally poor countries. In the late fifties and early sixties entrepreneurs invested in expensive courses, often of so-called 'championship standard', at Penina, Vilamoura, and Vale do Lobo on the Algarve and Sotogrande, Atalaya, Guadalmina, Nueva Andalucia and Los Monteros on the Costa del Sol. Courses at Pals and Santa Cristina de Aro were in play on the Costa Brava and Mallorca had a couple of nine-hole layouts.

The Seventies

Further expansion of facilities in resort areas continued in the seventies until the world's economies were thrown into reverse by the quadrupling of the oil price by the Arabs in late 1973. The effect was near and actual bankruptcy for a number of developers who had got their forecasts and timing wrong and were therefore left with land, infrastructure, golf courses and other facilities, and partly built properties as buyers failed to come forward. Many projects in Spain were badly affected; some in Portugal also suffered from the uncertainty following the overthrow of the Fascist regime and the advent of inexperienced democracy at the same time.

In spite of the economic downturn and the problems of some developers, more attractive resort courses had been added to the existing attractions of the Algarve and the Spanish Costas. Others were created on Sardinia, Corfu and Rhodes, in Italy, Greece and Austria and, more optimistically, in Morocco. Only a few were built in France, then in decline as a destination for quality tourism, as demonstrated by the closing of our consulate on the Riviera due to lack of demand for its services.

During the past decade golf has taken off in Germany and Sweden, with an effective doubling of the numbers of courses and players. The game has grown spectacularly in other European countries too, with France leading the rest in numbers of courses constructed. Japan's golf growth has kept pace with its economic power; and its keen players have travelled outside Japan to use resort courses wherever they meet their demanding standards. The effect of all this national growth has been to increase international demand for popular Portuguese and Spanish courses. Long waiting time, indifferent staff, clogged fairways, heavy wear on turf and temper, green fees which escalate unreasonably: all of these criticisms have been vigorously made over the past few years, when supply has been unable to cope with ever-increasing demand.

Course Standards

As a direct result of all this pressure more courses have been built, are under construction or are on the drawing board than at any other time in the game's history. It would be remarkable if all these new facilities were well sited, well conceived, well planned, well built, well funded and well maintained. But the business of golf development is not as consistent as that.

Some new complexes, like some of the now-famous golf resorts of the sixties and seventies, are simply in the wrong place. Some are poorly conceived and planned. Some may prove to have been poorly built and maintained. A few certainly have courses which are punishing for the average golfer, when pure delight should be the objective, with long uphill, cardiac-arrest fairways, penal rough, intimidating and unnecessary lakes and bunkers and long treks from greens to tees. Some of the new complexes repeat the mistakes of those planned earlier, with poorly integrated housing minimising the benefits of living on a fairway. These are usually the outcome of an inexperienced developer falling into the hands of an experienced and strong-willed golf architect whose intention is to build a monument to his ego, regardless of what the customer wants. A number of examples can be seen where fairway-fronting apartment buildings are so badly conceived that views of the course are unobtainable from half the units. One developer sited a building alongside a course but placed it in a hole excavated to conceal the property from his own villa: seven years later some of these apartments were still seeking purchasers.

The Ideal Golfing Property

Clearly there is a great choice of locations and specific properties open to you if owning a home on a foreign golf course represents your ideal. There is now a wide selection of resort homes within easy reach of courses too, without actually being within the golf complex. Now that the hinterland of the French Channel and Atlantic coasts is well served for courses the hunt for the ideal foreign property for a golfer can begin at Calais and follow the French, Portuguese and Spanish coastlines until slowing down at the Italian border. The Balearics now have attractive eighteen-hole courses to add to the earlier nine-hole facilities; Sardinia has a couple, Tenerife three and most other larger islands within three or so hours' travel time of the population centres of Europe have at least one course. This wide choice of new and resale property associated with golf will get even wider as development and demand progress.

With all this variety on offer how do you apply your critical faculties to golf property? The importance of location in the general sense is covered in Chapters 1 and 2 so is judgement of estates in resort areas (see Chapter 5). Put simply, property on a golf resort carries a premium price: you and only you can decide whether or not this premium price is worth paying for the extra benefits of living on or near a golf course. Now the odd fact is that 70 per cent of people who buy homes on golf courses don't play the game! This statistic was first revealed in the USA where the integration of golf and housing has reached an advanced state of sophistication. I can confirm that it is equally true in Europe in my personal experience as a golf development consultant. This means that not only golfers are prepared to pay a higher price for the advantages of living on a course but also mainstream buyers find the environment so appealing that they too will pay more than average prices for homes with the benefit of being near a green space with sporting and social facilities.

The fact that fairway living appeals to more non-golfers than golfers underpins the market for course-fronting property. Golf courses generally improve environments, real estate values and saleability of homes. But some golf property is better than average; some is worse than average and some is outstanding by any criteria. It follows that if property around golf courses has general appeal, in other words, if more non-golfers than golfers buy it, then general criteria can be used in judging its quality or otherwise. Elsewhere in this book there is sufficient guidance on this for repetition to be unnecessary. However, there are some important points of difference between golf-course property and resort property generally, in practical as well as social terms.

The big plus for most people who are attracted to this kind of environment is being alongside a massive permanent green space. An eighteen-hole course can be constructed on about 50ha (125 acres) and the distance from start to finish is likely to be around 7km (4¼ miles). This vast area is maintained by somebody else at no cost to the householder unless he is a member of the golf club. In resort areas it is seldom necessary to be a club member to enjoy the facilities of the bar and restaurant, and some non-golfers are therefore drawn to such places by the residual snobbism which sometimes remains associated with golf.

A more understandable benefit of owning a home on a golf complex is that a clubhouse in a resort is invariably welcoming. Meeting people from other countries and backgrounds, easily and without formality, is a major benefit for today's socially mobile and more confident expatriates. There is not likely to be the outdated and humiliating investigation of one's pedigree by a purple-faced colonel or someone similar, before being allowed to buy a drink in the clubhouse as still applies in some 'traditional' clubs here in Britain. In Europe they are fundamentally friendly places.

It can be argued that if non-golfers are the main category of buyers on golf complexes then they should be the people to buy the less attractive homes, without course views, which are a feature of poorly planned golf developments and most are in fact poorly planned in the sense that the benefits of the enormous green area are not usually fully exploited in the masterplan for the development. However, a living-room and a terrace overlooking the course is the strongest selling point to a buyer who can't get, can't afford or doesn't want sea views from a resort property.

Clearly, a non-golfer is hardly able to judge the qualities of a golf course; but he will be able to appreciate that there are some important factors to be taken into account when considering the attractions of one course complex against another. Golfers may have personal likes and dislikes to be favoured, and they really should be indulged as owning a home in another country is truly a question of what pleases you.

The Ideal Golf Course

Some fundamentals should be accepted by developers and their golf architects at the concept stage. Early land-use analysis should acknowledge the fact that a golfer should be able to choose what length of course he wants to play: this means that allowance should be made for long tees, as much as 40 or 50m from back to front, so that the lady golfer, the high-handicapper, the straight-hitting but ageing player, the single-figure amateur and the touring pro can all enjoy the course.

The loss of a golf ball causes different reactions according to personality. Some golfers are like some motorists, who undergo personality changes when thwarted behind the wheel. But playing golf is not about thrashing around in the rough, becoming increasingly frustrated, with playing partners becoming irritated, and those behind wanting to be waved through, while searching for a ball which is hardly worth the effort. So who needs rough which is really rough on a resort course? What possible purpose does it serve? Slow play is the curse of the popular resort courses, and a lost ball is almost invariably the reason for the delays.

Trees, shrubs and even flowers should be included in the golf architect's palette, to give year-round colour and shape to the areas between fairways, behind greens and tees, and to create undulations and focal points on flat terrain. But trunks and stems should be trimmed of growth below 1m (3ft 3in) or so to allow for balls hit off-line to be easily spotted for the same reasons that rough can be eliminated in practice. Many elderly British courses have 'blind holes' and there are some sloppily planned resort courses which also suffer from this defect. Out-of-sight landing areas are no longer tolerable. And all hazards should be clearly visible. Muddy, fairway-level pit bunkers should be things of the past. Sand-traps carved out of softly curved mounds can be seen, can be drained and give delight to the eye.

Whether you are a golfer or not you should be able to spot the signs of an inadequate specification or poor construction; and poor maintenance can also be seen by the naked and untrained eye. Boggy areas of fairway; bare, compacted paths; worn tees and ragged edges to bunkers; over-used pin positions, creating maddening domes around the holes; parallel long holes running east and west into the sun; stones, known as 'floaters' working their way to the surface under fairway turf, causing danger to wrists and clubheads: these and other tell-tale indicators should be considered when judging one complex against another.

Who owns the golf club? This question seldom suggests itself to British people contemplating buying property around existing courses as we are accustomed to members owning courses as debenture or ordinary shareholders, or local authorities owning public courses. In Europe either of these situations is possible. But many are developer-owned; some are owned by hotel companies, airlines and banks; some, particularly in France, are owned by commercial organisations in 'chains' like departmental stores and are operated with businesslike efficiency, far removed from our own semi-professional routines.

Ownership of the courses and ancillary facilities should be established early when considering buying a home nearby if you want to be able to enjoy some of the facilities. Clearly use has to be paid for; and the terms of membership or daily fees may or may not be appealing to you. In some cases, when buying a home on an existing or new golf complex, membership privileges may be included in the purchase package offered: you will need to exercise judgement on how to value this sweetener.

There are now hundreds of golf courses in the resort areas of Europe. Not all of them have integrated housing; not all of the housing is *well* integrated. But there are thousands of homes for sale at any time. The choice is, therefore, wide enough for anyone determined to live on a fairway in another country to find what he wants.

Marinas

The choice of property on a marina is not so wide. With the exception of Florida, which has a never-ending supply of marina-fronting homes, the resort areas are notoriously short of villas and apartments overlooking moorings.

The great majority of marina developers have seen marinas simply as places to park boats. Usually, creating a marina involves a few years of negotiation with government departments in order to agree the formalities of leasing part of a seabed from the state and the technicalities of constructing massive, wave-resistant harbour walls to enclose the facility. The leasing of the seabed means that neither the harbour walls nor anything within them can be sold freehold: this fact has been a barrier to integrated housing developments on what is effectively reclaimed land; it follows that all homes offered for sale would be leasehold according to the local laws unless the developer owned all of the existing coastline fronting or overlooking the marina.

Even where the marina developer has owned the original waterfront there are many instances of poor planning similar to the usual errors made in the case of golf complexes. The common fault is to build over-large apartment blocks in a form which gives no marina views from most of the units. One notorious example at Manilva on the Costa del Sol almost bankrupted the developer: most of the apartments overlooked the noisy and dangerous coast road rather than the yachts and therefore proved unsaleable within the timescale forecast. At Santa Eulalia in Ibiza a luxurious apartment building on the marina was planned to give most of the units a view of an untidy backstreet. There are many instances of the saleability of homes being jeopardised by placing an unnecessary road between them and the waterfront. A normal fault is to put potentially noisy bars and restaurants beneath highly priced residential property.

Marinas, like golf courses, have traditionally upgraded tourist and resort development. Some are actually listed as specific tourist attractions, visited annually by millions, to the discomfort of those who own what were originally intended to be highly desirable homes. Clearly, if you are intent on buying a property on or overlooking a marina you will need to be aware of some of the potential disadvantages as well as the plus points.

High-density Developments
Unlike a golf complex, a marina development is normally planned to a high density. Waterfront cafés, bars and restaurants can be considered normal ingredients in the property mix. Some have very comprehensive boat maintenance and repair facilities. Some have few homes and many berths, with car parking on a grand scale. Some are attractive to owners of 'gin palaces' and arms dealers with aircraft carrier-sized boats with helicopters at the ready. All of these factors guarantee a high ambient noise level. If you need something

close to silence for your eight hours' sleep then you are unlikely to get it in such an environment.

On the other hand, sailors are usually sociable, and you may not be bothered by all the activity associated with a successful marina of this kind. Indeed, the lively atmosphere at all times may be a major attraction for you. But not all marina developments with integrated housing are noisy: you may prefer to find one which allows you to enjoy the softer sounds of wind in the rigging and the water lapping the hulls. Port Grimaud in the South of France is an example of a marina arranged Venice-like to give a mooring alongside one's home: it has a lively centre in season but most of the homes built on man-made canals are free of the disadvantages mentioned above. The less-stylish Spanish equivalent is Ampuriabrava on the Costa Brava. It is significant that these and other similar marina developments were planned with resort property as the priority rather than berths for boats.

No statistics are available to show what percentage of buyers of marina homes actually sail. However, anecdotal evidence suggests that a similar situation to the percentage of non-golfers who buy property on golf complexes applies to buyers of homes on marinas. The facilities of a marina are less important to buyers of homes than the general environment: the water, moored boats rocking gently, others coming and going, sails being raised and lowered, and a choice of friendly bars and cafés out of earshot. Clearly the quality and comparative prices of the homes are important too.

The Future
Future trends point to more marina developments on the Port Grimaud pattern, with housing on canals cut into existing low-lying land rather than on reclaimed land within harbour walls on the seabed. From Gibraltar north, where the negligible rise and fall of the Mediterranean does not assist such development, some marinas and housing have succeeded, with locks to manage the water levels. There are some other successful developments mixing boats and homes on French and Swiss lakes; more can be expected.

Serious sailors will have clear ideas about what facilities they consider essential for their use and what they consider desirable. Mooring charges, services, berth leasing, maintenance and repair facilities, rentals of boats not in use are easily discovered by experts. Standards vary widely.

Golf complexes and marinas represent growth points for future resort development, offering opportunities for owners of homes in other countries which have, for some, greater benefits than living on estates which have no theme or focal point. Those who are likely to be attracted to these preserved environments will willingly pay the premium property prices required.

8

CONVERSIONS AND RENOVATIONS

The traditional resort property of the British middle classes was a country cottage a few hours' drive away from their everyday home. The upper classes had town houses and country estates around ancient piles. For some of us old houses, however primitive, are simply magnetic. Others have irresistible urges to convert derelict farmbuildings into unique homes. But, except in the most inaccessible or inhospitable locations, these powerful impulses can no longer be indulged in the UK. Across the Channel, from Calais to Algeciras and the toe of Italy, the natives generally prefer a new apartment or villa on the coast or an apartment or chalet in the mountains to the local equivalent of a country cottage, especially one which needs an amount of tender loving care to make it comfortably habitable.

The increasing demand from British lovers of old homes is being increasingly satisfied in various areas of France, in Cataluna, Alicante province and Andalucia in Spain and in Tuscany and Umbria in Italy. Portugal north of the Algarve is also attracting curious explorers. Sardinia is yet to be invaded by those seeking romantic rural peace but it will surely happen. Old homes on the Balearics are now almost as hard to come by unimproved as they are in Britain. Few farmhouses on Malta or Gozo are offered for sale direct from the farmers. From time to time specialist agents have tried to create business from the sale of old houses in Cyprus; they have had trouble putting together a worthwhile inventory – problems of supply rather than demand.

Converting a potentially attractive old property into a home in Britain is practical enough: all you need is average commonsense, flair and imagination, time, patience and access to more money when the set budget is inevitably exceeded. How practical is it to buy and convert or renovate an old property in another country?

Practical Considerations

A number of factors come into play. Is the property very easy to get to, at the drop of a hat, from your home in the UK? Is the work to be carried out cosmetic, a face-lift, or is it structural? Does the work include the provision of basic services (water, electricity and sewerage)? Is the road access to the property acceptable or must it be improved? Are you intending to add to the volume of the property? Do you intend to do-it-yourself, do-none-of-it-yourself, or mix the two approaches? Are you in a hurry?

Location

It has been made clear that location, location and location are the three most important factors concerning real estate of any kind at all times. What this means to the converter/renovator is clearly that the property is easy to get to, usually by car rather than by plane (because country living really does need a car outside the door at all times for a feeling of well-being), and is not more than a day away from Britain in travel time. Island living involves modified criteria in this as in other factors because driving to your island home is hardly practical; but you would in any event have to solve the problem of transport locally for full enjoyment of any kind of resort home on an island.

A certain feeling of remoteness may be an essential part of the location, location and location criteria in your case; but during the conversion/renovation programme the disadvantages of such isolation would soon become obvious if you were the anxious type and were leaving the work to somebody else. Living on site while the work is carried out is an option to be considered. Supervision, monitoring or simply worrying about it all assumes that you will be there frequently unless it is physically impractical to be so. Only you can decide how well your future home fits the profile of your personality. And you will have to live with the consequences of having picked a place which carries practical penalties while being made habitable; it would reduce later fun if you tired of the journey before you had completed the work on your retreat.

Do It Yourself or Employ an Expert?

Cosmetic work like decoration, minor replastering, the replacement of non-structural woodwork, erecting shelves and reshaping or replanting gardens and outdoor living space is usually part of the attraction of the ownership of old homes. Rarely can the dedicated converter/renovator keep his hands off the tools. Primitive forces are responsible for this syndrome: it is unrelated to the excuses, delaying tactics and downright deception which are sometimes employed when similar tasks are scheduled on, in and around one's everyday home. Such work usually becomes part of the pleasure of initial visits to your resort home; for some it becomes a semi-permanent evolutionary process – in other words, a way of life. If it is not part of the pleasure of owning an old home in another country to be able to tinker with it then you are unlikely to sign the necessary purchase contract in the first place.

Structural Work

Structural changes, repairs and improvements are not to be considered beyond the capabilities of truly dedicated amateurs. Clearly available time needs to be added to interest and ability. In any event professional advice is needed for questions of foundations, walls which are cracked or bowed, floors which have fallen in and roofs which require retiling or reslating if pitched or rebuilding if flat. If reconstruction of a pitched roof is necessary then advice is essential: sometimes local regulations require insulation as standard when reroofing.

Face-lifts are a different matter, requiring more dedication and some basic skills if doing it yourself is the intention. The ability to communicate clearly, monitor and supervise is essential if the intention is to hire suitable contractors to do the work for you. Replacing windows, inserting new windows in new openings, removing non-loadbearing walls, re-laying floors of timber or tile, upgrading bathrooms and kitchens, repairing ceilings and exposing beams are within the competence of somebody bringing commonsense to the job. Plumbing and electrical work is best left to experts. New window openings involve simple skills in rustic building (the insertion of lintels for example) and making good use of the techniques employed when the place was built. Removing a non-loadbearing wall involves a commonsense judgement about whether or not it really isn't carrying a load. If you have the slightest doubt then take advice and shed the blame if more of the property comes down than you intended. Re-laying floors is a basic process: rot or wood-borer damage in supporting timbers is easy to spot; two people jumping up and down on the floor in question will help you to make commonsense decisions about what needs to be replaced, using standard and safe chemical treatment against future trouble where necessary. Solid floors, if being replaced, should incorporate a damp-proof course, laid according to manufacturer's instructions: sheet plastic can be simply laid. You should think carefully before using old tiles or stone flagstones as hardcore: sensible restorers are best advised to keep anything which can possibly be recycled. The existence of cellars add an element of excitement and danger to the rethinking of floors.

Bathrooms and Kitchens

Upgrading bathrooms and kitchens in rustic houses leads to imaginative or strictly functional solutions. It is not difficult to buy a bathroom package almost anywhere in a small town in Europe complete with the name of a friendly installer; the same applies to kitchens. On the island of Gozo, for example, luxurious kitchens have become affordable status symbols for many of the local people: they are placed in the houses as additions to the existing kitchens; the new ones are kept for special occasions (if used at all) while the original kitchens continue in everyday use! If you have flair then bathrooms in old houses can become matters of art rather than clinical cleanliness. And little flair is required to create simple, appetising kitchens with dining space around country tables, with country chairs, with old floorboards or tiles on the floor, rough-plastered or tiled walls, beamed and plastered ceilings (or planks where they are the local treatment) and basic preparation facilities. Wall-hung storage out of the reach of ants is often sensible. Outdoor eating areas alongside such kitchens are easy to create and easy to appreciate.

Ceilings

The approach to repairing ceilings and exposing or featuring beams is similar to that mentioned for timber floors. Jump about until satisfied that the timbers will last as long as you need them to, or until you feel unsafe. Unless you are obliged by your ambitions or the condition of the property to undertake major structural work the commonsense plan should be to make the minimum changes needed for a civilised simple life.

Heating
What kind of heating you install will depend upon when and how you want to use your bolt-hole. Do you require central heating, or will open fires supplemented with spot or background heating suffice? For many such a decision carries little urgency: it can be taken later in the light of experience. For others, concerned with the greater sensitivity to cold which comes with ageing, heating is priority number one.

Extensions
Adding to the volume of the home generally requires formal approval and the obligatory use of an architect; so does any physical change which is likely to alter the external appearance of the building. It is, in any event, sensible to talk personally, or through an interpreter, to the mayor of the community in which the property is situated, and to neighbours within sight of the property. The value of good public relations should never be underestimated. You are the alien in their midst and you are almost certain to be welcomed as routine; but you should not risk ignoring protocol even if you want to get the work under way without delay. Usually an informal approach, asking if permission is needed, will result in the mayor and his friends visiting the site, offering six different solutions, accepting a few drinks and suggesting that you get on with it before the weather breaks. Failure to act in this straightforward and courteous way may result in lack of co-operation or worse.

Local regulations
There are increasingly rules which apply to some valued old properties, intended to preserve characteristic local architecture or features or to maintain compatible use of traditional materials. The use of stone and slate in Brittany is one example; the use of Franka stone in the Maltese islands is another. In some locations the size of windows is seen to be important to the community. In others, the use to which the property will be put is more important: de-ruralised farmhouses in Umbria and Tuscany are usually substantial and desirable but if they are not de-ruralised they are of no use at all to you because you would not be able to live in them.

Mains Services

Septic tanks are more common on most of the Continent, and on most of the islands, than they are in the UK. It is likely that modernising your property will entail the question of whether or not a new septic tank is necessary. The traditional hole in the ground may no longer be acceptable. If this subject is to be considered then the mayor and neighbours should be parties to the debate for obvious reasons. In some localities wells are the source of water supplies not utility companies. Water rights may be shared. Tanks and pumps may become important factors in your future lifestyle.

Electricity may or may not be important to you if it is not already connected to the property. If you need it and it is not yet connected the costs of bringing the supply to your home may shock you. Spanish utility companies have in the past been rapaciously commercial when asked to supply; but government pressure and threats have resulted in more acceptable quotes latterly. France has an efficient distribution system but the countryside is often defiled in all directions by the most obtrusive network of gigantic pylons in Europe, for many an environmental disaster.

Intermediaries

It is clear that you will need to rely initially upon the advice of an experienced estate agent and a lawyer when buying an old rustic property in another country. But your own judgement will be critical – you will have only yourself to blame if you pick the wrong property. If you speak enough of the language to be able to communicate your wishes clearly then you could enjoy sub-contracting the essential work to local specialists (general builders as we know them rarely exist elsewhere). If the work is structural or involves building extra accommodation then you will almost certainly be obliged to employ an architect: one of you at least must be able to speak the other's language. Contracts for work to be done should be crystal clear; sometimes you will not get a local mason, carpenter, plumber, plasterer, roofer or electrician to quote in writing let alone sign a contract but unless you employ an architect your judgement in such cases is a matter for you alone. . .

There is no doubt that some intermediaries have appeared in those areas of Europe which have become popular with the British for the purchase and conversion/renovation of comparatively inexpensive old properties. Some have proved to be helpful, taking the time-consuming load off those people who are more interested in the end result than in achieving it by personal input. Some in Italy particularly, have made themselves wealthy by exploiting the trusting by massaging up conversion costs and generally stealing money from anyone who has retained them. They have often been granted Power of Attorney to formalise the connection. Agents who operate under codes of conduct, are licensed and well established can usually be relied upon for fair advice prior to making a sale and after if you retain them to do so. Architects are bound by tight rules. Cowboys cannot be relied upon and should be avoided at all costs.

Unique Properties

There are some special properties which need special attention. The classical Loire châteaux are outside the scope of this book, but there are châteaux and châteaux. Some early buildings covered by this elastic word were indeed castles made to withstand sieges and some remain in private hands. Occasionally truly magnificent, robust examples come on to the market at prices which still seem low compared with those of rather commonplace city centre or choice suburban family homes in Britain. The middle-period, middle-range French châteaux are not quite ten-a-penny but there are thousands of them, often with land, and many are on offer, again at prices which attract raised eyebrows. Then there are what should more properly be called *manoirs*, often run-down country houses in a few hectares with outbuildings and mature trees, at prices which are as much (or as little) as much grander châteaux. Such properties in France flooded the British market in the eighties and plenty found buyers before the UK domestic market went into decline at the end of the decade.

The special attention which should be accorded princely property of this kind may be obligatory. Before buying a châteaux of any kind you should check and double check whether tough ancient monument regulations apply. These rules govern what you can and cannot do to the place by way of physical changes. A handful of British architects are *au fait* with the French ground rules.

There are castles in Spain too. At the last count there were two and a half thousand of these very solid but somewhat unreal buildings of varied vintages and styles. They are about practical defence rather than picturesque country living, the result of eight hundred years of warfare between the Moors and the Christians. Most of them are in the area most fought over during the Moorish Conquest, named appropriately Castile: the land of castles. Some are *paradores* (state hotels); some are museums or much-visited monuments; some occasionally are placed discreetly on the market by distressed owners.

Other special properties in Spain are the abandoned villages. In mountainous parts of Cataluna particularly, off the main roads, there are small collections of houses built of random stone, usually on hills but sometimes on rock outcrops, which are Iberian equivalents of the ghost towns of the Wild West. The asymetrical houses prop each other up, following the slopes, small-windowed, with stones placed upon the roof tiles to keep them in place when the wind gusts. Cattle and sheep roam between the houses. Cobwebs curtain the windows. People are rare. These spooky villages are part of the aftermath of the civil war of the thirties. British people often have no real conception of what the Spanish Civil War was about. Brother fought brother. People starved. Hundreds of thousands died. It was the army versus the people. The people lost and many who survived ran away to other countries and fought against the Nazis there. More died. Others made new lives outside Spain. Hence there are abandoned villages in parts of Spain. Those which are being converted and renovated for the delight of the current generations usually have problems of title – to be expected – but are timeless, tranquil and traditionally sited to command valley views. Naturally they appeal to the romantics of all nations. They are amongst the most magical places in Europe.

There are some fortified villages in Tuscany and Umbria which are even more attractive than the abandoned villages of Spain. Some of them have been offered internationally during the eighties. Others have been sensitively and sometimes artistically rehabilitated to create homes of great emotional appeal.

There are millions of old homes of various qualities and conditions in Europe and on present and future resort islands. The market for converted and renovated well-sited old property is perpetual.

9

REMOVALS

Owning a home abroad should be fun, however you define the word. But you will know that moving from one home to another in this country is not fun by any definition. Uprooting is upsetting. So how do you avoid the anguish of moving all your belongings from one country to another? There is a simple but brutal answer: don't do it!

A sound case can be made for selling up here 'lock, stock and barrel' and buying everything you need locally for what will be in reality a new life. What you cannot sell can be given to friends or relatives or donated to favourite charities.

Depending upon personal tastes, it can be argued that European furniture and furnishings are better designed and made than those normally found here except in specialist designer outlets. 'Out-of-town' showrooms are the norm in Europe, lower land costs making huge hangar-like buildings economical for the display of thousands of square metres of furniture. The choice is usually wide, both in traditional and modern styles. Prices are broadly comparable with those in the UK. Browsing amongst such a selection can be fun for some particularly if your tastes have evolved since furnishing a family home here.

Many of your electrical goods will have been imported into the UK. Is there any sense at all in packing them carefully and re-exporting them expensively possibly back to where they came from in the first place? Better surely to buy kettles, toasters, mixers, fridges, dishwashers and washing machines – if, in fact, you decide that you actually need them – where you know they will be compatible with local power supplies and water pressures, and with guarantees that start on day one of your new life.

Gas cookers are easily crossed off the list of essentials as many parts of Europe exist on bottled gas, making expensive conversion necessary. And your TV set would be better off staying in a receptive home here rather than costing money to be taken to another country to cost more money for conversion to receive local channels.

Curtains and fitted carpets will obviously remain. Garden and other tools and equipment are more likely to benefit new owners here than you there. Books, pictures and other collected treasures are more difficult to leave behind; so are valued and possibly valuable carpets and some items of furniture particularly antiques and heirlooms.

So should you sell it, put it up for auction, give it to a friend or relative or become a benefactor of a charity? Or can't you possibly bear to be parted from it? These are hard but vital questions and they have to be answered before you get too far with your removal plans. In fact, sentiment usually wins over logic, and the majority of people take what they cannot be parted from rather than what they cannot sensibly do without.

One man I know took his Flymo to Portugal 'so that I can look at it from time to time, knowing that I'll never again need to use the damned thing.' He and his wife live in a beach apartment with no garden. Another, with a villa high above a Balearic bay, has a terrace furnished with appropriate local cane chairs, settees and tables. But his living-room looks like the officers' mess of an élite regiment somewhere in the East before the war: comfortable, sagging sofas; old Asian rugs and carpets; and faded group photographs of boxing teams and classes of young officers he had trained at Sandhurst. And a once-famous actress, now 'resting' and ageing gracefully, has light local furniture in her villa; but her walls are covered with photos and paintings of her features as they once were, as a kind of shrine to somebody else.

Given that the process of selection depends upon whether or not you want an item, rather than whether or not you *need* it, an experienced international remover will soon help your concentration: his estimate will be based upon distance and cubic metres carried.

Choosing an International Remover

Moving furniture and effects from Britain to another country has only a superficial resemblance to doing the same job within the UK. It is as far from the 'Up your end a bit, Charlie' scene as international estate agency is from our traditional domestic variety. Put simply, the knowhow required is quite different. The fundamental advice is therefore, as always, to deal only with competent professionals, as in all other aspects of owning property in another country (see Useful Addresses for the address of the British Association of Removers).

It follows that you will only want to entrust your carefully selected valuables to an expert at overseas removals rather than just any common or garden remover whatever his reputation in your area. Such an expert will know that his everyday staff can cope with the complex and demanding job of finding their way through frontiers and the customs forms and formalities which still guard them.

How do you choose a remover? As in the case of choosing a property and an agent, you should start with a checklist.

Checklist

1 Does the remover regularly deliver to the country you will be moving to?

2 Does his price normally include genuine door-to-door service?

3 Does his price normally include professional packing?

4 Will special items, like antiques and paintings, be given special attention?

5 Will the job, or any part of it, be sub-contracted? If so, under what circumstances and to whom?

6 What method of transport will be used: air, road and sea, rail, containerised etc?

7 Does he offer a 'shared container' service, which can sometimes reduce costs and speed delivery?

8 Does he have storage capacity in Britain and in the destination country?

9 Can the remover guarantee to obtain and process every necessary piece of official paper required to secure easy and legal passage of your valuables?

10 Bank guarantees are sometimes needed to accompany imported goods. Does the remover handle these formalities if necessary? At what rate?

11 Is full insurance cover included in his offer, door to door?

12 Given the state of flux of European Community regulations, is the remover up to date with current requirements?

13 Does the remover take trouble with your personal requirements? Does he listen and respond to what you are saying? Does he tell you how to get the best deal from him? Can you comfortably see your most prized possession being packed, loaded, moved a few thousand

kilometres across sea, land and frontiers, and being unloaded and unpacked by this man's staff in your new home? Can you happily place your goods in his hands with confidence?

Estimates will undoubtedly vary and you should obtain more than one, unless you have a powerful reason not to do so, such as a personal recommendation from a friend or relative who has been moved by the company recently. It hardly needs emphasis that the cheapest quote is not always the best; but it cannot be taken for granted that a low price means a low quality of service. You will have to make the choice based upon your own judgement of whom you feel most happy with.

Finally, door-to-door service takes on a greater significance when one door is a few thousand kilometres away in another country. Remember that the remover has to find it. Very precise instructions are needed, and a map and where to get the key if you will not be on the spot to receive the delivery. New property on new estates are seldom numbered; often roads have no name signs. Old village houses often have no number or name. Farmhouses and barns in countryside and isolated property generally need the most detailed description to make for trouble-free delivery. Sometimes carelessly, and sometimes deliberately (because not all owners of overseas homes are innocent) removers are misled about access to the point of delivery. Essential information is sometimes overlooked or deliberately withheld. Please don't make their job more difficult than it already is.

10

MANAGEMENT OF INVESTMENTS

Planning your financial affairs well in advance is essential and my advice is to take expert advice. The friendly chap in a local bar is not a reliable source of guidance! You do not, of course, have to take expert advice on how to make your investments work for you. But there are some basic principles best discussed with professionals even if you wish to manage your investments yourself.

Taxation

If you intend to live in Andorra you will live tax free but if you intend to live anywhere else covered in this book you will have to pay some tax. Some countries encourage foreigners to settle with tax incentives or special treatment of one form or another. Any real estate agent will draw your attention immediately to any such benefits because they sometimes help him to sell property. But real estate agents are not tax advisers: they can only state the obvious. You will, therefore, pay tax wherever you go to live outside the tight borders of Andorra.

You must consider your position *vis-à-vis* the UK tax authorities. Like thoughts about health, thoughts about tax tend to lodge firmly in the back of the mind of those planning to go away: the back of the mind is the wrong place for such thoughts. Early consideration and thorough research can save money: sometimes you can legitimately arrange your affairs so that you actually make money too. By leaving it too late you can conversely pay more tax than would have been necessary simply because you took the wrong decisions or took no decisions at all.

UK Residency

You will be considered to be a resident of the UK for tax purposes if you place your foot upon British soil during any tax year if you are a non-working expatriate. This is not a serious problem unless you have failed to arrange your affairs according to the rules.

The rules which you need abide by are clearly (in civil servant's English) intended to prevent anyone paying less tax than the law requires – and ignorance is no defence. Your professional advisers will know what these rules are at any one time and they will be able to tell you the implications of any intentions you may have. If you remain resident in the UK then all of your income, regardless of source, all of your capital gains, wherever and however made, and all of your assets given to or inherited by others, no matter where the assets or the beneficiaries are located, are liable to the taxation regulations as they apply in detail at the time. Some people sometimes express surprise when this simple situation is brought to their notice.

The question of whether or not you would be regarded formally as 'resident' is subject to less than precise answers from experts because our tax legislation does not define the word in such common usage. The 'foot on English soil' image used earlier applies in some cases: 183 days – six months – spent in the UK continuously or on a number of visits during any one tax year applies at all times. If you spend ninety days only in Britain during a succession of tax years you will also without question be considered 'resident'. However, and this is where the ill-defined word is perhaps useful to the taxmen and the government, there are some exceptions allowed on a case-by-case basis. If you have worked abroad and intend to retire abroad you may be one of the exceptions – but only if you can prove it at all times – even though you have placed both feet on English soil frequently.

It is quite clear that if you live partly in Britain and partly in your retreat abroad you are 'resident' as far as the British tax authorities are concerned. You will pay tax accordingly by the British book on whatever you make, no matter how you make it, at the rates which apply.

It follows that your investments will be made against the background of your existing experience: your interest in a home abroad will simply be one of your assets but will not otherwise change the way you look at investments. Net rental income will, of course, be treated as income. The ill-defined status of 'resident' as far as the Inland Revenue is concerned refers to a tax year – not to a longer period.

Permanent Residency Abroad

Another condition without legal definition is that of 'permanent residence abroad'. The Inland Revenue, again on a case-by-case basis, can grant this status generally to those who have taken the decision to leave Britain, have sold their property here and have bought a home in their host country, not intending to leave Britain permanently but for a few years usually planning to return. Clearly the word 'permanent' does not mean what you would expect when applied to tax regulations.

Domiciled Abroad

Less flexible and generally more interesting for those who plan to quit the UK for good is the status of 'domicile'. The do-it-yourself or 'ignore it' school of expatriate living abroad has a lot to answer for in this situation. Many who left the UK in the seventies and eighties thought that they were no longer of interest to the UK tax authorities simply because they no longer lived here. But most of these optimists retained some sort of domicile in Britain which kept them trapped into our tax liabilities. This miserable condition was commonly the outcome of the very bar or café habitué's advice which you have been warned against. Advice of a professional quality would have made it clear that even leaving your toilet bag in your daughter's house would have provided proof that you had a pad available to you in Britain whenever required; and this is a costly mistake which a professional would have warned against.

The questions of status have been highlighted because until they are resolved according to your immediate and long-term intentions management of your investments remains academic. When you have made a number of decisions: whether the foreign home itself is your major investment overseas; whether you wish to make a number of investments in your host country; whether you want to play the Madrid Stockmarket the way you play Newmarket; whether you wish to invest solidly in one of the many plans produced by British-based financial services companies, after considering your tax responsibilities; you should be able to settle down to the fun of watching your investments fall in value, soar or stagnate. But the motto here, as in selecting your foreign home, is that nothing should be forever: do not get locked into investments which you cannot escape from.

A shaded terrace overlooking a spectacular view with a glass of something local within reach is not the place to get an ulcer.

11
HEALTH

Health is not a top priority of those who talk of motives with agents selling overseas property. Often the subject is not mentioned at all. But it is one of the major underlying reasons why people buy a resort home. Naturally, whether you discuss it freely or not, staying fit enough and staying alive long enough to enjoy your new life to the full is really what it is all about. Wanting a less pressured and more relaxed lifestyle, with more exercise, eating and drinking well but wisely and spending the maximum amount of time out of doors contribute to the all-important health factor.

Your body will need servicing and repairing as well as more careful driving as you grow older. It makes no sense to put this practical factor into the back of your mind as the majority of those who commit themselves to buying a home in another country for part- or full-time living do. Force yourself to plan this aspect of your future life so that it cannot become a worry later.

There are a number of options. You may simply rely upon the social services here and where you will be living. You may have set aside a hefty sum for your future healthcare. You may intend to join a local private clinic's treatment plan when you get around to it. But reciprocal healthcare arrangements via our NHS are based upon your acceptance of local standards in your host country. We can no longer claim that our system is the best in the world and any nation's healthcare system is subject to economic and political influences. Waiting lists are waiting lists in any language. Abroad, as here, money, the quality and quantity of staff and nursing levels are the obvious factors: less obvious, unless you have personal experience, is that nursing and practical care are geared to local cultural practice.

Medical Insurance
The local private clinic will provide the equivalent of BUPA-style accommodation and will accept payment before you leave as long as it's cash, cheque or credit card. As in the UK, surgeons,

anaesthetists, lab staff, physiotherapists etc present their own bills for immediate settlement.
   Medical insurance comes in many forms.

In-house Plans
Many private clinics run their own 'in-house plan' which covers treatment and surgery for acute medical conditions and, for example in Spain, work out at about £1 per day (subject always to upward inflationary pressures): this limits you to treatment in the group of participating clinics.

Host-country Plans
Medical insurers *in the host country* offer medical plans which provide for treatment and surgery at most private hospitals throughout that country.

UK Expatriate Plans
UK medical insurance companies, provident associations and friendly societies offer a variety of international medical plans to *permanent expatriates* for any area of the world which can include treatment back in the UK. These can be broadly divided into two types:

(a) An annual contract.
(b) An ongoing contract renewable at your request.

The relevance of a UK medical plan offering an on-going contract could mean little in the euphoria of embarking on a new lifestyle but private medical insurance is for the treatment of new, acute conditions and accidental damage. Those conditions which you already know about are not covered (although some plans bring them into cover after a period of stability); so the golden rule is to join at the earliest moment before any new conditions are diagnosed, and to pay on time every year to safeguard continuity of cover.
   Annual plans might seem more attractive as they can be approximately one-third cheaper than on-going arrangements; but some cease cover when you reach the age of seventy and others may decide that your previous year's claims were a little too high, adding a premium loading or even excluding future treatment for specific conditions.

UK Travel Plans

These are very useful to owners based in the UK who visit their overseas properties several times a year. There are many variations and the number and length of your trips will influence the best value plan for the forthcoming year. For those making more than two trips in twelve months an *annual travel plan* will offer good cover, eliminating the need to arrange separate cover for each trip (a maximum period of one hundred days for each visit is usual).

Choosing the Right Plan

European Community changes have encouraged medical insurers from both sides of the Channel to buy into one another's firms. A totally flexible, refundable and transferable Euro–Medical Plan for mobile and mature people will be marketed when costs have stabilised and standards equalise.

In the mean time, how do you work out what you need? You have to find out what is available and what makes you feel comfortable. This means asking the right questions. What is your preferred country's national healthcare structure? What are provisions like in practice? What is the usual standard of the rooms, the equipment, operating facilities and such like? Will you be fed and washed, or are these family tasks? If your command of the local language is less than total (under pressure it could improve dramatically – or not!) could this be a problem? What does the UK Department of Health advise regarding reciprocity at the time you need to make your plans?

Spain's healthcare provisions make it essential that all travellers and permanent residents budget for comprehensive private medical cover for peace of mind. France has a three-tier health insurance system and more structured hospital treatment facilities. Standards elsewhere vary. But if you are used to private healthcare in the UK and would not relish the idea of waiting months for a planned operation anywhere then the various private arrangements available should obviously be considered.

You will need to find the time to carry out this essential research, looking at the fine print of the UK's and your host country's medical insurance plans before coming to a decision. A serious international estate agent will be able to point you towards some of the answers to your questions. Medical care brokers and insurers are another source of information; but they have usually vested interests in selling the services they represent. An agency known as Healthcare Database Services provides an independent analysis of all the available plans: increasingly, they are being used to take the legwork out of the necessary research for intended buyers of overseas homes, saving time and energy.

Your future lifestyle depends upon feeling good. Make the enquiries now if you intend to spend more than a couple of weeks a year in a holiday home which you let for the rest of the year. Your decision should hold good for the rest of your lifetime and be flexible enough to enable you to enjoy it fully, wherever you are.

12
SELLING UP

Nothing is forever and you should think seriously about how easily you could expect to sell your resort home before you contract to buy it. This is fundamental not frivolous advice.

Market Demand

The probability is that the demand for resort homes in attractive areas of various countries and islands will continue to grow with occasional fluctuations. The demographic changes identified over the past couple of decades certainly ensure a steady stream of prosperous and active pensioners able to live where they please. The so-called middle classes are in any event earning more and keeping more. The increase in value of the average home in Britain during the mid-eighties has had a remarkable effect upon the level of inheritance benefits as well as enabling 'trading down' to release substantial funds for the purchase of second homes abroad. Redundancies on generous terms and voluntary early retirement are further factors which underpin general demand. And this demand comes not only from the UK (we are almost bottom of the demand league) but also from all other European countries. Demand from the ex-Eastern Bloc countries has yet to evolve into buying power but inevitably it will. All of this should give a degree of comfort if you have bought wisely or if you plan to do so.

Clearly there are fluctuations in this generally upward curve of demand for resort property. Countries, resort areas, specific locations, towns and areas go out of fashion. Golf courses and marinas make other areas fashionable; motorways and other access improvements affect localities and even regions. Political and social changes affect demand from time to time. Economic factors here, or abroad, can influence demand short term for good or ill: interest and exchange rates; the relative health of the property market here; how the stock market is performing; whether or not business confidence is high; whether or not government-to-government relationships are good also come into the picture.

Factors Influencing Property Sales

You can have no influence whatever over external considerations. But you can, by following the advice given earlier, choose your property intelligently, with an eye to its future saleability.

Regular Maintenance

You can also sensibly prepare for an eventual sale by keeping your property in good order and ensuring that your property taxes and other obligations are at all times paid when due. Essentially, your initial purchase documents should demonstrate that you bought the property in an orthodox manner, with properly imported funds; that the price recorded officially accorded with acceptable local custom and law (rather than risky expatriate custom and lore); and that the transfer of ownership to you was properly registered in the local equivalent of the Land Registry and wherever else necessary.

Future Development

More and more resort property will be created to add to the current supply as authorities release more land zoned for building in the existing and new resort areas. Concern for civilised environments generally, density controls, protection for areas of specific environmental importance, and the encouragement of high-quality development rather than mass-market projects are increasingly factors which are affecting and will affect what is built where. But there is no doubt that more land will be zoned for resort development within acceptable travel time from Europe's major population centres. And there is no doubt that developers will continue to risk time, effort and money to create new projects which they will promote internationally.

Finding a Buyer

When you decide to sell your resort home you will be competing with other individual owners who, like you, want to sell when you do; and you will be competing with developers who have to sell according to their forecasts and they are likely to be promoting their products aggressively and internationally. You would, therefore, sensibly conclude that you will have to compete with thousands of resort homes also looking for a buyer. With a vast selection of property for sale from Turkey to Le Touquet why should the prospective buyer choose yours?

Firstly, assuming that your paperwork is completely in order, you should think about the likely characteristics of your buyer. The simplest way to do this is to think about yourself. What are your characteristics and interests? How did these factors lead you to the country, area, specific location and actual ruin, country or village house, ski apartment, marina home, fairway or waterfront villa, house grouped around a pool with others, or low/high-rise apartment overlooking the Mediterranean. It will help you to draw the profile of your potential buyer if you can be quite clear about your own reasons for selecting the property in the first place. You will be looking for a buyer who reacts as you reacted and for similar reasons. The way in which you present the property to such a potential new owner should be reasonably easy and you should begin to define and refine your 'selling points' in order of importance according to your judgement of priorities. What appeals to you should appeal to someone like you.

Marketing

Having analysed the kind of buyer you aim to attract how do you propose to handle the marketing? Do you have the time and interest to do it yourself? The point has been made that no qualifications are necessary in order to sell resort property in another country to the British. You are not obliged to use an agent. But selling the property yourself really does take time and effort – and it costs money directly and indirectly – and you will in effect be temporarily in the business of international estate agency. Having profiled your prospective buyer you will then have to decide how you find him. If you are clear that he is like you then you should be able to find him through the same medium which led you to the property in the beginning. Clearly he is likely to read similar publications to those which you read.

You should be able to remember what it was about the original advertisement which attracted you to find out more about the property. If it was a few lines in the classified section of a national newspaper or a general or specialist magazine then you may initially be happy to follow the same simple advertising route. From reading the current advertisements you will easily select the wording which appeals to you. The basic information should be what it is, where it is, how much it is, and where and how you can be contacted, ideally at any time. You should budget for sufficient classified advertisements to bring you fifty enquiries at least, because you should reasonably work on the classical conversion ratio of two sales from one hundred enquiries for well-sited, well-built and well-promoted resort property in another country. You will not, of course, know how well your advertisement pulls until you have measured the response to the first insertion. This response will be affected by the state of the market and the other factors mentioned earlier in this chapter. It will also, clearly, be affected by the asking price of your property.

Setting the Asking Price

How do you set your asking price? In the case of mainstream resort property where there are other similar homes on an estate or in an apartment building then checking the prices of any on the market is relatively simple: you look and ask and decide on the level which you feel confident you can sell at happily. You should not assume, as human nature often suggests, that your own place is worth more than the others of a similar size, location and specification. Competitve homes around yours which compare in appeal, whether new or for resale, should also guide your price decision. If your home is non-standard, not on an estate or in a complex, or is an individual property of any kind then you should either pay for a valuation from a local professional or you should have a brave stab at judging the market price yourself. Property valuation is, in any event, something less than an exact science; amateur valuation naturally carries risks which you are either prepared to accept or not.

Property Details

Assuming that you have listed the 'selling points' of your home, how do you present them to prospective buyers? If you are to do a reasonable do-it-yourself marketing job then at the very least you will need the following:

- Good, clear photographs of the property (not at all the same thing as casual family snaps)
- A location map to show the area and its facilities
- A 'how to find it' map

- A clear description of your home expressing what you found and still find attractive about it and its surroundings etc
- A simple plan of the accommodation, showing the dimensions of the rooms and land if any
- A list of the legal documents, tax receipts and any other official paperwork in your possession.

Brochures from the local tourist office add something to your own material; they are usually readily available. The material should be put together logically in a dossier. And you should be ready to supply at least fifty of these dossiers to enquirers. You may be able to eliminate timewasters who telephone you in response to your advertisement by asking them the basic questions:

- Are you in the market now or are you thinking of buying in the future?
- Is this in the area you prefer?
- Is it the kind of accommodation which you need?
- Is the price within your limit?
- When could you visit the property?

When the enquirers have received your material you should then follow up your mailing by telephone for maximum efficiency, with an offer to answer any questions prompted by the material. Plainly, you have some key questions for them at this point. 'Are you interested in the property?' 'Shall we meet to talk about it?' 'When can you visit the place?' 'Shall we set a date for your visit, so that we can meet there?'

When you reach the point at which some prospective buyers are interested enough to visit the property then you will have to plan the way in which you would best like to present your actual home to the people whom you hope will live in it after you. There are some advantages at this stage in opting for the do-it-yourself approach. You have only one property to sell and you will give it your full attention.

Viewing
There are still plenty of estate agents who will say fatuously upon showing a prospective buyer a room with a bath, a shower, a bidet, a lavatory and a washbasin: 'This is the bathroom.' What you should say is, for example, that the water pressure is strong, that the water heater is effective, that you only need the radiator on for a few weeks a year and that the plumbing does not groan or knock when you turn on the taps or flush the loo. It follows that a demonstration

of these basics helps prove your points. If none of these statements is true then you should either say so, not mention them, or think of something else to say, according to your nature.

Your home is best presented with the basics first: hall, bathrooms and kitchen, then the bedrooms, and finally the dining-room or area, the living-room and the terrace, balcony or patio. At this point you should offer the prospective buyers a comfortable seat overlooking your view, indoors or out, in sun or shade depending upon the relaxed point you wish to make. Conversation should then take place with a drink in hand according to taste. You should lead the conversation through your various selling points concerning the country, the area, the locality and what specially appealed to you when you bought the place, what if any changes you have made and why you are now selling. If you can at this point arrange for a few favoured friends and neighbours to join you so much the better. The key word here is conversation: this should not be a monologue – the buyers should be encouraged to talk about their expectations and interests. If you plan the sequence well a meal together on your terrace or wherever is most attractive within the home, or locally in a restaurant where you are well known should enable you to get to know each other suitably.

If you live permanently in the property then the planning of your marketing will need to be adjusted so that you carry out the advertising and mailing and the follow-up routines from afar. Clearly, the do-it-yourself approach is cheap and effective only if you do not cost your time and effort into the marketing and if you are willing and able to devote yourself seriously to the task. Many people consider that it is a simple matter to sell their valuable resort property; that a queue of buyers will appear, desperate to secure such a prize, with money in hand; and that the whole process will be concluded in no time at all. If it was as easy as that then there would be nothing to support the thousands of estate agents in the resort areas and in Britain and elsewhere who provide a service which the vast majority of buyers and sellers need – and willingly pay for – at commission rates which seem high by the standards of residential sales here.

Using an Agent

International estate agents and those licensed to sell in resort areas charge much higher commission rates than we are accustomed to paying in Britain. You should allow 10 per cent of the purchase price before tax. You will know, having bought a home in another country, that VAT or the local equivalent, or a buying tax of some kind is levied by most governments on the transfer of ownership of real estate. Some people, out of touch with reality or tempted to shave a few points off everything they buy, become argumentative or even abusive when told that the standard terms for selling a secondhand home are either side of this 10 per cent rate. If such commissions are likely to cause you pain then the solution to the problem is plainly to market your home yourself. Estate agents will sometimes tolerate awkward buyers but they seldom welcome difficult sellers.

How do you choose the agent who will give you the service you need? Firstly, you have been warned off buying from friendly expatriates in bars: under no circumstances should you be tempted to sell through them either. If you decide to use a local agent then make sure that he is properly licensed if the law requires it, or is a member of a legitimate trade body if the law does not require agents to hold a licence. If you are unimpressed by the agent's office, display material, staff or personality then go somewhere else. It is essential that you have confidence in him personally: he will effectively be representing you and you are his client, not the prospective buyer. He will tell you what he considers a reasonable price for your property. He will, if pressed, tell you how long it should take to sell the home. It is wise to ask him twice, emphasising that you would prefer a realistic rather than an optimistic answer. He will expect you to sign a written agency agreement. You may be asked to sign a Power of Attorney (under whatever local name) but never give anyone Power of Attorney unless your lawyer confirms, in writing, that it is both essential and safe to do so. Having signed an agreement you then wait patiently or impatiently for the buyer to be found.

If you do not live permanently in the property then the agent will need keys to gain access. If you are not happy to place the keys into the hands of your agent, and his staff, then you should find an agent in whom you have the necessary trust. Reliable neighbours are sometimes given this responsibility but sales have been lost by this routine: if the key is not available when the potential buyer calls then the agent will, quite reasonably, take the buyer elsewhere.

There are clear advantages in giving your property to an agent who is on the spot. He is around during or outside working hours; he knows how to sell the locality; he may have associations with agents in other countries who send him potential buyers; and he lives and works in the area in which your buyer would be living if he bought your property – sometimes a suitable curb on sharp selling practices. However, estate agents in the resort areas sometimes have such an agreeable lifestyle that they do not diligently chase the chance of making another sale. The unhurried pace of life in your chosen location may well have been a major reason for you having selected it originally but you may feel happier to think that the agent you favour with your business is dedicated to the pursuit of profit at all times.

Instead of granting selling rights to a local agent you may prefer the simple commercial approach of a British agent who specialises in your foreign locality and who is happy to accept instructions to sell desirable resale property to potential buyers whom he may already have on his list. A phone call to a number of specialists will enable you to decide which ones you should visit: their response to your phone call is indicative of how they would receive calls from potential buyers. Visiting the shortlisted agents is essential unless distance makes it too difficult for you. You should take or memorise the selling points which you have prepared, and the supporting paperwork so that you can effectively present your property clearly and in such a way that the agent has the full picture. You will need to convince the agent that he can sell your home profitably and in a reasonable timescale. You can be sure that he will react positively to the challenge of selling a well-sited, well-built, well-maintained and well-priced property in his chosen area if the documentation is in order. Anything short of enthusiasm on his part requires an explanation. The market may be flat. He may feel that the property would be difficult to move. There may be too many similar homes on the market in the area at the same time. He may prefer to offer new property. Whatever the explanation for anything less than firm interest you should respond accordingly and go elsewhere.

The people you select will do all of those things which you would have done had you decided to market the property yourself but with some variations. It is unlikely that your property will be individually advertised unless you make specific arrangements for this to be done. It is not likely that the agent will spend as much time in your property with a potential buyer as you would have. But he may actually accompany the prospect from the UK to the locality on an organised inspection trip. Or he may make arrangements to meet the prospect locally if independent travel has been fixed. Alternatively, the agent may have an association with a local agent who will attend to the potential buyer. Spanish regulations do not permit anyone to show a home for sale to a prospect except its owner or a licensed agent but this rarely causes difficulties because no legitimate British agent would contravene this requirement.

Legal Advice

Unless you were unhappy with him at the time it is reasonable for you to instruct the same lawyer to handle your sale as dealt with your purchase. He is likely to be clear about any legal or fiscal changes which have taken place since your original purchase. Capital Gains Tax, under whatever local name, is payable in Europe. 1 Community countries regardless of whether or not the property is your only, principal or second home. Some countries outside the EC do not levy any form of Capital Gains Tax on non-resident foreign owners in order to attract buyers of resort homes. Others are even more generous. But you should be aware that governments exist partly to make new laws and sometimes these new laws are enacted in order to remove tax concessions when their purpose has been achieved. They may have been a contributory factor in your selection of the country as the location of your property or domicile originally. Your specialised lawyer will be up to date on current legislation on this and other relevant matters.

Repatriating Your Funds

Your lawyer will also know when and how you can repatriate your sale proceeds if that is what you wish to do. Greater freedom of capital movement within the European Community means that you are given considerable choice about where to transfer your capital if it is not to be used to buy another home. Advice on this is outside the scope of this book. However, you should have enjoyed the whole process of dreaming about, considering, selecting and living in your resort home. You should have picked the perfect place for your own personality. You should have had fun, because owning a resort home is about nothing else. You should have fond memories and an enriched spirit as a result of your ownership. And, if you bought wisely, you should have made a reasonable profit as a bonus on top of all the other benefits which you have enjoyed.

Part II

The Countries

13

ISLANDS

We are told as children that we are an island race. The brainwashing begins at school in the most elementary history lessons. This actually means no more than the fact that Britain is surrounded by water. Most people are quite unaffected by this phenomenon one way or the other. In any event, more Dutchmen, Belgians and Danes live closer to the sea than do most British people. However, some are deeply affected by this fact and a piece of land surrounded by water has an almost mystical effect upon them. This condition is recognised but no rational explanation for it has ever been advanced. How could there possibly be a rational reason for wanting to live on the Falklands? Or Lanzarote? Deep in our psyche there may be something atavistic and aquatic to explain this illogical attraction. Or the answer may be a cellular defect like those with an extra chromosome which dooms them to a life of criminality.

Whatever the cause a simple cure is available to some who are not permanently affected by their condition. Buy a home on an island and live there for a winter: your condition will either be confirmed by the experience or you will leave without a backward glance, having placed your island home on the market to await another romantic. However, nothing is forever; and if you are compelled by some inner urge to buy a home on an island then buy wisely so that you can sell readily if you need to. There will always be a steady supply of island-lovers.

If you have the urge then it is best tempered by practicalities. Assuming that travel time to your island is acceptable to you (or unimportant if you are retiring) then getting on and off should be easy enough to enable you to come and go just when you feel the need to do so. Ideally it should be a stepping stone – not Alcatraz! But even a stepping stone should not be too small for comfort. Getting on and off a small island easily by plane could mean that you can never escape from aircraft noise. And the five winds of the Mediterranean mean that flightpaths often have to be changed to accommodate their vagaries. Islands and wind are, in any event, synonymous and you should choose the location and orientation of your home accordingly.

In this chapter some islands within reach of the UK have been omitted from those described, not because they are unattractive but because they are impractical places to live. Madeira, for example, took more than a century to move out of the category of an island for rich eccentrics when access by plane became easier in the eighties. Its neighbour, the beach-fringed delight of Porto Santo, was opened up for development by its new airport during the same decade. Both are, however, isolated.

Sicily is isolated by reputation: it is omitted from this chapter because it has an image which deters any but the very curious would-be property owner. Change is expected to be as slow in the future as it has been in the past.

The Greek islands will undoubtedly become the up-market playground of the future, representing the Mediterranean's expansion area. Ease of access will be the pre-condition as elsewhere. But, at present, practical home ownership by foreigners on these magical islands is hardly an easy option. Rhodes and Crete are similarly considered out of the mainstream in spite of their size and current tourist industries.

The Turkish islands await a period of credible democracy before they can be considered locations for resort development. The same applies to the other potentially fascinating area for civilised living – the islands off the coast of what we still call Yugoslavia. There are, in the mean time, plenty of prime locations for those who are unable to resist island living.

The Canary Islands

This group of islands off the African coast in the Gulf Stream are the stuff of legends. Are they the remains of Atlantis after a series of earthquakes and volcanic eruptions many thousands of years ago? Where did the Guanches, the original fair-skinned, tall, blue-eyed, fair-haired inhabitants come from? They lived a Stone Age existence in caves, embalmed and mummified their dead and originated a staple food and children's games which still exist on the islands.

The first European and Arab visitors to the Canaries a couple of thousand years ago were impressed: they gave them the name

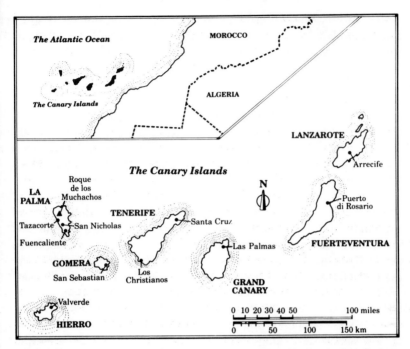

of the Fortunate Isles. The natives were friendly and the climate benign. Seven major islands of different character spread over a distance of 480km (300miles) of the Atlantic were on the routes to other more important places, without being worthy of conquest until the fifteenth century. Then the Spaniards took the best part of a hundred years to overcome the apparently primitive Guanches. Clearly the cave-dwellers were no pushover and the conquest was further complicated by the appeal of the islands to Portugal; naval battles between the two maritime powers were frequent until the dispute was settled by treaty, leaving the Spanish a clear run in their campaign to subdue the islands. One by one the Canaries fell to the Spaniards with Tenerife the last to be overcome.

While the battles for La Palma and Tenerife were still raging the first of the truly famous visitors to the Canaries was loading supplies of food and water on newly subdued Gomera for his attempt to find a shortcut to the East by travelling west. The tradewinds which took Columbus to the Americas later took Spanish enterprise in the same direction, including bananas for planting in the Caribbean and Canarians who settled in Central and South America. The economy of the islands developed from their geographical position, as staging posts, and from their climate and fertile soil, as producers of sugar (until hit by undercutting from the new colonies in the Caribbean), Malmsey wine (well publicised by Shakespeare and Voltaire) and bananas and other early fruit and vegetables for growing European markets.

The prospect of loot inevitably attracted pirates, privateers and Horatio Nelson by the end of the eighteenth century. Hoping to capture a Spanish ship with a cargo of treasure in the harbour of Santa Cruz de Tenerife, Nelson lost his battle with the defenders, 226 of his sailors and his arm. His name is remembered in Santa Cruz by a street named after him, Calle de Horatio Nelson.

To assist the islands out of their economic doldrums in the mid-nineteenth century the Spanish authorities enacted a far-reaching law which conferred upon them Free Port status. This act enabled the ports of Santa Cruz and Las Palmas to achieve international importance. Georgian sash windows on some houses on Tenerife testify to the growing number of British traders who had business in the islands. Tourism of a sort began to follow trade and the Yeoward family shipping line from Liverpool began offering three-week cruises taking in Lisbon, Madeira and the Canaries at a first class fare of 8 guineas (the family is still active on the islands as shippers, plantation owners and developers, with a street in Puerto de la Cruz and a school bearing their name).

In the twenties the Spanish Government granted the islands the title of Provinces of Spain, separating them into two entities, with Santa Cruz as capital of the four western isles and Las Palmas as capital of the eastern group. In the mid-thirties the Spanish Government sidelined a troublesome young general by giving him a command away from the centre of events, appointing him Captain General of the Canary Islands. Plotters came to him, however, resulting in his agreement to support a revolt against the elected government. With the help of a British businessman, who hired a British plane and pilot, General Franco flew from his base on Tenerife to the Spanish enclave in North Africa, mobilised his Spanish troops and Moorish mercenaries and began the Spanish Civil War. Franco soon assumed leadership of the insurgents and won the conflict with practical assistance from Hitler and Mussolini. His victory and his obligations denied the Allies use of the Canaries during the many battles of the Atlantic.

After fifteen years of international isolation Spain was given membership of the United Nations as part of the horse-trading which proved necessary during the Cold War between East and West. Trade and tourism flourished in the islands, with some benefitting more than others throughout the sixties and seventies. The ports of Santa Cruz de Tenerife and Las Palmas on Gran Canaria thrived: within ten years the tonnage handled by Santa Cruz doubled. Hotels and tourist complexes were built; airports were built or upgraded; different crops were planted to accommodate the tourists' tastes and those of European markets. With a more confident democracy in Spain during the eighties the Canaries were granted political autonomy.

The various and varied islands have obvious climatic and other advantages to attract buyers of resort property. The larger and more developed of the seven main islands have all the necessary services and facilities for a civilised lifestyle and in some areas all the usual problems associated with rapid and careless tourist development. But if your future life includes exercising curiosity about history and nature, and if you intend to use your future home as a base for exploration and mild adventure, then the islands off the North African coast hold enough interest and variety to enable you to enjoy life to the full.

Gran Canaria

The name is misleading: two other islands in the group are larger than Gran Canaria. But it looks grand enough from any angle with its high point 2,000m (6,000ft) above sea level; and its population of 600,000 is as many as that of the other Canary Islands put together. Its capital Las Palmas is the largest city of the islands, the largest port and the administrative centre of the province: it has a population of around 350,000.

Gran Canaria has magnificent beaches, some of black and some of blond sand, rocky coves and towering cliffs. It has Sahara-like sand dunes, ideal as locations for filming Westerns; vast banana plantations; productive agricultural land; plains; valleys; forested uplands and jagged peaks. It is possible to become red-nosed from the sun on a south-coast beach and red-nosed from the frost on a mountainside during the same day. It has a few boring stretches of landscape and many breathtaking vistas.

Gran Canaria was commercially colonised by the British in the

1880s. Shipping companies developed the port of La Luz and settled the island with owners' families happily enjoying the climate and the natural beauty, building the first golf course on Spanish territory and watching the port grow into one of the most important in the world. Rust-streaked tramp steamers from Greece, immaculate cruise-ships, oil tankers and Russian fish-factories line the docks today and their crews take shore leave in the cosmopolitan city of Las Palmas: part resort, part working city and part bazaar for the islands importing free-trade goods. Pidgin English is the common language between the sailors from every seafaring nation and waiters, barmen and shopkeepers. This lively city is regarded by foreign homeowners on the island as a bonus to be added to their lives on the hillsides or along the varied coastline.

Columbus was the first notable sailor to make use of the port in 1492, on his way, he thought, to the East Indies. He returned in 1493 having discovered the Americas. He is well remembered in the Casa de Colon (the House of Columbus) which was where he stayed as guest of the island's first governor Pedro de Vera. The house, built gracefully around a patio, is now a museum commemorating the exciting period of Spanish adventure with displays of nautical artefacts of the time.

Las Palmas contains most of the artistic and cultural relics of the island's past. Operas, orchestral concerts and plays are regularly staged. In addition to tourist tat all the needs for civilised living can be purchased here. Lawyers, bankers and medical services consistent with the requirements of over half a million people also exist. All-night discos swing for those who need them. And the vast open-air café in Santa Catalina Park opposite the pier is one of the wonders of the world, serving all nationalities at all hours.

But Las Palmas is clearly not all that Gran Canaria has to offer anyone living or staying on the island. The motorway south from the capital mercifully enables you to pass a stretch of boring countryside quickly until mountains loom enticingly in the distance before reaching the famous 16km (10 mile) beach of golden sand. Stretching from San Augustin to the lighthouse at Maspalomas this beach, on the southernmost tip of the island, is halfway to Miami in character, with hamburger joints, high-rise buildings, a casino and all the other usual development to be expected along an accessible big beach.

The dunes of Maspalomas are, however, unspoiled. This freak

of nature is spectacularly and sometimes blindingly beautiful. The coves beyond are being developed less rapaciously with property on a more human scale. There is a golf course in the hinterland and a marina at Puerto Rico. At this point the road leaves the coast for practical reasons – the terrain is simply too rugged – and heads inland. If you are of a nervous disposition this is the time to retrace your route rather than tackle the hairy mountain road with its miles of bends.

The northern coastal area is greener for the same reason that the northern coastal area of Tenerife is greener: there is more rainfall. This is banana country and central to the coast is the island's banana capital, the attractive old town of Arucas, dominated by an enormous, out-of-scale cathedral built this century in neo-Gothic style. Plantations cover the hillsides, sloping to the sea for mile after mile.

Inland are caves, some inhabited, complete with water and electricity, in magical mountain settings. There are more caves near the coast, hundreds of them in a kind of cave-dwellers' village, where maidens were confined, according to legend, until they were thirty-five years old when they were permitted the choice of either leaving the colony to marry or remaining forever.

Residents regard the black-beached Puerto de las Nieves as a romantic spot to visit between the formidable cliffs of the western flank of this coastline. It has a small fishing fleet in a maze-like harbour and is below the town of Agaete about 1km (⅝ mile) inland.

The centre of the island is reached by careful driving over hairpinned mountain roads. Dramatic scenery, pine forests, sheer drops, panoramic vistas, almond blossom in February, old towns and the unreal crater, 1km (⅝ mile) across, of Bandama, with a farm, surrounded by green fields, over 200m (655ft) below on its floor: these and other delights await the adventurous motorist. There is a romantically sited, isolated, state-run parador at Cruz de Tejeda for those wishing to rest from the concentration of driving.

As a place to live permanently or semi-permanently Gran Canaria is big enough and interesting enough, with great contrasts of rural peace, mountain isolation, beach activity and the benefits of a lively city, to commend itself to anyone who is not moved by the Balearics or the other somewhat less civilised Canaries. Santa Brigida, half an hour or so inland from Las Palmas, in the hills, with a soft climate, is still favoured as a location for permanent living. The coast is the coast and will always appeal to those who need to be by the sea.

Lanzarote
By the standards of almost anywhere else you could imagine this island deserves ridicule as a place to buy a resort home. It resembles a slag heap as featured in the brochure of a company which specialises in the rehabilitation of derelict land.

Lanzarote has a volcano for each of its 300 square miles. It has black volcanic ash instead of topsoil and its beaches look like coal dust. There is no natural water except the dew. Those visitors who make the trip to the Montanas de Fuego (the Fire Mountains) to see the 'badlands' of spiky rock and desert never book a second trip. Beneath its surface the island is actually on fire: a local gimmick is to ram a metal pipe into the ground, pour water down it and watch the jet of steam blast up into the air. The wind-blown dust scours.

But it has its admirers. Massive investment by the Rio Tinto group, ERT Union Explosives Rio Tinto SA, in the early seventies was intended to create 'Europe's finest development' on 8km (5 miles) of ocean-front on the island's south-east coast five minutes' drive north from the capital Arrecife. This group was Spain's largest private company at the time and it had the capability to produce an ambitious masterplan and implement much of it in advance of property sales (but the intended twenty-seven holes of golf designed by British golf architect John Harris still has eighteen holes unbuilt). A five-star hotel was built to set the up-market image. A Lanzarote-born artist, Cesar Manrigue was appointed aesthetic director. No less than thirteen hotels were planned in the first phase and thousands of villas and apartments. A staggering 30km (18½ miles) of roads had been built by the mid-seventies. Electricity generating plants, sewage purification plants and desalination plants were constructed. But, as with other over-ambitious projects aimed at a poorly understood market, sales did not keep pace with expectation. Inevitably changes were made; sites were sold off to other developers; the largest private company in Spain ran into difficulties. The upshot was that Costa Teguise took shape at a slower than intended rate and remained a construction site for many years longer than early purchasers expected.

But there is more to the island than the sum of its unattractive natural features. Its geographical location gives a guaranteed year-round climate which is never cold nor too hot. Humidity is low. It was settled by the Spanish in the fifteenth century and its inhabitants, about 60,000 in number, are traditionally fishermen and farmers who eat, drink and make merry with gusto. Its capital is bright and lively with the most important fishing port in the Canaries as its focal point. The old capital, Teguise, is almost entirely sixteenth century and is a designated national monument, with a fifteenth-century castle and a restored palace as a centrepiece. The island's high point is 675m (2,000ft) above sea level. Much of the land is, in fact, strangely farmed: individually planted vines and tomato plants in bowls of volcanic ash, like craters, are an almost hypnotic antidote to the general air of desolation. And there is an oasis-like Valley of the Ten Thousand Palms in the north of the island near Haria.

Large areas of Lanzarote are surprisingly fertile and green from crops which rely on the porous volcanic cinders to absorb the nightly dew. Green is also the general colour of the sea in the island's many lagoons and grottos. Some of the caves have become renowned for their size, natural grandeur and man-made enhancement. Los Verdes, originally an outlet for molten lava, is a tunnel some 7km (4 miles) in length opening to the sea. In the Jameos del Agua grotto the sculptor Cesar Manrique has created a romantic restaurant overlooking the clear water, with soft mood music and lush landscaping to complement nature.

Nature needs complementing on Lanzarote. Where man has created a visual change the appearance has almost invariably been improved. White houses in Moorish-looking villages; geometrically planted vines, tomatoes, potatoes and onions; the white glare from salt-pans; some resort building (height limits apply) in keeping with tradition, with white walls and green-painted woodwork externally; oversized swimming pools and areas of lush landscaping: these provide the visual relief to the otherwise harsh environment.

Sun-worshippers find Lanzarote close to ideal for their purposes; so do enthusiastic bathers. The beaches along the south-eastern facing coastline vary in quality and colour but are generally wide and deep reflecting the slope of the land on this side of the island. The quality of development is mixed beside the clear water of the Atlantic. Facilities are provided for underwater swimming, sailing and fishing from boats both inshore and deep sea. Surfing conditions exist on the northern side of the island.

There are local Spanish and international restaurants with the benefit of fresh, high-quality local fish, fruit and vegetables. Most meat is imported. The local wine is strong at 20 degrees and sweet in the Malmsey manner; every other imported drink imaginable is available at reasonable prices from the many supermarkets which have been established to serve the appetites of the holiday visitors.

Holiday property – either villas, apartments or grouped housing – is the standard here rather than homes for permanent or semi-permanent living. Lanzarote is almost 58km long and 21km at its widest (36 × 13 miles) a little larger than Ibiza with a similar number of inhabitants. It is therefore large enough to be considered as a living space by expatriates. But you would need to satisfy yourself that you could literally live with the landscape and the less than comprehensive facilities.

Tenerife

The approach to Tenerife is impressive at any time, either by sea or air. But to fly into the island when the cloud stops halfway up Mount Teide, and to see the conical top of the highest mountain on Spanish territory rising sunlit through the cloud from a hundred miles out, with its snow-cap glistening brightly, is an experience to be remembered. Teide is Tenerife, reaching 3,700m (12,140ft) above sea level, and like an iceberg there is more of it below the surface. It is three times the height of Ben Nevis and from sea level to summit has climate and vegetation which varies from sub-tropical to that of the Highlands of Scotland.

Physically, the island is enormously varied: high, forbidding cliffs, broad bays and narrow inlets; black, grey and khaki beaches; interminable banana plantations on gentle slopes; productive, well-watered fields of tomatoes and potatoes in the valleys; pine, beech and eucalyptus woods on Teide; misty heathland with stone outcrops; and sharp and unwelcoming rock formations in volcanic deserts. At sea level unbelievably exotic flowers and shrubs thrive; lichen and damp mosses grow above the tree line.

Tenerife is the largest of the Canaries at 1,265sq km (790sq miles). Few of the 450,000 inhabitants live on the mountain as the capital, Santa Cruz, accommodates over 200,000. Most of the remainder live and work along the fertile northern coast and amongst its valleys. More and more are now being pulled towards the employment opportunities created on the south coast by the opening of the new airport there during the eighties, the construction of the new coast road and the consequent boom in tourist development in what was previously an underexploited area.

The island's climate throughout the year has been its attraction for centuries, beginning with the visitors who arrived during the days of sail and culminating in the holiday development boom along its south coast during the eighties. It is indeed 'springlike' by the standards of our own climate, with only about 7°C difference between the average of high and low temperatures, ignoring the effects of altitude. Morning cloud cover over the north of the island is comforting for some and irritating for others. As in other resort islands sea breezes are bracing at times. The climate is regarded as healthy by long-term residents particularly those who are members of the old-established English Club overlooking Puerto de la Cruz, founded in Edwardian times by earlier settlers.

It would be correct to refer to the climate in the plural: there are many climates on the island; the north is wetter and more inclined to cloud cover than the drier, breezier south; and the altitude determines the temperature. It is therefore perfectly possible, at almost any time, to get into your car and drive somewhere else to experience a climatic change and a change in the vegetation too.

Overlooking Puerto is another demonstration of the equable climate of Tenerife: the Gardens of Acclimatisation, known more colloquially as the Botanical Gardens. Created by Royal Decree in 1788, this marvellously managed collection of flora was used practically to acclimatise plants, shrubs and trees from the New World before being transplanted in the gardens of the Old World. But the soft climate results in exotic flora in more everyday settings too. Any roadside verge or garden is likely to smell and look good with mimosa and honeysuckle, palms and pines, frangipani and jacaranda, poinsettia and bougainvillaea and the appropriately named Bird of Paradise flower.

The fact that the island is effectively and efficiently the market garden of Europe is another demonstration of its climate. Tenerife tomatoes occupy shelf space in your local Marks & Spencer's and potatoes from the island are to be found in every greengrocer's in Britain. Banana plantations have centuries-old traditions and give a tropical lushness to the landscape below the slopes of Teide. Those who were children during the blockaded forties may recall the excitement when the first consignment of bananas for some years got through the cordon of U-boats. The story made headlines; queues formed; and children had to discover how to get past the unfamiliar skin to reach the fruit – these welcome symbols of normality came from Tenerife. Paradoxically, Franco is reputed to have allowed a number of ex-Nazis sanctuary on Tenerife after World War II on condition that they adopted a low profile; some, it is said, went into the banana business, building homes in the middle of their plantations, and protecting their privacy with gun-wielding guards and unfriendly dogs.

Tenerife is shaped like a ham hock with the port and capital of Santa Cruz, the old capital of La Laguna, the old airport, the old golf course and most of the population at the tapered end. This was where most of the island's life was concentrated before mass tourism brought about demographic changes. It remains the centre of commercial and administrative activity; but most of the millions of visitors travel in the other direction after arriving at the new airport 50km (30 miles) away and many fail to make the journey from their holiday hotels or apartments to this end of the island.

Development of the southern coast during the earlier boom in the sixties and seventies was inhibited by awkward access from the old airport. The new airport, located almost as far south as it's possible to go, and the infrastructure which serves it, had the intended catalyst effect on this part of the island even before it opened for use in the early eighties. Growth has been spectacular, generally directed at the lower end of the mass market. As a result Playa de las America now joins the list of resorts – Torremolinos, San Antonio, Benidorm and Magaluf – which are best left to the young, noisy and sleepless.

There are, however, some outposts of civilised resort development here. A couple of golf complexes on the optimistically named Costa del Silencio are too close to the flightpath for nervous putters; but the environment is improved by 50ha (125 acres) of fairways, greens and tees. The principle of big beaches meaning low-grade development and small beaches meaning higher-grade development applies along this coastline. Generally, the nearer you get to Los Gigantes the higher the quality of property: towering cliffs mark the limit of the coast road and the end of practical resort projects. The choice of property from the airport to Los Gigantes is plentiful in the holiday-home range and limited in the permanent-home range although this situation is likely to improve as the result of the usual evolutionary trends in resort areas.

The evolutionary trends of the previous generation can easily be seen in and around Puerto de la Cruz, the original point from which Canarian wines were shipped to Britain. In the late fifties and early sixties packaged tourism to the Canaries effectively began here; so did the sale of resort homes for those looking for a sea view in almost eternal spring. Four five-star and twenty-one four-star hotels indicate clearly that, in the case of Puerto, packaged tourism was not for the masses looking for two weeks in the sun in August. Puerto was for the well-off wanting a month or two of winter sun while being cared for as if they were on a cruise-liner. There is an English School, an Anglican Church, and a British Club and Library, all of long pedigree, and a casino. There were no easy ways to enter the sea for bathing – not a priority for the earlier clientele – until it became commercially obvious that the hotels should aim for year-round occupancy: then an ambitious lido was built on the waterfront to provide artificially what nature had overlooked.

Puerto is a bazaar, selling the usual tourist tat from narrow-fronted shops, with a tiny fishing harbour, an attractive main square and an old quarter of narrow streets and elaborate doors and balconies. Property around the town for sale to newcomers is generally well built but lacking in eye appeal compared to other resort areas around the Mediterranean. But to some the orderly suburban atmosphere of the bungalows and apartments, with neatly nurtured gardens is comforting and appealing.

La Orotava is a pleasantly situated city behind Puerto in the lush, broad valley of the same name. Steep streets, graceful parks, houses dating from the sixteenth century with intricate craftsmanship on balconies, doors and windowframes, and flowers everywhere: these give the city its unique identity. Most of the old property is clearly well loved by its occupants. Some venerable houses reach the agents' inventories but not for long.

The long northern coast is given over to banana plantations and efficient market gardens, occasional fishing ports and a few tourist developments. With the focus now on the sunnier southern coast further large-scale development in the north is unlikely. The expansion of Puerto was due to the proximity of the old airport in the north. The new one is about an hour and a half by car from Puerto and there is no direct route. But the growth in tourist development in the south has been primarily at the lowest common denominator end of the market: some is truly appalling by today's supposedly more civilised standards. If the north coast is to be left alone it will become a more agreeable place to live. A long ride to and from the airport is hardly a disadvantage if you only need to make the journey rarely. Holiday accommodation needs to be on the south coast and easily accessible from the airport. Homes for more permanent living are better located on the north coast until residential quality development begins to be created inland away from the disappointing ambience of the big resorts, and until overall facilities match those of the Puerto area.

Local produce is of the highest quality and the fish from the Atlantic is staggering in its variety compared to the normal selection offered on our fishmongers' counters. Tenerife is not a gourmet's paradise but nobody dedicated to the pleasures of eating should be bored by food without flavour; and complaints about small portions are never voiced. Local restaurants serving local dishes need to be sought out. Gofio was the staple ingredient in prehistoric times on Tenerife, and today it is added as a thickener to vegetable soups and stews: it is toasted wholemeal or maizemeal. Potatoes baked in salt in their skins and eaten whole with the piquant sauce, mojo picon (oil, garlic, hot peppers and saffron), are a simple delicacy for those who have forgotten the flavour of real spuds. This hot and tangy sauce is the local accompaniment for Sancocho, the famous sea-bass stew. Grilled swordfish steaks, octopus cooked in various ways, all the usual shellfish and some which will be new to you are all readily available.

All the customary brand-name wines are available on the island, but local wines should be specifically sought out. In the days of Good Queen Bess wines from the Canaries were on the Court's dining-table. Sweet Malmsey and Muscatel are no longer fashionable drinks but they add something special to simple desserts. Non-tourist bars and restaurants still offer wine from nearby, often in a jug or a handy bottle, drawn from a cask in the cellar. Acceptable rum is distilled on the island and a banana-based liqueur has some fans. Supermarket shelves on Tenerife carry a greater selection of beers, wines and spirits than you are likely to find in your best winemerchant and bargain prices are still the norm.

There may be some truth in the oversimplification that the British buyer of property on the northern coast, like the clientele of the four- and five-star hotels there, was likely to be a conventional, conservative character; and the buyer of an apartment on the southern coast was likely to be a self-employed scaffolder. This snobbish attitude is changing as the resort property business on the island continues to evolve. Fortunately Tenerife is large enough to accommodate the brash southern resorts and the more sedate and older spots around Puerto.

Fuerteventura

Fuerteventura is considered the resort island of the future. The same opinion was expressed in the early sixties, the early seventies and the early eighties. It is 96km (60 miles) from the North African coast, about 2,000sq km (780sq miles) in area, and looks from the air like a long, long sand dune which belongs in the Sahara rather than in the sea. The island was originally a green and pleasant land before it was overgrazed by imported cattle, sheep and goats: now it is parched and eroded with occasional oases of palms, stunted eucalyptus, potato patches and tomato plants.

Not a lot happens here either for the 25,000 or so locals (who prefer to be known as Majoreros like their primitive ancestors) or for the visitors who arrive by charter plane. But it will eventually be a resort of some special identity if the golf complexes and up-market developments mooted ever materialise.

The island's capital and major port used to be called Puerto Cabra which means Port of the Goat. Developers with an eye to the future potential of the island arranged for it to be changed to Puerto de Rosario which means Port of the Rosary. This was a presumptious change for an unassuming, if not scruffy, little town. But eventually you can be clear that the town itself will change to fit its new name when the inevitable development of Fuerteventura takes place. Serious money tied up speculatively in very substantial tracts of the coast effectively ensures that it will happen.

By the late eighties around 20,000 British were holidaying on Fuerteventura annually for the usual couple of weeks in the sun. This compares with 1 million travelling to Tenerife and over a ¼ million enjoying, or at least visiting, Lanzarote. The island clearly has the potential climate and space, beaches and unpolluted sea and now, with its airport, the ease of access which are the essential preconditions for civilised development in the nineties. When resort property on Fuenteventura is seriously marketed in Britain you should not expect it to be cheap.

Gomera

Gomera will have its airport and it will therefore change from being an add-on, day-trip destination from Tenerife to a place where people plan to stay put for a while. Twenty-five thousand locals have, of course, stayed put without the benefits and dis-benefits of tourism of the boom years. But the capital San Sebastian does have an incongruous eleven-storey skyscraper as a symbol of outdated modernity.

Reached by ferry from the terminal at Los Cristianos on Tenerife after a forty-five minute trip Gomera looks dull and uninteresting throughout the journey and San Sebastian too seems to be without immediate appeal. Its claim to fame is that the intrepid Christopher Columbus left finally for the New World from San Sebastian harbour in the Old World. He is reputed to have left his girl, Beatriz de Bobadilla, in this port too. She was the wife of the Count of Gomera, who was himself relaxed about fidelity (he was killed by the family of his native mistress). The fact that Columbus returned to Gomera in 1493 and 1498 adds a certain credibility to the stories of his liaison with Beatriz.

The island has another minor claim to fame: its mountain crags are many and the mountain people have evolved a whistling language on a similar basis to the Swiss yodel to enable them to communicate across the valleys. This is a real language, with a vocabulary sufficient for transmitting gossip or jokes. The highest point of Gomera is a modest 1,500m (4,900ft) above sea level; but the valleys between peaks are deep and a whistled conversation is clearly easier than a journey round miles of bends.

Gomera is 365sq km (146sq miles) in area. The terrain is rugged and planted with crops where practical. The few beaches are easier to reach by boat than by car or foot. The people have a charm and independence associated with their somewhat isolated island living. As a place for a resort home Gomera is suitable only for the self-sufficient. Speculation in land is now rife as a result of the news that the airport will happen.

La Palma

La Palma is not and will never be a beach resort. It is effectively a mountain in the Atlantic with its high point, Roque de los Muchachos, at 2,400m (almost 8,000ft) above sea level. It is 725sq km in area (280sq miles) 40km (25 miles) long from north to south and 25km (15½ miles) across its widest point and has a population of 80,000. It is the most north-westerly of the Canaries and is less than half an hour from Tenerife by plane.

It is considered by some to be one of the most beautiful islands in the world. Undoubtedly it is the steepest with the highest mountains within the smallest landmass. Topography affects everything on La Palma: the road from the airport to the capital Santa Cruz de la Palma is, in part, cut through a tunnel in the wall of an extinct volcano which is over half a kilometre in length. Another road takes you steeply to the largest natural hole in the world: the crater of an extinct volcano nearly 9km (5½ miles) across and 700m (2,300ft) deep. Unlike some of the other Canary Islands it is predominantly a green island: there are the inevitable banana plantations, palm trees, pine forests, almond trees and vineyards producing a well-regarded Malmsey wine. The coastline is short of good beaches, which has prevented its exploitation as a resort area, with the exception of the west-coast area near the port of Tazacorte. Volcanic eruptions in 1949 and in 1971 have left solid rivers of lava flowing into the sea near San Nicholas and Fuencaliente in the south.

Old colonial houses with colourful external woodwork and modern buildings of compatible scale give the port and capital of Santa Cruz its identity. This clean town has a population of 15,000 with facilities and services to meet the basic needs of the islanders. The true beauty of the island is not enough to justify La Palma as a location for holiday, semi-permanent or permanent homes for foreigners unless independence and self-sufficiency are your characteristics and the simple life is what you are looking for. But if you have chosen Tenerife or Gran Canaria as your future home in the sun then visiting La Palma for breaks is a bonus just minutes away by plane.

El Hierro

El Hierro was well known to travellers for a couple of hundred years until Greenwich was accepted as the standard meridian. It was the original point of 0 Longitude recognised by chart and mapmakers generally. Since that time it has returned to obscurity.

Seven thousand people live on the island in 270sq km (107sq miles) of land. The approach is bleak, either into the airport or the harbour near the capital Valverde, the only capital in the Canaries not to be relocated on the coast as the threat of piracy receded centuries ago. Valverde has a population of 5,000 and is a basic, no-nonsense town with few attractions for the visitor.

The terrain is part volcanic and part attractive green countryside with stone-walled fields, banana plantations and pinewoods. It is likely to remain a peaceful backwater for visitors from the other more civilised Canaries rather than be developed as a resort destination for the simple reason that there are more profitable places for investment in the next few decades. The island's dramatic cliffs and views and its spectacular sunsets and the odd appearance of Mount Teide rising above the nearer island of Gomera all give it an identity to be enjoyed for short breaks.

Corsica

If you stand beneath a statue to the island's most famous son and ask a Corsican about Napoleon you are likely to have a short conversation! You will be told that the statue was erected by the hated authorities from Paris and that Napoleon was a traitor to his people. He identified with *les continenteaux* and he did not return. Like the Sardinians across the straits Corsicans feud amongst themselves, often violently; but they forget their family quarrels when the opportunity arises to direct their fiercely nationalistic feelings towards the mainland French. Corsicans who have been jailed in France for bloody or petty crimes are fêted, sometimes as heroes, when they return to their native villages. A degree of blind optimism is required by anyone considering Corsica as a place to buy a resort home.

The nineties began where the eighties left off, with further demonstrations of Corsican feelings against foreigners who regard the island as a potential location for hotels, holiday complexes, second homes and golf courses. Four new projects were bombed by masked raiders of the National Liberation Front in the early weeks of the year. A course designed by Trent Jones was attacked, action considered somewhat extreme even by the many critics of this golf architect's work. The list of ruins to be visited on the island had earlier been increased when the Club Méditerrané development was finally abandoned, having been regularly wrecked by nationalists. And not only the French and not only developers receive the wrath of the locals: an Italian was shot by a fisherman simply for exhibiting one of his national characteristics – he was considered much too noisy!

Merely making money is much less important here than the expression of personal liberty. Corsicans prefer to do things their way and sometimes this means not doing them at all. One result of this attitude is that the island has not been developed as elsewhere in spite of its many physical attractions. Villages remain timeless. Seas remain unpolluted. Big beaches and small coves remain empty. Forests and fields remain as they have done for centuries. The maquis, ablaze with wildflowers, is not trampled underfoot by hoards of visitors. Unlike elsewhere in the accessible Mediterranean the Corsicans are just not interested in changing their life with more tourist dollars. That is not to say that some development has not taken place. New four-star hotels are being built at Bonifacio (before this the largest hotel on the island had just a hundred rooms); other small towns on the coast have small hotels of varied quality; Propriano is a scruffy resort best visited once out of curiosity. Ajaccio, well sited on a wide bay, south facing, but squashed on a strip of buildable land below a mountain, is best seen from across the water, where its high-rise apartments are not so obviously of poor quality. Calvi, north facing, is an attractive resort, with a fine beach, fine restaurants and an almost thirties' South of France ambience, backed with hilltop villages, vineyards, farmland and wild maquis. Bastia, the island's second city, has a working port of some charm but the appeal of the city itself holds the attention only momentarily. Porto Vecchio in the south actually swings in season when the Italians arrive.

But the cities and towns of Corsica are not amongst the island's attractions: the remote and peaceful countryside, the uncrowded roads and waterside, the coastal and mountain scenery and the lack of accustomed commercialism have a strong appeal for some adventurous visitors. Robust food and wine, with old-fashioned flavours; rustic courtesy and an absence of commercial flunkeyism; simple stone homes grouped in ungentrified villages: these basics have an appeal for some of a romantic nature.

The Corsicans do not, however, like their visitors to stay too long. A resort home is about fun. The risk of having a bomb in your bath is not generally considered acceptable by potential buyers of resort homes whatever the unspoiled and unique selling points of an otherwise delightful location. The Corsicans believe that the island is theirs. They do not need you or your money. Developers who have attempted to create projects which would benefit the local economy have usually packed up and left for places where they have been welcomed or at least tolerated. Corsicans do not consider that working in an hotel, serving foreigners, is a job which carries respect. Bus drivers regard a timetable as a curb on their liberty. There is absolutely no enthusiasm locally for exploiting even the relics and treasures of history: the Fesch Museum in the capital Ajaccio, which houses a renowned collection of Italian paintings, has been closed for renovations for almost a decade.

It is reasonable for the Corsicans to decide what they do or do not want for their island. They have made it clear that they do not welcome exploitation and change as they see it. They do not want you as a resort-property owner.

Cyprus

Many of the big names of early history visited Cyprus. They read like a roll-call of the early greats: Homer wrote about the island in *The Odyssey* and *The Illiad* (one of the first of many writers to have 'made' places by publishing their impressions of them); Alexander the Great ruled in 334 BC and was succeeded by Ptolemy; Cleopatra and Mark Antony continued their affair in Cyprus; Paul the Apostle was there in AD 45 with St Barnabas, the island's patron saint; the foster-mother of Mohammed is allegedly buried there; and our own King Richard the Lionheart was the first to dabble in real estate, taking the island in 1191, selling it to the Knights Templar, repossessing it when they were unable to hold it, and reselling it to Guy of Lusignan later.

Neolithic Man lived on Cyprus eight thousand years ago and the signs of occupation still attract the world's archaeologists. Classical Greece as we know it was effectively centred upon Cyprus by 1500 BC. After Ptolemy the Romans and the Byzantines ruled for a thousand years: Byzantine buildings, wall paintings and mosaics remain today to augment the rich remains of past civilisations on the island. Ownership passed between powerful states of the maritime period: Venetians, Turks, the Spanish kings and the Arabs. Turkish rule ended when the island became a British Protectorate in 1878.

Greek and Turkish Cypriots have never co-existed happily. Independence from Britain was fought for and won in 1960 and much blood was spilled on the way, some of it British. The republic remained within the Commonwealth after independence but the internal warfare between the two communities continued. The island was invaded by Turkish troops in 1974 and divided the territory by creating a separate state north of the capital Nicosia, including the then successful resorts of Kyrenia and Famagusta. Foreign property-owners who had homes in the Turkish zone were effectively dispossessed. No attempts to bring both communities together have so far succeeded.

Middle East conflicts during the eighties have made the island the centre of international activity, intrigue and occasionally negotiations for the release of hostages held in the Lebanon. The Lebanese war resulted in many Lebanese businesses and business-men relocating to the commercial calm of Cyprus.

The island is 9,250sq km (357sq miles) of which more than one-third is Turkish. The population is around 650,000: 80 per cent Greek, 18 per cent Turkish and 2 per cent of other nationalities, including 4,000 or so permanent British residents. The British bases on the island have educated hundreds of thousands of service personnel in the pleasures of living on Cyprus, with the exception of those who were preoccupied with survival in the years of conflict. For historical and practical commercial reasons English is widely understood by those local people who have had regular contact

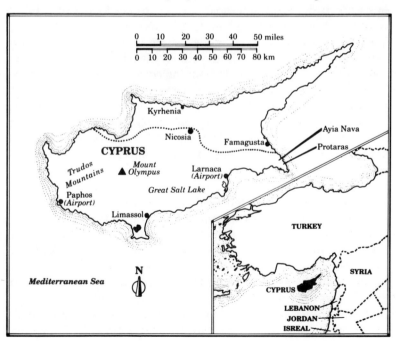

with foreigners. However, a knowledge of Greek, especially in the country areas, helps integration and adds to the overall enjoyment for anyone planning to spend more than a couple of weeks a year on Cyprus.

The island's climate is its major attraction for buyers of resort property. Midsummer temperatures along the coastline are sometimes too hot for comfort through the middle of the day outdoors – in the nineties (around 35 degrees C). But you don't have to be on the coastline and you don't have to be outdoors through the middle of the day: 340 or so days a year of sunshine, with winter temperatures in the 40–60 degree F range (5 degrees C) can be enjoyed inland if you remain below the snowline in the Trudos Mountains in the centre of the western half of the islands – or the southern part as the Cypriots prefer to call it.

The southern, Greek Cypriot two-thirds of the island covers an area of 5,500sq km (2,200sq miles). The high point is Mount Olympus at almost 2,000m (6,400ft) above sea level. There are two international airports, Larnaca and Paphos at either end of the southern part, which means that nowhere is much more than an hour's drive from the normal point of arrival on the island. The flight time from Britain is about four hours.

The position of the island in the eastern Mediterranean has been historically important but in the eighties it has become even more so. Cyprus is 64km (40 miles) from the coast of Turkey and 122km (76 miles) from Syria. Given that the traditional conflicts between Greeks and Turks are a permanent part of Cypriot life they are overshadowed in scale by the endemic problems of the Middle East. Given also that the necessary presence of the United Nations Peace Keeping Force from the sixties has put some welcome cash into the local economy at the grassroots level, this too is nothing compared to the economic benefits which have flowed from the destruction of commerce and trade in the Lebanon and the constantly shifting political centres of gravity in some of the Arab states.

Cyprus has provided a stable base from which the Lebanese business community has been able to operate, with an immediate and direct contribution to the local economy from the purchase of luxury homes, business premises and all the additional expenditure which results from the need to relocate. Embassies have had their status upgraded and their staff consequently increased. Governments-in-exile, opposition groups, rebel factions with adequate funding and exploiters of turmoil have established bases on the island for its convenient location and its civilised facilities: its up-to-date telephone system has been widely praised, for example. Even 'safe houses' have been bought here by the intelligence services of those countries who have a vested interest in the future of the Middle East, in Iran, Iraq, Lebanon, Syria, Egypt, Israel and Libya. All of this expensive activity has underpinned the cashflow of the airlines, the operators of the five-star hotels and property developers who have opted for the luxury market.

Tourism has progressed unevenly. In the eighties, strikes by Spanish hotel staff increased the growing disillusionment by British tour operators with the lower end of the market which they had themselves created around the costas. Somewhat cynically they switched their business from time to time during the eighties to Cyprus. Cyprus was aiming higher, at the up-market end of the trade, but the salesmanship of the very experienced British tour operators enabled them in some cases to close deals, short term, with Cypriot hoteliers, use the deals against the Spanish hoteliers, and subsequently switch to Spain again at attractive terms. Most of the resorts against which the operators were acting were created in Spain in the fifties. Paradoxically, the architectural identity of those resorts chosen by the tour operators in the eighties in Cyprus although built much later, had a fifties atmosphere. The standard of architecture in Cyprus, except for its ancient buildings, is unfortunately uninspiring, anonymous with boring façades being the norm. High-rise buildings are, however, now forbidden and four storeys in height is the maximum permitted. More five-star accommodation has been created on the island as a direct result of 'business need' rather than the demands of tourism. And there is evidence that greater expectations are beginning to result in more attractive designs of resort property being offered in the nineties.

The food and drink available on the island is higher than the standard required by mass tourism. There is a basis of Greek cuisine overlaid with influences from other Mediterranean cooking. Like the Spanish tapas or the ristafel of Indonesia, the meze is a selection of small dishes from which you help yourself: keftedes (spiced meatballs), kebabs of pork and lamb, stuffed vineleaves, houmus (crushed chick peas, garlic, sesame seed paste and olive oil), moussaka, various fish dishes, salads and cheeses, particularly those made from goats' milk, are everyday delights available in the bars, cafés and tavernas. Glorious meat stews are a surprising feature of country kitchens in such a climate.

The grape varieties are so numerous that you would have difficulty in remembering the names and flavours of all of the hundred or so grown on the island – both dessert and wine grapes are profuse. Many small vineyards still make their own wines; others supply highly professional producers who have pedigrees which stretch back for centuries. Besides the well-regarded table wines, Cyprus 'sherry' is renowned even when compared with the traditional Spanish invention; brandies are also revered – especially those of great age – and the local version of the famous Greek spirit ouso, flavoured with aniseed, is addictive either neat or with ice and water.

The food and drink is clearly a result of the climate, the fertility and the traditional economy of the island. So is the appearance of the countryside away from the coastal resorts. On the slopes of the Trudos Mountains there are impressive forests of Corsican and Aleppo pine, cedar, cypress, juniper and the golden oak. Citrus trees blossom in early spring; so do the spectacular wild anemones and cyclamen in the meadows after the almond trees have flowered in February. Fruits load the trees in the citrus groves in summer and fields of barley and wheat add to the warm colours everywhere. Melons ripen in the sun. Gnarled olive trees provide the fragrant oil and objects of almost pagan worship by the country people: the trees are said to ward off evil spirits by families who have traditionally needed all the good luck they could get in earlier times.

By providing work, and the opportunity of comparative wealth, tourism and resort development has distorted traditional patterns. Population has shifted away from isolated village communities into growth areas, leaving some potentially useful and appealing old homes of more interest to foreigners than to local young people. But not until the late eighties has any organised attempt been made to seek out and offer these properties to the British market. The purpose-built villa was the standard product for sale to the British buyer until the eighties, when a wider range of property was made available for the international markets on the developing coast.

Amongst regular visitors to Cyprus are the pink-and-white flamingoes which grace the Great Salt Lake near the historic town of Larnaca. This is the point of arrival for most of the island's human visitors, into the international airport, and Larnaca is itself a progressively developing centre for tourists, with a lively seafront scene, a marina and beaches with watersports facilities.

Ayia Napa and Protaras on the headland on the south-east corner are now thriving beach resorts, both with clear water and silver sand backed by attractive countryside and projects of varied quality of architecture.

Nicosia, the capital, is on the new border and the contrast between the old part of the city and the newly developed areas is extreme but compatible: Venetian walls and narrow streets, kebabs roasting over charcoal, craftsmen's shops, nightclubs, restaurants and hotels like the Hilton, the Ledra and the Churchill are just across the 'Green Line' from Turkish mosques. At the time of forced partition Nicosia had to rehouse the thousands of Greek refugees from the Turkish-occupied sector.

From Nicosia the new motorway to Limassol has linked the capital with the island's second-largest town, much favoured by Arab visitors, with a number of five-star hotels and some vigorous nightlife. Property development continues to boom here with a selection which starts with homes in the million pound range on some estates, with stunning Mediterranean views and marble everywhere. There is a wide choice in the middle range of prices too. The high-rise buildings of the decade from 1974 give parts of the town a dated look by the more civilised standards of today but the quality of construction, as opposed to the quality of design, is generally impressive.

Cyprus has a justified reputation for well-built property. Many of the major construction companies on the island were almost wiped out financially by the partition of the seventies. The recovery has been dramatic and is a demonstration of the commercial abilities of Cypriot businessmen. That most of the construction companies are developers too, and remain essentially family firms, gives a solidity to the property scene. The more imaginative homes now being planned show that they are reacting positively to the style criticisms which have been levelled at earlier examples of their projects.

Developers are not only concerned with the growth of the property business along the coastline: the lower slopes of the Trudos Mountains are being selectively exploited for those who want to establish themselves permanently or semi-permanently on the island and this includes some of the hundreds of thousands of Cypriots who have spent all or most of their working lives in Britain. Evening chill, requiring sweaters and sweet-smelling log fires, is regarded as a plus point by those who prefer to see the sea and the built-up coast from a comfortable distance. Villas and complexes of grouped housing are the usual product here.

Paphos at the south-west corner of the island was a small fishing community dominated by a castle about 80km (48 miles) from Limassol. Now it has its own airport and has progressively been developed under government encouragement as a controlled resort area. The locality has a wealth of historical connections: Alexander the Great used the castle; Cicero governed here; and St Paul was one of the local preachers. The atmosphere of the town is more compatible with things Cypriot than the more international resorts elsewhere on the island; as a result it has been a favoured area for retired British people and other nationals.

Given the encouragement which the government has directed towards the purchase of resort homes by foreigners, and the straightforward real estate laws and practices, buying a home on this island in the sun will continue to appeal to British middle-of-the-road retirees and those who want to live for extended periods in a favourable climate. Travel time from the UK at four hours plus is, however, a deterrent for those who are seeking a holiday property for use periodically for the occasional couple of weeks' break unless rental of the unit on an organised basis is part of your plan. It follows that the criteria for selecting an easily and profitably let holiday home should be carefully observed here as elsewhere.

As an example of the government's attitude to foreign buyers of resort homes they levy no Capital Gains Tax upon resale by non-Cypriots; other attractive tax benefits apply to investment income arising from capital imported by foreigners who take up residence; there is no Capital Transfer Tax; and finally there is no estate duty payable by UK expatriates domiciled in Cyprus provided they had acquired their property in Cypriot currency external to Cyprus.

The island will continue to progress as the Cypriots are determined and businesslike. The layouts of estates and the architecture generally continue to improve as developers take on board the criticisms which have been voiced. Government control of height and density in newly developing areas will continue to be maintained. It is reasonable to assume that the major contractors and developers will continue to be keen to protect their family names, many of which were founded in the thirties and forties. The climate will continue to be benign. Cyprus has many solid attractions as a resort area for the British who have no personal reasons for regret about the terrorism of the past. Enosis – union with Greece – is dead as an issue and so are its protagonists.

There is, however, one cautious note amongst the generally solid basis for buying homes in Cyprus. Some old family construction businesses began in the eighties to produce the Deeds of Transfer to their buyers with great slowness. Under no circumstances should you accept a condition which allows this to happen to you. Take independent legal advice and insist that deeds are produced as promised; otherwise you should reserve the right to a full refund of purchase monies plus interest and damages.

Ibiza

In ancient times Ibiza, Formentera and the islets around and between them were known as the Pitiusas: the Pine Islands. They were considered a separate group from the larger Balearic Islands of Mallorca and Menorca. The pines have gone from Formentera but the small but well-formed mountains of Ibiza are still green with these old trees. Approaching the island from the sea or by plane you will be struck immediately by the physical differences from the other Balearics: it is greener, with many cliffs and coves and many houses scattered throughout the countryside.

Ibiza is 572sq km (220sq miles) in size with a coastline of some 170km (105 miles) in length and a population of almost 70,000 which is doubled at the height of summer. The Spanish coast is 83km (52 miles) away and North Africa is only 220km (138 miles) to the south of the island.

Ancient mariners preferred to sail within sight of land; so the trade route of the western Mediterranean was from Carthage in North Africa to Sicily via Spain's coast and the islands. Discovering salt on Ibiza 2,500 years ago the Carthaginians settled, bartering the salt and the fish it preserved for other minerals along their trade routes. The Carthaginians were competitive exporters. Ibiza's soil was found to be non-toxic and its clay ideal for practical pottery. The amphorae made on the island were early examples of hygienic packaging, much prized for the transportation of wines, oil, fish and other foods.

After five hundred years of rule from Carthage the Romans came and stayed for the next five centuries. True to their nature they built good roads and viaducts, levied ever-increasing taxes and gradually enslaved the population. The first visitors from Northern Europe, the Vandals, became instantly popular: they massacred the corrupt Roman officials and cancelled all debts. The Vandals remained for only a hundred years.

Over the next three and a half centuries the island was occupied by a variety of foreigners – Byzantines, Moors, Christians under Charlemagne and even Vikings – until the Moors began five hundred years of rule in AD 901. The physique, music, traditional dress, customs, architecture and agriculture of Ibiza's people can be traced directly to this period.

With the advent of Catalan and Christian rule in the thirteenth century the islanders ceased to be on the receiving end of one form of piracy after another: they began to give as much as they had received. For the following few hundred years they produced their own corsairs who became popular heroes from their inspired swashbuckling. Overlooking Ibiza harbour is the only known monument funded by public subscription to the fond memory of a much-loved pirate.

By the end of the first half of the present century the island had become sleepy, ignored and impoverished, and parents who cared for their children sent them off Ibiza into Europe to enable them to earn enough to buy food enough to thrive. But in the early sixties this simple unchanged lifestyle began to draw a more gentle invader: the flower people, who were usually American and usually wealthy. The beauty of the island, the contrast with high-pressure city living and the renowned tolerance of the people began to spread by word of mouth. Artists, writers, craftsmen, musicians and 'simple-lifers' came, followed by international business and show-business person-alities who wanted to slow down. Some settled permanently; others found homes to retreat to as needed. Tourism followed this trend. Elsewhere tourism preceded it.

The tourist boom of the sixties transformed the local economy. The airport, opened at that time, was rebuilt in the mid-eighties and now handles over 1 million passengers a year. But the crude over-development which has ruined most of the Mediterranean's popular resort areas has scarred little of Ibiza's rugged coastline.

Long stretches of the island's dramatic coastline are preserved for the enjoyment of future generations. The whole of Ibiza Old Town is designated an ancient monument. Tough but enlightened planning controls prevent high-rise overbuilding in areas of out-standing natural beauty and the Law of the Coasts enacted in the late eighties prevents building within 100 metres (110yd) of the shoreline generally.

The development of certain designated areas is not, however, discouraged, provided that the new quality norms are observed: indeed, high-quality projects in approved locations are encouraged. New marinas and golf courses of international standards have been approved in recent years to broaden the earlier limited appeal of the island for home buyers. Farmhouses for conversion and isolated detached villas have attracted discerning buyers from the sixties but until twenty years later no attempts were made to provide property for the mainstream buyer of resort homes, with some exceptions at Cala Llonga and Santa Eulalia. The island has benefitted from the taste of many of the earlier converters and builders with the result that Ibiza has more outstanding – and expensive – resort property than any comparable area around the easily accessible Mediterranean.

The style of the old country property on the island was Arabic, traceable like the famous Ibicencan hound to Egypt, with cubes of masonry, small windows, flat roofs and sheltered entrance porches. These basic features inspired the progressive modern architects of the Bauhaus design school in Germany in the twenties and can be seen to influence the work of many distinguished architects of that period and later. The shapes are specific to Ibiza and are another point of difference between the various Balearic Islands. Tiled roofs are rare. With the exception of hotels and apartments built in the sixties for the tourist trade most modern property on the island echoes tradition either directly, as reproductions of the Arab farmhouse, or indirectly, as modern homes based upon ancient shapes, materials and principles.

But there are some parts of the island which should be visited once *only* during the season. San Antonio, set around a magnificent bay on the island's north-western coast, is hardly ruined by high-rise development – most of the package-tour hotels and apartments are across the bay from the town – but in season it is ruined by people: usually young; usually boisterously drunk; and usually, but not invariably, British. Football hooligans seem to spend time there between soccer seasons. High spirits evolve here into rowdyism and violence regularly every night in July and August resulting, in the summer of 1989, in the death of a local waiter. Most mass tourism to Ibiza is concentrated around this unfortunate town.

Santa Eulalia, the second of the island's coastal towns, is much more agreeable. Also set on a bay, south facing, the town was not swamped by tourism in the sixties and seventies. It was prosperous enough, as its fertile hinterland and dozen banks for twelve thousand inhabitants will testify, to do without the masses. It did, however, have an attraction for the new settlers at that time and many bought homes in the surrounding plains, including a number of internationally famous celebrities from stage and screen and from the sports and city pages. The town built its Paseo Maritimo as late as the mid-eighties and had the sense to restrict it to pedestrians only.

Ibiza Town, on a spectacular site overlooking a natural harbour, is ancient, well preserved, and, in the streets below its ramparts, like a souk in season. After tourism the fashion business is the island's most important trade and local sales are made nightly in these streets during the season, with boutique after boutique offering clothing and accessories which range from the outstanding to the outlandish according to taste. Bars and restaurants add to the atmosphere. The higher you walk through the old city walls the quieter it becomes and the quality of the bars and restaurants improves. Some of the old mansions in the old town are now millionaires' pads.

The three main towns of the island, and their clear differences one to the other, exemplify the contrasts within this comparatively small island. San Antonio is appalling because of the people it attracts. Santa Eulalia is appealing because of the people it has attracted for centuries. Ibiza Town is physically stunning and commercially vibrant on many levels.

Traditional dress is still worn by older women in the fields and in the towns and villages. Modern fashions are worn by younger inhabitants and visitors and some of the clothing is extreme by any standards. Ibicenco males are macho in the Mediterranean manner. Gays of all nationalities are accepted without problems outside their own bars, restaurants and beaches. Traditional music and dance exists alongside world-famous discos. Local lamb, cooked in a variety of age-old dishes, and the island's special flans are full of flavours never found in supermarket meats and sweets. There are more excellent restaurants of international standard than can be found in any other resort area around the Mediterranean. Farmhouses which have remained unchanged for centuries exist within sight of others which have been lovingly restored. Luxurious modern homes also exist scattered throughout the countryside as well as fronting the ocean.

Foreigners, and the new ideas and habits they bring, have been accepted on Ibiza for two and a half thousand years. But this is not an island for prudes. Tolerance is the way of life for Ibicencos and nobody should contemplate settling on the island unless they too possess this quality.

As elsewhere there is a difference between north and south. Distances are short – the island is about 50km by 25km (30 × 15 miles) – but the southern half is more favoured for living than the rugged north. The coast between Ibiza Town and Santa Eulalia is attractive, with many choices of properties, between millionaires' villas, low-rise apartments and complexes of grouped housing, some of which have spectacular views of the islands between Ibiza and Formentera.

Major roads on the island are excellent: after decades of neglect they were rebuilt at central government cost during the mid-eighties. At this time the general hospital was built on a hill behind Ibiza Town, making the island medically self-sufficient for the first time in its history. The odour from Ibiza harbour on otherwise balmy summer evenings was cause for comment from visitors until twenty-five centuries of the town's effluent was no longer augmented daily in the mid-eighties: the new sewage arrangements coincided with luxury development around the bay. Mains sewerage is the norm now in urban areas. Water and electricity supplies from the utility companies are generally available except in the remote countryside.

The infrastructure and facilities of Ibiza have been progressively upgraded to the point where the island is prepared for further developments of resort homes. The development plan for the island, announced in the late eighties, preserves most of Ibiza from urbanisation. The pine-clad hills, which have a high point of 475m (1,500ft) above sea level, will remain undeveloped except where they have been specifically designated otherwise.

Formentera

Formentera, seen from most high ground on Ibiza which has a southern outlook, is reached by ferry from Ibiza harbour and elsewhere. It is a magical place to visit at the end of a ninety-minute boat trip through the islets but the trip and the visit are more likely to encourage the purchase of a boat than a property on Formentera. It has long, undeveloped beaches, a few holiday hotels and complexes, and very few homes which could be considered suitable for permanent or semi-permanent occupancy by anyone looking for more than isolation from all things representing real life.

Mallorca

Island-lovers argue about which approach to Mallorca is the most dramatic. Is it by sea from Barcelona, along the wild north-western coast, below the towering mountains, round the Isla Dragonera, turning at Cabo Cala Figuera into the vast Bay of Palma, with the US Sixth Fleet at anchor for added effect; or by air from Barcelona or Valencia, in winter, low through the snow-dusted peaks, crossing the almond-blossom-dusted plains scattered with windpumps and watertanks, then heading out above the bay before banking for the approach to the airport, giving the only attractive view of high-rise Arenal – from above?

But all can agree that you should certainly see the mountains first. You and they have come far. They rise 900km (560 miles) away in Andalucia behind Cadiz in the Atlantic and continue under one name or another until they fall into the Mediterranean at Cabo de la Nao near Javea at the most easterly point of the Spanish peninsula. The mountains resurface in miniature as Ibiza, drop deep beneath the sea again, and emerge finally as a rugged chain of peaks that runs for 100km (62 miles) along the north-western coast of Mallorca from Dragonara to Cabo de Formentor. Seven mountains exceed 1,000m (3,280ft) above sea level with the high point, Puig Mayor, at 1,445m (4,750ft).

This mountain range gives the island its identity, covering some 20 per cent of its area, and tempers its climate, providing a wall against the cold north winds from France. Thus protected most of the island enjoys an average winter temperature of 10°C and an average summer temperature of 25°C, moderated by soft prevailing winds from the south. Locals allege that it only rains for short periods on seventy-five days a year, usually in November and December; but with 80 per cent of London's rainfall the island has downpours rather than drizzle. When I flew into Palma to a snow-covered runway on the first day of Lent in 1983 I was told that it was the first time in twenty-three years that snow had settled. However, regardless of the fact that Mr Chopin, during his famous visit, was obliged to play the piano at breakneck speed to warm his fingers, Mallorca has higher-than-average western Mediterranean winter temperatures. This physically attractive island has suffered badly from its 'success' as the most popular holiday destination in Europe. All the worst clichés about the desecration of the Mediterranean coasts apply to Arenal and Palma Nova either side of the capital, Palma; and Magaluf is a gross example of the now-discredited sixties' form of resort development. Even with due allowance for Spain's urgent need for foreign exchange and jobs, at the time, the ruin of the landscape around accessible large sandy beaches is indefensible. Now that the callous commercial pressure from our own tour operators to produce lowest-cost packages has abated, and the autonomous government is actively encouraging a higher grade of tourism and development, many recent and planned projects are far removed from the earlier mistakes – philosophically as well as physically. The cheapjack image of the island has changed during the last decade.

Only short stretches of the long coastline were badly marred by lowest common denominator, high-density, high-rise desecration in any case. Low-quality high-rise hotels and apartments are out of favour; today's entrepreneurs react by creating low-density, low-rise complexes which reflect this change in demand, offering more choice in the range of quality. Much of the varied coastline is still in the ownership of the Ministry of Defence; some cannot be developed because of its protected status; and the remainder, if zoned for development, is now subject to the Law of the Coasts, enacted at the end of the eighties to prevent building within 100m (110yd) of the waterfront. The change in attitudes and expectations cannot obliterate the effects of earlier *laissez-faire* postures. But it seems clear that the authorities, at least some civilised developers and those in the market for well-placed and well-planned property are heading in the same direction on the island of Mallorca.

The island is physically attractive enough to merit more thought in its development than it had in the past; and its history and traditions provide further attractions to anyone considering Mallorca as a place to live permanently or semi-permanently. Its easy access from any European population centre is one real benefit from its popularity as a holiday destination; property-owners can travel to Mallorca readily and economically because Palma airport is the most used in all the Iberian Peninsula.

As with any inhabited island the origins of the earliest inhabitants are mysterious. There is evidence that people were living on Mallorca in 5000BC. Visitors must have spread word about the islanders' specialist skills because the Carthaginian forces contained valued units composed of Mallorcan sling-shot marksmen during the Punic Wars: these mercenaries preferred to be paid in wine and women rather than money.

The Romans came, saw, conquered and remained for over five hundred years. The Moors occupied the island for four centuries. There was much activity by pirates and other marauders and the Catalans attempted to take Mallorca during the twelfth and thirteenth centuries. The last of the Moors in Mallorca surrendered to the Catalan kings in 1232. A period of democracy well ahead of its time followed, with the establishment of a separate island kingdom, until it was incorporated into a unified Spain by Ferdinand and Isabella in 1492 around the time when the Moors were finally driven from Spanish soil.

This was a period of adventure for newly unified Spain and the Spanish began seriously to explore and colonise. Christopher Columbus began his leading role in this expansionist phase by successfully persuading Ferdinand and Isabella to fund his attempt to find the East Indies by travelling west. All of this is history of course, but it does have a little-known connection with Mallorca. We are taught that Columbus was an Italian who discovered the Americas while looking for somewhere else. Spanish historians now dispute this and they are supported by a discovery made in archives in Budapest. 'If Columbus was Italian,' their argument runs, 'why couldn't he speak Italian? But he was, it seems, fluent in Castilian Spanish and Catalan.' His name was not even what he claimed it was and nor did he come from Genoa. He was in fact Juan Colom from Genova in Mallorca. He upgraded his name from Juan to the more resounding Christobel – his name is, in any event, Christobel Colom in Spanish – before doing his famous marketing exercise on the royals to fund his discovery of the shortcut to the Spice Islands. Now the mystery is compounded by the documents in Budapest which seem to place his birth in a specific farmhouse in Felanitx near Genova on the island of Mallorca.

The island has always been better known for those who have visited it than those who have left it for somewhere else, in spite of the Columbus connection. But there was another local who went west to leave his mark on America. Father Serra, a Franciscan friar and teacher, founded a mission in what is now San Diego. While mopping his brow one day in 1769 he exclaimed: 'Cal de forn!' meaning 'hot as an oven'. His exclamation became the name: California is therefore Mallorcan in origin.

Before the advent of packaged tourism the last-known case of forced removal from the island occurred a couple of hundred years before the naming of California by the voluntarily exiled friar. Corsairs abducted twenty-four women from Andraitx in 1578. About forty years later English ships landed troops on the island. They were, they claimed, only looking for something to drink. After four days of fighting with the locals they left. This was not Magaluf in the eighties but Arta in the 1620s.

Reflecting a period of calm and prosperity many palacios were built by the nobility in Palma in the mid-seventeenth century. Approached through arched double doors from the street, with the famous local feature of a patio entry court, from which stately stone stairs lead to expansive first-floor living-rooms, with stabling and servants' quarters below, a number of these fine properties remain to give distinction to the Palma street scene. Some are still family homes for the remnants of the Mallorcan nobility. One on the city outskirts at Marivent, suitably renovated and made secure, is the resort home of Juan Carlos, and is periodically visited by Prince Charles and family.

Troubles throughout Europe seem to have made the local nobles rich from war profits for the next couple of centuries. The island also attracted wealthy refugees from these unsettled and dangerous times and places, including those escaping from the French and other revolutions and Napoleon's later expansionism into the peninsula. More magnificent homes resulted from this demand, some of which were built as manor houses or fortified estates in the countryside – rare for Spain (and never available on the open market). First-floor living is a feature of these properties as in the city palaces in Palma. To give scale to this influx, it is estimated that by 1811 the total number of refugees from the French Revolution and Napoleon's arrival in Cataluna amounted to a staggering 40,000, most of whom were aristocrats or clergy. This was the year in which Sir John Carr published his snappily titled book: *Descriptive Travels in Southern and Eastern Parts of Spain and the Balearic Islands.* As elsewhere a book by an enthusiast made the island more widely known. Distinguished visitors began to call. Even the adverse publicity from Georges

Sand's uncomplimentary account of her stay on the island with Chopin failed to stem the trickle; nor did reports of slight earthquakes, famines, droughts and occasional plagues in the middle of the nineteenth century deter adventurous travellers.

More distinguished visitors came, some, like a British group who created the island's railway in 1875, to invest; others, like a mysterious Middle-European count, to write the standard work on the islands – in nine volumes. The railway, as elsewhere, prospered and expanded and wilted and was pruned until it finally ceased as a serious operation in the seventies. The count returned to the island ten years after his first visit in 1867; by then he was an Archduke of the Austro-Hungarian Empire and built a great villa at Miramar, filled it with nobles, writers and scholars and became a successful enthusiast for all things Mallorcan. By the end of the nineteenth century many visitors had written favourably of the island as an appealing backwater. Even the newly established British Consul felt compelled to write a book about Mallorca. As a consequence it began to cease to be a backwater.

Things began to change when an Argentinian businessman with flair, dynamism, money and taste bought the whole of the Formentor Peninsula and planned and built one of Europe's outstanding resort hotels on a spectacular site, with the intention of filling it with the rich and famous. To attract attention, Sir Adan Diehl rented space on the Eiffel Tower to advertise his Hotel Formentor. Various stars were persuaded to patronise his place, including the ubiquitous Aga Khan, the future Prime Minister of Britain, Winston Churchill, and the future, if brief, King Edward VIII.

Other entrepreneurs followed Diehl's lead. By the end of the first decade of this century Palma's Grand Hotel was thriving and the Fomento del Tourismo had been established to promote the island's attractions to foreign visitors who arrived there under their own steam, by cruise-liners or by ferries from the mainland. But not until 1925 was international business actively sought except by the enterprising management of the Hotel Formentor. Palma soon had half a dozen hotels of quality (all now closed) which relied upon the increasing numbers of cruise-passengers who decided to spend part of their winter in Mallorca. The English predominated to such an extent that ot the locals 'foreigner' meant 'Englishman'.

By the time the Army in Spain rose against the government in 1936 Mallorca had thirty hotels for foreign visitors. Italians rather than Englishmen then became the normal visitors for the duration of the Civil War as the island served Mussolini's airforce as a base for bombing raids in support of Franco. The island's most influential son at this time also supported the rising against the government. Juan March, who reputedly liked the smell of three things – melons, money and women – was a local boy who made good, originally as a smuggler, adventurer and businessman generally, until his wheeling and dealing made him an influential figure in commerce and politics in Spain in the twenties and thirties. He funded Franco's uprising (and reputedly backed some factions in the government as a side-bet) emerging after the Civil War as a respected banker and owner of the oil and petrol monopoly in Spain. His name remains as Banca March (now partly owned by NatWest) and as creator of the impressive collection of exotic plants on the island.

The airfield from which Mussolini's bombers flew to bomb the civilians of Barcelona and Ibiza and other targets was expanded for the flood of tourists in the late fifties. The main terminal was built in 1967 and the charter terminal in 1972 to receive the millions of passengers who were attracted to the island. Both terminals were rebuilt to high standards in the late eighties.

Millions of package tourists mean thousands of hotel rooms to accommodate them and during the expansion of facilities in the sixties hotels were, at one time, being opened at the rate of one every two days. The numbers of tourists and their needs have distorted the older patterns of life and commerce on the island. The deep and fertile topsoil in the central plain, fed by underground water, made for productive farming from traditionally small farms, 8ha (20 acres) being the average holding. But Mallorca now imports most of its food from the Spanish peninsula. There are signs of neglect in the countryside; farmers are ageing; labour costs are higher than on the mainland; sons no longer want to follow fathers into back-breaking customs; and therefore crops which are traditionally labour intensive are disappearing.

Some other traditional production has benefitted from visitors where mechanisation has lowered labour costs. Shoe manufacture, which began in the eighteenth century, still thrives, although affected by intense competition from countries with low wage economies. The artificial pearl business established in the thirties, using glass, fish scales and oyster shells in its processes, still produces and sells millions of pearls each week. Red wine is still fermented at Benisalem and white wine still comes from Felanitx – where Columbus may have been born – in viable quantities.

Ancient and modern history and the economic and social changes which have flowed from it provide a rich and varied mixture to retain the interest of anyone wishing to settle on the island from any British background. Permanent or semi-permanent living has no built-in boredom factor unless you literally have no interests or hobbies.

Mallorca is more cosmopolitan than almost any other resort area, and any other part of the peninsula. Visiting symphony orchestras and international stage personalities can be enjoyed along with pop groups and folklore events. Culture, however defined, is available in the capital and elsewhere. The standard of living is exceeded in Spain only by Madrid and Barcelona. Shopping facilities range from the stylish boutiques around the main streets of Palma and Woolworths and C&A to backstreet corner shops. Restaurants of all qualities and prices from the international to the local and the 'fast food' categories can easily be found. Golf courses and marinas exist in variety and more are planned.

Plugging into the traditions of the island can be rewarding if you have the required curiosity. Fiestas have a religious basis but not necessarily obtrusively so. Traditional dress is now worn only on folksy occasions, but dances, music, singing and the instruments which accompany them still live; the bagpipe-like instruments have particular charm. Some superstitions remain: the ability of some gypsies to read your fortune from an examination of the soles of your feet; the power of menstrual blood to attract wandering or future husbands when used as an ingredient in cakes or alcoholic drinks; the use of stewed bulls' testicles to perk up male potency – these are a few of the special ancient customs which still command respect! The local language – akin to Catalan with Moorish and other influences – now flourishes after being banned by Franco for forty years.

Cockfighting, illegal since the mid-fifties, can be found by those determined enough to do so. Bullfights are staged in season. So are trotting races, which are traditional to Mallorca. There is excellent football and professional pelota in Palma. There are excellent sports complexes of a better standard than we are used to in Britain. All water sports can be indulged.

The traditional food has little resemblance to that served in tourist hotels or restaurants. Paellas, the locals claim, are better than those found in Valencia. The local equivalent of pizza, cooked in farmhouse ovens, is a delight compared with the manufactured variety. Rabbit stew (containing raisins and almonds), roast suckling pig, sobraesada (a red, spiced sausage using the best parts of a pig rather than the remains as here), turrones (a cross between nougat and halva), the light, flat spiral of the ensaimada (a sweet bun, best eaten at breakfast, dipped into hot, thick drinking chocolate): these are just some of the delights of Mallorca. Less easy to like is the aperitif, palo, made from carob beans.

Mallorca is about the size of Cornwall: 3,600sq km (1,400sq miles). It is about 95km (60 miles) across its widest point. It has a population of around half a million; most live in Palma or its immediate area. Clearly it is big enough to support all the requirements of a civilised lifestyle. There is enough variation in the terrain, coastline and property available to give a wide choice to anyone looking for a permanent, second or holiday home. Prices, as you would expect, reflect all the criteria mentioned elsewhere in this book. More farmhouses, with a few hectares of land can be expected to become available as the farming community ages. New developments are better controlled and planned than many earlier

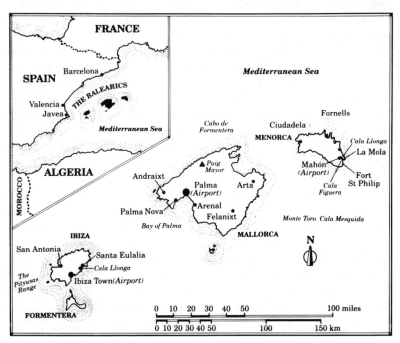

efforts. But some older developments enjoy better positions; others are affected by too-popular beaches and twenty-four hour noise during the tourist season.

Mallorca has all the facilities and natural advantages for the broadest spectrum of potential buyers of resort property.

Menorca

Expatriates who live in Menorca claim that it feels more remote than it is. It has a shorter holiday season than Mallorca or Ibiza. It is not served by charter flights throughout the year. Topographically it is unlike either of the other Balearic Islands: the road through Menorca from the old capital of Ciudadela to Mahon effectively marks the geological split personality of the island, part being an extension of the mountains of Andalucia, like Mallorca and Ibiza, and part being an extension of the Pyrenees. It is rare to find anyone from Menorca who has visited Ibiza and vice versa. It is nearer Sardinia than Madrid. Menorca is 48km (30 miles) long by 19km (12 miles) wide and has 216km (135 miles) of coastline. Its population is around 55,000.

This small island has two kinds of countryside because of its two geological origins. This contrast is best seen from the island's high point, Monte Toro, 363m (1,200ft) above sea level, almost halfway between the old capital and Mahon. Looking north across undulating grassland with some high points and rock outcrops to the rugged and indented coastline, with its great bays either side of the village of Fornells exactly due north, you could feel that this was Pembrokeshire in the Mediterranean. Uniquely in the Mediterranean, the grassland is grazed by cattle: there are almost as many bovine as human inhabitants. To the south is a stony plateau tilted generally towards the sea, deeply cut in places by seasonal watercourses. Limestone walls around fields, and some remarkable prehistoric remains of massive stone slabs and columns lead the eye to many small coves and beaches, with some areas of marshland.

It has to be said that Menorca has a less benign climate than Mallorca or Ibiza. It is unprotected from the wind from the north, the tramontana, which blows, sometimes with ferocity, for around 120 days intermittently, from October to April. This wind hits the northern coast of the island spectacularly at times and provides the reason for the deep fiord-like indentations along the shoreline. Trees here grow at a 45° angle away from the tramontana, like life-sized bonsai. Voluntary settlers accept or actually enjoy this wild weather which often arrives out of a clear blue sky.

Like the other Balearics the island was on the trade route of the western Mediterranean in ancient times; so Greeks, Carthaginians, Romans, Vandals, Byzantines and Muslims came and sometimes settled until the Catalans conquered the Balearics in the thirteenth century. Periods of relative calm followed periods of local and international turbulence. When the island's population was decimated by various plagues, during the fifteenth century, King Alfonso V pardoned prisoners on condition that they went to Menorca and stayed there. The people of Ciudadela fought the people of Mahon (there remains today antagonism between the old and new capital and many of today's inhabitants of Ciudadela do not visit Mahon and vice versa).

Various Muslim fleets sacked Ciudadela and Mahon during the sixteenth century. The authorities commissioned the same Italian architect, Juan Bautista Calvi, to fortify the entrance to Mahon harbour and Ibiza Town. Massacres, pillage and slave-raids by Muslims continued into the seventeenth century, until the might of the Crescent powers waned. Conflict between the island's main towns continued but the superior harbour at Mahon finally resolved the question of which was the capital of the future. By the time the British arrived in 1708 Mahon had won the local battle for status.

For reasons of balance of power in the Europe of the time, which now seem ludicrous, Britain, France, Austria and the Netherlands were all involved on one side or the other in the War of the Spanish Succession. The Spanish Empire then included what is now Belgium, parts of the Americas, Sicily and most of Italy amongst other possessions. There were two claimants for the Spanish throne. Mahon harbour was then considered the best in the Mediterranean. A force of British troops supported by Spanish and Portuguese set out from Mallorca to take Menorca for the supporters of the Austrian claimant to the Spanish throne. The fact that the French supported the rival claimant, and that Menorca was an ideal base for monitoring the activities of the French fleet based at Toulon, were added attractions.

The thirty-five-year-old military genius, Major General James Stanhope, led and planned the campaign for the conquest of Menorca. Stanhope always claimed that the success of his campaign was in great part due to the support his troops received from the local people. His real problem was to capture the impressive Fort St Philip, created by Calvi one hundred and fifty years earlier as a deterrent to Muslim raids. This he achieved by a mixture of frontal attack and low cunning, using artillery, horseback charges and messages attached to arrows, offering a couple of gold pounds to deserters. The reply was quick in coming from the garrison's commander asking, effectively, what was in it for him?

British rule, consolidated by transfer of sovereignty of Gibraltar and Menorca under the terms of the Treaty of Utrecht, was exercised by Sir Richard Kane, an Ulsterman and professional soldier who was progressive and enlightened for the period. Inevitably the island's old establishment and clergy based upon Ciudadela engaged in trials of strength with him from time to time usually based upon the needs, as they saw them, to preserve the Catholic authority over the island's thought processes. With the support of Whitehall Kane saw off such challenges. Meantime he was winning the battle for hearts and minds with the people.

Kane built the island's main road from Mahon to Ciudadela via Alayor, Mercadal and Ferrerias and financed it and other projects by imposing a tax on alcohol. Much of this road remains and still bears its originator's name. The wine produced on the island at the time was, incidentally, compared by the British and the French visitors to that of Burgundy, until phylloxera destroyed the island's vineyards at the end of the last century. Kane drained the wetlands around Mahon and made them suitable for horticulture and orchards, controlled production and prices of food in the local markets (food of all kinds was in short supply at the time), and introduced from Britain new varieties of crops, cattle and poultry. He also controlled the sometimes riotous activities of his forces of occupation.

Kane's successors did not enjoy either his reputation or his achievements. One, 'Red' Anstruther, so nicknamed for his florid complexion, was actually recalled to London, after which he quickly produced the island's Alcohol Tax from his back pocket. Another tried to top up the British Navy's manpower needs by use of the Press Gang amongst the island's able-bodied males on the basis that they were, of course, British subjects: they took a different view and won after the spilling of some blood. Yet another had the opportunist idea of introducing Greek traders into Menorca to perk up the commercial climate locally: they traded as expected and developed salt-pans and even mined for coal, and actually created a Greek community with its own church in Mahon, to the disgust of the Catholic hierarchy.

By the mid-1750s British rule on Menorca had become somewhat slack. The forces were then commanded by General Blakeney, an amiable man much given to the pleasures of the punchbowl. He was lacking in ambition, being eighty-two years old at the time. The once impregnable Fort St Philip had fallen into disrepair due to the shortage of funds and interest. When word came that the traditional enemy, France, was constructing further ships at Toulon for an adventure against Menorca Blakeney called a council of war, only to discover that almost all of his officers were on leave in Britain or had not even taken up their posts on the island. Meantime, Admiral Byng had been dispatched from Britain with reinforcements. The French arrived on the island and set about a relaxed campaign to take the strongpoint of Fort St Philip. After a couple of months they succeeded. Admiral Byng came, saw, fired a few cannonballs and went away: he was shot after a superficial trial in March 1757 for lack of diligence, in the classic phrase: 'to encourage the others'.

General Blakeney, who spent his day in bed at the height of the siege of his garrison, returned to Britain to a baffling hero's welcome. The French victor, the Duc de Richelieu returned to Paris with the recipe for mayonnaise picked up locally by his chef from a lady in Mahon.

The French were well received by the populace, particularly the old families and clergy of Ciudadela who were much taken with the newcomers' manners, fine clothes and compatible religion. But when they left after thirteen years not much remained except the attractive village of San Luis to remind us of their occupancy.

The British returned in 1763 – except for the Governor Sir Richard Lyttleton who preferred to run the island from his home in Richmond, Surrey – under the terms of the Peace of Paris, the Spanish and French having been defeated in the Americas. Once again the islanders welcomed their new rulers. The Greek traders, expelled by the French, also came back. A Jewish community was also established and was also opposed by the Catholic authorities as they had previously opposed the Greeks. The greatest relic of this period of British rule is the enormous parade ground in the town, now Villa Carlos after Charles III of Spain but then named Georgetown after George III of England.

War broke out again fifteen years later between France and Britain and Spain allied itself to the French cause a year after,

in 1779. Seven thousand French and nine thousand Spanish troops
came ashore at Cala Mesquida and proceeded to blockade the British in Fort St Philip. The British garrison survived incredibly for
six months before being forced to surrender as they were literally
wasting away. The Spanish demolished the highly effective Fort St
Philip in 1782 for reasons which seemed good at the time. When
the British came back yet again in the late autumn of 1798 Mahon
surrendered immediately to General Stuart's forces: the island fell
without the loss of a single invader's life.

These final four years of British rule added greatly to Menorca's
prosperity. The needs of 12,000 troops for accommodation, food
and relaxation and the needs of the navy for supplies and dockyard
repairs put money into the local economy. The five days spent on the
island by Nelson during his only visit in October 1799 still benefits
the economy.

As a result of wheeling and dealing Menorca was again traded by
treaty in 1802 and returned to Spanish rule, but not to the liking of
the inhabitants, who chaffed under the more centralised government
from Madrid. Trade which had flourished under the British fell off,
adding to the local discontent. The days of the British began to seem
like 'the good old days'.

When Napoleon installed his brother Joseph as King of Spain six
years later discontent led to strife throughout Spain. Like Mallorca,
Menorca received an influx of wealthy refugees from Cataluna as
Napoleon's forces entered Spain and Mahon expanded to accommodate them. Spain and Britain were allies during the Peninsular War
and the British fleet again used Mahon harbour as a valued base
against the French. The commander of the British Mediterranean
Fleet was then Lord Collingwood – Nelson's second-in-command at
Trafalgar – and he conducted his campaign from Mahon. His house
is now a well-regarded hotel between Mahon and Villa Carlos.

As in earlier conflicts the local people stood by their traditions
of not getting involved in wars themselves. Freedom from military
service has always been regarded as a basic freedom on Menorca.
Emigration to the Americas and North Africa; riots and the
destruction of public records; even hurried marriages; these have all
been ploys for the avoidance of military service until Franco's harsh
regime made conscription unavoidable from the forties onwards.

The decline in local prosperity followed the decline in Mediterranean wars throughout the nineteenth century and this too

encouraged emigration. But there were some bright spots. The authorities having dismantled Fort St Philip on the south of the harbour entrance decided to erect another fortress, La Mola, on the other side of the entrance fifty years later: This ambitious project created a great deal of employment. Further work was generated by the introduction of shoe manufacture into Ciudadela in the mid-1850s. The island settled into a lifestyle of moderate affluence by the standards of many other less fortunate areas in the Mediterranean and this continued until the start of the bloody Civil War.

As in some other parts of Spanish territory which are physically isolated and have close-knit communities the local people do not discuss the Civil War with foreigners. Neighbours and families were split. Supporters of the elected government and supporters of the army revolt died in gun battles; some were murdered. When the military rose, with the backing of some families from Ciudadela, the revolt was put down by the majority, and the island remained in Loyalist control. The island was blockaded and shortages of food and other commodities, except for wheat and milk, prevailed. But it was not invaded. Some bombs fell on the island from Italian planes based in Mallorca, and a deal was struck between Franco and Mussolini which yet again traded sovereignty of Menorca in exchange for other advantages.

At the end of the Civil War the British came back, if only temporarily, on an errand of official mercy. HMS *Devonshire* carried Franco's emissary to Mahon a couple of months before the formal end of the war on 1 April 1939. The agreed terms of surrender involved HMS *Devonshire* carrying 450 Republican sympathisers to France while the occupation by Franco's troops was subject to token resistance only. A possible massacre was avoided. Later, when the British were concerned about Italy joining Germany in the Axis a suggestion, backed with threats from Churchill, persuaded Franco to renege on his agreement to transfer the control of Menorca to Mussolini.

It is considered by some commentators that the residual goodwill of the islanders towards the British rests mainly upon the fact that Churchill spared them from yet another change of sovereignty without their agreement. Others say that the reminders of British rule in the appearance of the countryside, Georgian townscapes in Mahon and Villa Carlos, door-knockers, door-latches and sash-windows (unknown before they were introduced during British rule), and words like 'bottle' and 'table' which remain the local language are more responsible for making British long-stay visitors feel welcome. Holiday property on the island is generally suitable for its purpose. Homes for permanent or semi-permanent use are ideally planned to account for the rough weather which hits Menorca from October to April: this is a matter of commonsense assessment by potential buyers. Your agent is unlikely to mislead you if you have carefully spelled out your needs and have demonstrated that you have done your homework.

It follows that the exposed north coast is not the place for year-round living unless you select an appropriate site and an appropriate property. But the less exposed south coast is primarily given over to holiday homes (with some well-built exceptions) and you will know from comments made elsewhere in the book that holiday complexes do not always provide the most suitable setting for long-stay visits or permanent living.

The island's farmhouses are rightly treasured, with or without an hectare or two of land. Old houses in Mahon and Villa Carlos are also becoming collectors' items: those in Ciudadela rarely reach the agents' windows (like Palma's palacios, the aristocratic mansions in the old capital are never on the market). Mahon itself, and either side of its spectacular 5km (3 mile) long inlet, is arguably the most appealing general location for property for permanent use, particularly after the imaginative and practical upgrading of many of the capital's services and facilities in the eighties.

Apart from some spectacularly inappropriate hotels which have permanently scarred the appearance of some magnificent bays, and some early substandard villa developments, the island has been spared the usual development excesses. No new hotels are contemplated in the island's current zoning plans and height and density controls are enforced. Some over-ambitious projects, often without the needed consents, remain as reminders of less sophisticated times. Current projects generally show respect for the low-key appeal of the island. Overall, facilities are adequate for a full and active life.

The Maltese Islands

From the air the deep blue sea around the islands looks more attractive than what seems to be flat barren land and crowded towns which form a continuous urban sprawl. A closer look reveals that every patch of land which can be cultivated is cultivated, and that the crowded houses are built from stone the colours of honeycomb, often ornately carved. Malta island accommodates around 350,000 people on what is essentially a piece of softish rock no more than 27km (16 miles) long and 14.5km (9 miles) wide. There are no mountains, rivers or lakes. Undoubtedly, beauty is in the eye of the beholder and to some Malta is indeed beautiful.

Paradoxically, the earliest inhabitants of the islands were farmers who preferred them to Sicily 93km (58 miles) to the north. Various local civilisations waxed and waned, leaving remarkable architectural monuments of massive dressed stones, which are thought to be the oldest buildings in existence – some were created six thousand years ago using lifting techniques unknown to us. The growth of maritime trade made the Maltese Archipelago strategically important because it was on the way to almost everywhere in the Mediterranean. Phoenicians, Carthaginians, Romans and Greeks all established trading posts on the islands.

Christianity first came to the island of Malta in AD 60 when St Paul came ashore after his shipwreck. The Romans, the Byzantines from Constantinople and then the Arabs ruled until Roger the Norman reconquered Malta for Christianity. Control by many of the then European nation states followed until the renowned Knights of St John became rulers, protectors and benefactors in 1530.

For more than two and a half centuries civilised order was established under a succession of Grand Masters, bringing prosperity and justice to the islands until the Order lapsed into decadence. Thus weakened the knights surrendered to the forces of Napoleon Bonaparte in 1798. However, the French were soon beaten by the Maltese themselves, who rose against their invaders with the assistance of the British Navy.

Malta became a British colony and as such was ruled with the usual mixture of authoritarianism, paternalism and near-democracy. Full independence was granted in 1964. Ten years later the islands became a republic within the Commonwealth. A shared history for over a century and a half, a common language, a common experience in the heroic defence of the islands during the war, and even a tradition (somewhat voluntary) of driving on the left continue to link Britain and the Maltese Republic in spite of the tensions of the Mintoff years from 1971.

Tough and sometimes rough negotiations for better terms for the

Maltese for the leasing of their harbours and other facilities by Nato and the British led to soured relationships and more money and greater dignity for the Maltese short term. Links with the Gadaffi regime in Libya and decisions which were difficult for outsiders to understand had a longer term effect on the local economy. Tourism from Britain, for example, slumped and vacillated leading to over-capacity and unemployment for more than a decade. Visitors reached 700,000 again in 1980 only to decline by a third over the next four years: an overvalued Maltese Pound and sloppy standards are the accepted reasons for this drop.

Clearly, the apparently anti-British stance adopted by Prime Minister Dom Mintoff was matched by a reaction; and owners had a bad time as values of holiday and retirement homes dropped as buyers were hard to find. Some agents and developers went into other kinds of business. Meanwhile the sun continued to shine.

To put Malta into perspective it is only necessary to compare it with Ibiza, for example. Ibiza is about twice the size with about one-fifth of the population; the climate is comparable; so is the distance from North Africa. But Ibiza has over 1 million visitors a year. Ibiza has two official nudist beaches and all the rest are unofficial nudist beaches. It is forbidden for women to sunbathe topless anywhere in public on the Maltese Islands. Ibiza has a two-thousand year history of relaxed tolerance. The Catholic Church on Malta is reactionary; it is even more so on Gozo. Fiestas on Ibiza are secular; the Maltese equivalent are religious. There are hundreds of excellent restaurants on Ibiza; there are few on the Maltese Islands. There are hundreds of cafés and bars on Ibiza where families relax together over a drink to watch the world go by; there is no Maltese equivalent and families do not eat out or drink together in public. There are more outstanding resort villas on Ibiza than on any comparable location in the Mediterranean; there are few notable modern homes on Malta. Ibiza has many well-converted farmhouses, all detached and surrounded by fields; Malta and Gozo have many magnificently converted farmhouses, mostly terraced. Ibiza has one remarkable resort hotel, the remote Hacienda; Gozo has one of the world's best hotels, the low-rise bungalow Ta Cenc Hotel.

Further comparisons would only serve to emphasise that the Maltese Islands, the people and their customs are unsophisticated in the complete dictionary definition of the word. For some this is an enormous attraction. This appeal is reinforced by the real and open friendliness which is characteristic of the Maltese and the freely given smiles which are infectious. Visitors from the North of England often find themselves more at home more quickly in Malta than they do in the resorts of the south coast of their own country. As with Gibraltar, British visitors feel abroad on Malta, but only slightly.

The word 'barren' is used about these islands automatically, as a conditioned reflex. There is no doubt that the lack of trees, grass, shrubs and flowers – indeed, the obvious lack of interest locally in gardens and gardening – can come as a shock to visitors. In spite of the received wisdom about exchange rates and anti-British governments in the past few years having led to fluctuations in tourist numbers, and to small numbers of British buyers of resort homes, the real reason for uneven levels of visitors and purchasers is more likely to be the absence of greenery and flowers. Anyone who has made the trip to these islands can readily visualise the transformation which could be made by lush vegetation, palm trees, climbers and shrubs laden with colourful blooms and a few square kilometres of juicy green fairways. However, centuries of traditional indifference to this softening of the environment would need to be overcome for any noticeable change to take effect.

Fortunately local building skills have traditionally been outstanding, both in basic construction and in decoration. The feature of the landscape is the village church. The Church as an institution is powerful – 85 per cent of the population is said to be Catholic – and it shows. It shows everywhere because the village church is always cathedral-sized and would be appropriate in the main streets of Rome. Any visitor will be impressed, or even awed by these dominating domed and belfreyed Baroque buildings, paid for on the never-never by the subscriptions of the congregation. The quality of the stonework of old and new churches demonstrates the fine traditions which continue to be learned and practised, and this quality can be found also in the village houses currently being built throughout the islands.

The ancient city of Mdina is a fortified example of all the local building skills. Traffic-free, this silent city has many truly palatial buildings which have intricately carved masonry inside and out, some still owned by the Maltese nobility. The houses in Mdina very occasionally change hands; by word of mouth it is sometimes known that a 'decadent family' is willing to consider selling their collection of art, artefacts and furniture and the building which houses it.

Valletta also has palaces and finely crafted townhouses, most of which are now government offices, museums or galleries. The position of today's capital overlooking the historic and aptly named Grand Harbour is dramatic. The city can provide for all the needs of the island's population and for those of foreign residents, too, but sailors who remember the city when it catered for them in their thousands, when a substantial part of the British Fleet was always coming and going, will be disappointed by the air of calm and propriety.

Marsaxlokk, in the island's south east, is still a fishing village but it too has buildings – and inevitably a church – of a quality which would not look out of place in a major city in Europe. It also has a fleet of brightly painted 'Luzzus', the traditional Maltese fishing boats which are amongst the most photogenic in the Mediterranean. Besides the fine examples of architecture and building skills there are many less attractive examples of sixties' apartments built for the holiday trade and for foreign, mainly British, buyers and many villas which resemble over-ornate Edwardian bungalows, saved only by the fact that they are constructed from one of the best possible materials: the remarkable Franka stone.

For the British buyer of property on Malta during the nineties the 'best buy' will inevitably become increasingly scarce and costly. This 'best buy' is the farmhouse, built from massive cut blocks of Franka stone, with barrel-vaulted ceilings, ground floors usually intended for cattle rather than people, and flat roofs. These substantial homes are the true gems of the islands. Reproductions of these farmhouses, or modern buildings inspired by them, are more fitting than the mundane examples of sixties' apartments which are out of place on Malta and Gozo.

The drastic fluctuations in foreign exchange earnings from tourism and the purchase of resort property over the past few decades have clearly concerned the administration. New laws now actively encourage buyers of holiday homes and settlers. No rates and no Capital Gains Tax are levied against holiday or permanent homes owned by foreigners. Foreigners are permitted to buy homes which exceed LM 15,000: this is intended to keep lower-priced property for the Maltese first-time buyer. Controls exist to discourage speculation in property. One property per foreign family is the limit. Formal permission is needed for a foreigner to buy; this is sometimes withheld if the property is of historical importance or is in an area of historical sensitivity. Given the size of the islands and the size of the population, and the need to encourage foreign investment, a balancing act is clearly required, with understandable rule changes from time to time as necessary.

The Maltese Islands have major differences from other resort locations within acceptable reach of Britain. Elsewhere in this book reference has been made to the vital factor in your choice of where to buy your resort home in another country. The chosen location must feel right and give a lift to the spirits. Some who visit these islands can't wait to get off, visually bored by what they see as scruffy, bare landscape with natural slag heaps here and there, and terraced houses all of more or less the same colour, and plenty of them. Others see it differently: the rugged coast has some good beaches and coves; the sea is clear and reflects the usually clear blue sky; the people are almost invariably open and friendly; English is widely spoken; driving on the left seems voluntary but familiar; the street scene during religious festivals, trotting races and other public events is lively but without trouble; homes are usually twice the size of those in other resort areas; and the legal routines of property purchase

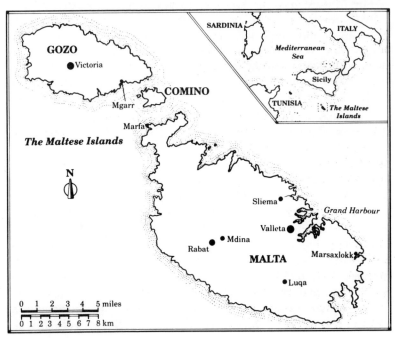

are protective of the buyer (Napoleon is said to have introduced the basics of his property laws during a busy six-day visit while the French occupied the islands).

Shopping on Malta itself is as comprehensive as in any large British town and the goods and produce are as familiar as at home. British TV programmes are shown normally on the local service. The streets clear when those locals with the appropriate 'boosters' to enable Italian TV to be received are at home to watch the very blue movies shown on the specialist channel. Craftsmanship is a bonus for anyone wanting special furniture or fittings to be made. Eating out opportunities are limited, compared with other resort areas, but local produce is tasty, especially the fish. Some local wines are palatable but the beer is excellent: there is a wide range of imported drink at acceptable prices.

Behind the ready smile is a pride, explained in part by the fact that the Maltese have never knuckled under their occupiers. There is the generally relaxed attitude to everyday life found elsewhere around the Mediterranean, but business is usually conducted formally, smartly suited when appropriate.

The Maltese Islands are easy to get to and easy to get from. Italy is a short ferry ride away; North Africa is a short hop away by plane and a short cruise by boat; given that this is the centre of the Middle Sea, Malta is the perfect base for anyone planning an active and mobile retirement in the sun.

Gozo

Gozo is a quarter the size of Malta with less than one-tenth of the larger island's population. Access is by ferry from Cirkewwa or hovercraft from Sliema on Malta to the harbour of Mgarr. Gozo is 6km (3¾ miles) from the main island and is less than 42sq km (26sq miles) in area. Nowhere on Gozo is more than a couple of miles from the sea. The island has its own identity: it is somewhat greener and much less crowded than Malta. The intention of the government is to encourage limited up-market development here during the nineties. A rugged coastline and curious flat-topped hills are the physical features; overpowering churches in each village, mysterious archaeological ruins, and the ubiquitous Franka stone provide the man-made features. But the island lacks a focal point: the main town Rabat, also called Victoria, is without attractions for the holiday visitor or the foreign homeowner. But its very absence of mainstream resort appeal is its appeal, for some. The Ta Cenc Hotel on the rocky south coast is a sprawling one-storey collection of stone buildings of inspired simplicity: used as a style-guide for future restrained development there is hope that Gozo will avoid the lowest common denominator overdevelopment which is no longer accepted by discerning buyers.

Sardinia

Anyone who has flown over this huge island – the second largest in the Mediterranean – will have seen vast mountain ranges dominating its centre. They have grandeur rather than beauty and serve as an awe-inspiring backdrop to the truly beautiful coastline. Many areas are still remote enough to remain unexplored. They make the stories of bandits still credible in the last decade of the twentieth century.

It is necessary to recognise banditry, however defined, as a subject still linked with the island in the minds of any visitor. The locals prefer to use the word 'outlaws' as a description of their traditional heroes or villains. Rustlers may be a better term for these people, who steal animals as a commodity in preference to kidnapping wealthy foreigners for a cash ransom. They have been doing it for centuries. Poverty and natural trust are part of the characteristics of the Sards, particularly those from the Nuoro district; but betrayal of this straightforward trust causes anger, leading to hatred and evolving occasionally into vendettas. Cattle, pigs, horses and sheep were and still are possessions easily stolen from the targets of vendettas; retaliation for the theft escalates into bloodshed; killings are not unknown, leading to sons making for the mountains to support themselves by whatever means practical. Outsiders are not welcome to involve themselves in these vendettas and that includes the police who try to enforce what the locals see as the alien laws of the mainland. Kidnapping foreigners is rare; but when it happens it makes headlines worldwide. Without doubt this factor has harmed the image of Sardinia as a resort destination and has resulted in little development relative to the size, climate and physical appeal of the island.

From Italy to Sardinia by boat involves about eight hours at sea today: small wonder that the island was settled later than more easily accessible islands. Evidence shows nothing man made on Sardinia before the end of the third millennium BC. But what remains of that period shows that the first inhabitants built massive fortified settlements – Nuraghi – over seven thousand of which demonstrate constructional and design skills which are remarkable in any period. Similar baffling buildings exist on Malta, Menorca and Cyprus. More sensitive qualities are shown in the delicate bronzes of the time. The truncated conical towers and massive defensive walls protected the early Sards until the Romans came, inevitably, and conquered the island in the third century BC.

Before the Roman Conquest Phoenician traders and Carthaginian armies established outposts and fought wars against the Sards and other potential rulers. During the seven centuries of Roman occupation they too were resisted by the Sards; by any modern criteria this remarkable period of guerilla warfare seems unreal and leads to facile assumptions about traditions of banditry and ambivalent attitudes to law enforcement. The Romans were literally on the island for what they could get out of it and left fewer reminders here than elsewhere in their overseas possessions of the time.

Over the next nine centuries Vandals, more Romans, Goths, Byzantines, Saracens and rulers of some of Italy's city states controlled Sardinia until the Aragonese King Alfonso IV took it during the time of Spanish expansion. Spanish rule was consolidated when the royals of Aragon and Castile united their families and their kingdoms. The Spaniards remained until Sardinia was handed around the powerful nations of the time under various treaties: the Elector of Bavaria held it for a few years; he lost it to Philip V of Spain, who swapped it for Sicily; then it went to the House of Savoy.

Vittorio Amedeo III proclaimed himself King of Sardinia and began his reign well, building roads and schools and introducing new laws; his son succeeded to the throne in 1730 and continued the progressive rule, but the next king passed the administration of the island to opportunists from Piedmonte. Unhappy times followed. Additional problems for the House of Savoy came with the loss of possessions and power to Napoleon. Succeeding kings lost more and more influence nationally and internationally, exploited the Sards and finally, after 140 years of ineffectual rule, the House of Savoy, and with it the Kingdom of Sardinia, lost its separate identity in a unified Italy in 1861.

The Sards had been occupied and governed by outsiders for

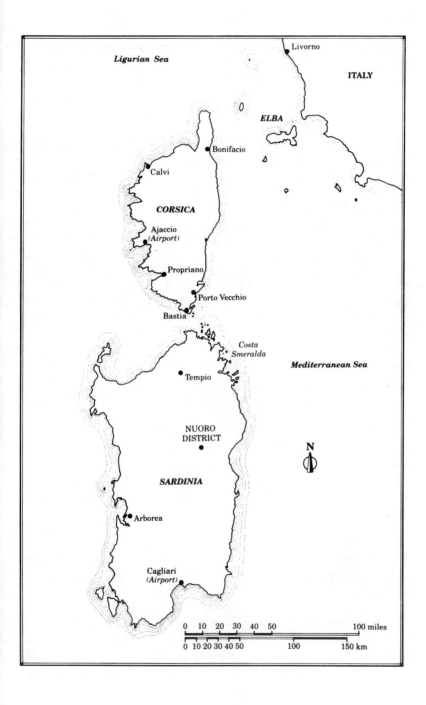

thousands of years. Union with a united Italy did nothing to change this until it became an autonomous region in 1948. It remained economically deprived in spite of some investment by entrepreneurs and central government: railways were built at the end of the nineteenth century; hydro-electric dams were constructed; irrigation was introduced in some dry areas; and Mussolini ordered the draining of swamps and the construction of the town of Arborea on the reclaimed land.

It can be argued that the last two invasions of Sardinia have had direct beneficial effects upon the people. American administrators during World War II dosed the island repeatedly and successfully with the then miracle drug DDT. This cured the centuries-old disabling sickness of malaria. Many homes carry a tribute to this practical side-effect of the war on the plaques and signs on their façades, which give the simple message: 'DDT 1944'. Tourism, admittedly not on the scale made possible by the length of Sardinia's marvellous coastline, has brought obvious benefits, and the potential for civilised resort development remains for future exploitation.

The original concept of the famous Costa Smeralda project on the magical coast at the island's northern tip was laudable. The Aga Khan was persuaded to invest in an enormous tract of virgin land with 48km (30 miles) of water frontage and 300sq km (7,500 acres) of land behind it. This vast area was intended to be developed as a luxury resort for what was then, in the early sixties, known as the 'Jet Set'. The estate has progressed over the years and contains some of the most impressive resort architecture outside the USA. Carefully controlled use of materials and some inspired designs have contributed to man's enhancement of the gifts of nature on this spectacular site. The golf course too is highly regarded, unlike the other Robert Trent Jones designs in Europe.

The concept of the Costa Smeralda project suffered from inherent flaws, according to some informed critics of resort development. Its target market, the Jet Set, was never quite numerous enough to take up the great quantity of property on offer: some 2,500 units (villas and apartments) only had been sold after twenty-five years. There is an inherent contradiction in creating an 'exclusive' development of such enormous size: unless there is a defined and small unity the word and the thought of exclusivity is untenable. The season is short and access out of season is awkward and time-consuming – if you do not possess a private jet! Banditry hardly helps promotional credibility when the internationally wealthy are the potential buyers of expensive property. Security is now part of the purchaser's deal – an obvious necessity which you would prefer to do without, given that a resort home is about fun. However, in spite of the conceptual flaws including its relative isolation from things Sardinian, the Costa Smeralda has many inspirational elements in its masterplan and in its individual buildings.

The potential of the island is outstanding, particularly if future development takes account of the mistakes made elsewhere around the Mediterranean. Sardinians like to eat and drink and make merry. Smoked sausages from Tempio and ham from wild boar are tasty traditional starters. Pastas have local rather than mainland characteristics. Country main courses are usually of meat: lamb, kid and suckling pig are simple specialities for visitors and everyday dishes for the Sards. Nearer the sea the fish dishes are renowned for fresh flavours, often enhanced by the use of local herbs. Crisp, thin dough baked in round disks is just one example of the many different breads available. Cheeses are sharp and tangy and are for some an acquired taste. Desserts are often honey based or sugary and are addictive. One of the mistakes made in the Spanish resorts is to internationalise the cuisine: it is to be hoped that future expansion of tourism and development here retains the local foods as part of the essential identity of Sardinia.

The local wines too are part of the powerful identity of the island. Full-bodied reds, famous whites, dryish rather than dry in the Italian manner, and a range of dessert wines provide the means for serious wine buffs and adventurous amateurs to enjoy their education in what the island has to offer the homeowner. It is said that it is not possible to buy a bad wine here: it is certainly not possible to buy a thin or weak one made in Sardinia. Local liqueurs are not outstanding but some speak well of the equivalent of Strega; there is also a local aquavit. These purely local products are unlikely to be modified to the point of anonymity to suit the supposed palates of the average wine buyer in our British supermarkets.

Festas are held throughout the towns and villages and are lively, sombre, noisy, quiet, religious and downright pagan in turn. Foreigners are welcomed and treated hospitably on these occasions if they show the slightest interest in what is happening. Some involve brilliant costumes; some make use of the island's impressive horses and horsemanship; some are very spooky.

Anyone considering buying a home here should sample them all in the same spirit in which they should sample all the wines.

Property on Sardinia is rarely aggressively marketed in Britain. The Costa Smeralda developers had an office in the centre of London for a short time. Some agents have offered homes there from time to time. Some developers have advertised in British publications periodically. All have promoted new projects aimed at the international market. Enthusiasts for homes on this fascinating island are usually obliged to do their own prospecting. Given the size of Sardinia, its topography, its varied food and drink, traditions and customs, and above all its people, taking your time to get to know it well in all its aspects makes pleasurable sense.

The legalities of property purchase are as for Italy.

14

AUSTRIA

Austria today has an image of political, social and cultural sophistication against a backdrop of natural beauty: well-ordered government with just an occasional hint of scandal; orderly people much given to taking coffee and cakes on café terraces; Nazi-hunters and neutrality; Strauss; opera and oompah bands; gluhwein, schnitzels, snow, ski slopes and lakes; Salzburg festivals, Klimt and Shiele; breathtaking scenery and clear mountain air; fairy-tale castles against forests and blue skies; and leather shorts and Tyrolean hats. The national symbol, after just one movie set in Vienna half a century ago, is regarded by some foreigners as the zither.

Austria is almost as central as possible in Europe. It borders Italy, Yugoslavia, Hungary, Czechoslovakia, Germany and Switzerland. Vienna was the seat of power in European affairs during the Austro-Hungarian Empire and it looks as if it still should be. The calm of today belies the country's history.

Austrian rulers used to throw their considerable weight about. They made alliances and wars, often in partnership with the British, often against Napoleon (who usually beat them), and won and lost territory in other people's countries with bewildering frequency. Maximilian of Hapsburg even became Emperor of Mexico until he was shot. In the early years of this century, however, Austria made an alliance without Britain which proved literally fatal. Horse-trading led to the establishment of two power-blocs: Britain, France and Russia; and Germany and Austria. Tension mounted and the armament factories worked overtime. The Balkans again came to the boil. While visiting recently annexed Bosnia, in what we still think of as Yugoslavia, the heir to the Austrian throne, Archduke Ferdinand, was assassinated by a Serbian student. This triggered off events leading to World War I. Austria was on the losing side. After the war a republic was formed.

Hitler occupied Austria with local support but against the wishes of the elected government in 1938. At the end of World War II Austria was effectively governed by Russia and the Western Powers until achieving total self-rule. The country has thrived since.

The reasons for interest by some British buyers of resort homes here are a mix of sporting, environmental and cultural factors. But the purchase of homes by foreigners is not straightforward in one important aspect. Strictly speaking, at any stage of the sale trans-action before title is registered in the Grundbuch (Land Registry) the sale can be challenged by an Austrian national. In other words, Austrians get preference in sales of real estate. Any offer for property made by an Austrian at the same price and on the same terms as that made by a foreigner will result in the sale being made to the Austrian. However, experienced agents offering homes in Austria on the British market take care to ensure that such difficulties do not arise. In many blocks of apartments the authorities, specifically the Land Commission, stipulates that a certain percentage of the properties may be foreign-owned. Provided the agreed percentage is not exceeded a challenge by an Austrian purchaser cannot be accepted. Where a property is already foreign-owned there is seldom difficulty in selling to another foreigner. As most properties of interest to foreigners are offered on the local and international markets simultaneously Austrians have, in practice, plenty of time to express interest ahead of the likelihood of any sale to a foreigner.

It follows that if the appeal of Austria is so strong that you must buy a resort home here you will need the services of a British-based agent who really does know what he is doing. All stages of the buying process require the sure-footedness of a mountaineer.

Areas favoured by British buyers tend to be around the festival city of Salzburg, in the countryside or in the villages which lie to the south or east of this historic cultural centre. World Cup skiing events are staged in the area during the winter season. The lakes and mountains hereabouts can be enjoyed at any time of the year, however, and year-round rentals are possible.

Having selected a suitable property, and having avoided a challenge from a local contender you will be happy to know that the legal processes for buying real estate are straightforward. The purchase contract is a binding legal document as elsewhere outside the UK. It is drawn up in German with an English translation. It can be signed either in Austria or in Britain. The 10 per cent down payment is only refundable if the sale falls through as a result of defective title or failure to obtain registration.

The contract of sale is normally prepared by a lawyer acting upon the instructions of both parties. He will need your Power of Attorney to act on your behalf. Mortgages can be granted to foreigners. The next stage is to sign the necessary legal documents to transfer ownership before an official at the Austrian Embassy in London. The signed contract of sale and the balance of the purchase price are then sent to the lawyer acting for both parties: the funds are placed in a trustee account. Registration of the transfer of ownership then takes place usually taking between four and six months. Finally the money changes hands when registration has been made.

Clearly, the restrictions on foreign ownership of a home in Austria are not off-putting to anyone determined to buy a property for fun in this clean and pleasant land. But it follows that practical guidance from a knowledgeable agent and a suitably experienced lawyer is essential.

15

FRANCE

The history of France over the past couple of centuries seems to indicate a split personality. Various Napoleons have risen, succeeded, failed and fallen. Outstanding democrats have presided from time to time. Membership of the Resistance seemed to increase tenfold after the war. There is little discrimination against blacks but North Africans are not even considered second-class citizens. The ratio of bathrooms to bedrooms is the lowest in Europe; architects still plan lavatories without washbasins; and, according to market research, a bar of soap lasts longer here than elsewhere. The size of apartments is generally smaller than anywhere else in Europe. And yet, culturally the French make the British seem barbaric. Paris is no longer the centre of the art world but it still shames London, particularly where official patronage of remarkable architecture is concerned. For a French businessman to understand art, music, literature, food, drink and women and to appreciate and discuss their qualities is considered quite normal: can the same be said of the average British businessman? It is a question of priorities, of course.

Except for office developments in Paris in the seventies, water company investment in the UK in the eighties and the Chunnel in the nineties our influence on things French, and vice versa, has declined since the end of World War II. Between 1963 and 1968 numbers of visitors from the UK to the South of France halved as Spanish tourism boomed: as a direct result our consulate in Nice closed in 1975. Somerset Maugham, Graham Sutherland, David Niven, Anthony Burgess, Dirk Bogard and Graham Greene were no longer everyday sights on the Côte d'Azur or the Riviera. . .

After the collapse of the old order following World War I the Riviera began to attract a faster and looser crowd. An observant visitor in May might have seen lunching at separate tables in sunny squares Lloyd George, Churchill and Beaverbrook; Cole Porter, Noel Coward and Beatrice Lily; Gertrude Stein, the Hemingways and the Scott Fitzgeralds; Picasso, Braque and Matisse; and the

Prince of Wales and his set. In 1925 an English solicitor opened an office in Monaco to service his clients who were buying homes on the coast. Three years later Grand Lodge in London authorised the founding of a Masonic Lodge in Nice.

Some argue that the dramatic decline in British influence and interest after World War II was responsible for the progressive debasement of the Riviera. Certainly it was French developers who created the monoliths but most of the villas designed for British and other blue-bloods in the last century were pompous and overblown piles saved only by attractive settings and good landscaping.

Now that the South of France is no longer ours what does it have to offer apart from outdated Victoriana and outdated sixties' blocks? The answer is: absolutely anything you want as long as you are prepared to pay the price. A million or two will still buy a majestically sited villa with sea and mountain views. Overpriced and undersized apartments on the busy coast road are always available. Rarely, romantic village houses are offered on hilltops behind Menton (which still retains an Italian ambience). Port Grimaud does not now die in September. The gap between St Tropez and Marseilles fills more each year with a variety of property for sale. A new generation of British people is being attracted to this area as a location for their resort homes. Golf courses are being built to attract those who would otherwise favour Spain or Portugal. Two centuries of tradition is now seen as important.

The traditional South of France is not, however, all of the South of France. The area from the Rhône to the Spanish border was unfashionable until the seventies. It had a reputation for malaria, killer-floods, saltmarshes and shallow lakes and a wind which could blow a baby out of a pram. It was a place to travel through, pausing only to drink the heavy red wines and eat the snails roasted over vine-clippings. Each summer thousands of French people did indeed travel through the region, on their way to spend their Francs on the burgeoning Costa Brava across the border. General de Gaulle was made aware that Frenchmen were spending money outside the country on holidays and second homes; so he initiated a state enterprise to develop the region with a chain of new resorts. Mosquitoes were eliminated by repeated bombings with chemicals. Flood relief schemes were planned and expensively implemented. Even the wine was upgraded and transported to Bordeaux for discreet blending. Massive marinas and resort developments were constructed from

the Carmargue to a point north of the ancient capital of Perpignan.
The results were mixed.

Tourism and resort development on a grand scale seldom
succeeds. Planning and architectural mistakes imposed upon
poorly conceived intentions remain to be seen along this coast.
Only now, decades later, are well-considered, human-scale projects
taking shape on this special coastline. The brutal architecture of
La Grande Motte is being softened slightly by the provision of a
golf course nearby. Other courses have been built, including one
in the naturists' Mecca of Cap d'Agde. But the region, with its
Catalan identity still proudly claimed, has many attractions for the
resort homeowner. Wines are made in great variety. The seafood is
outstanding. Visually dominated by the peaks of the Pyrenees, the
area attracted the great artists of the twentieth century: Picasso,
Braque, Gris, Matisse and Dufy lived here before they were able to
afford the Riviera property prices. Rennie Mackintosh made a small
living here in later life from his exquisite watercolours.

Not only new property is available here. In the early seventies
the French Government was obliged to cut production of *vin ordinaire*
which was this region's staple. The plan involved offering local
vignerons money to take vineyards out of cultivation. Enterprising
local agents associated themselves with Belgian agents in a venture
which spread happiness through the community: the surplus vineyards, with or without ancient stone houses or farmbuildings, were
sold to foreigners desperate for something in the south.

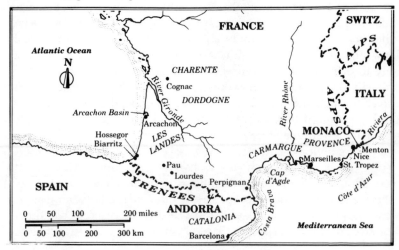

You should not expect English to be widely spoken here. The revival of Catalan nationalism in the region and across the border in Spain has rejuvenated the use of the Catalan language, although French is generally spoken as always. Increasingly, the young are looking towards Barcelona for inspiration rather than to Paris. The Sardanas, the magical music and dance which is peculiar to Catalonia, is as popular here as it is across the border. It is clear that many foreigners have bought homes in this region because it is almost Spain, with 320 or so days of sun annually and with ski resorts within a couple of hours. The fact that schoolboy French is readily understood is a bonus.

Further into the Pyrenees, in and around Andorra, Catalan, French and Castilian Spanish are spoken but more locals understand English in this autonomous anomaly because foreigners are necessary for the health of the economy. Andorra has its enthusiasts as a place for a holiday or more permanent home. The supply of building land is limited by its physical limits and contours: prices are not cheap except for duty-free goods. Its tax-haven status helps make Andorra a special case: highly priced housing is partly balanced for some by low or no taxes and a moderate cost of living for serious drinkers. Mountain resorts are either claustrophobic or represent freedom and wide open views as islands do: your psyche determines your opinion. In any event, escape is easy, with borders minutes away. But tax savings are not, alone, reasons for deciding where to live for fun.

Easier access to the central Pyrenees in the eighties and the staging of some 1992 Olympic events in Andorra are factors which will open up this attractive region to more potential buyers of rural or mountain homes. Property outside the ski resorts but within reach of their facilities can be found in the many small towns and villages where substantial houses requiring renovation can be bought for comparatively low prices. You would need to do your own prospecting through local agents and notaries.

For the adventurous hideaway hunter the wild, rugged and empty border country between Andorra and the Atlantic 300km (185 miles) away at Biarritz represents a challenge. Peaks a couple of kilometres above sea level are commonplace. Lakes and rushing streams; very wide open spaces; the frantic, and to some, the pathetic activity of Lourdes; Pau for the earliest European golf course; truly local food from farms, streams, lakes and shot out of the thin air. All this makes for a freshness which can be exhilarating if you are turned on by simple pleasures.

Biarritz is not what it was, in spite of new facilities, including golf courses and developments aimed at the newly free-to-buy Spaniards from over the border. But the area of coast north of the city has a special identity, and another golf course at Hossegor. Property here and along the lakeshore behind the coast is expensive. Further up the coast all the way to the Arcachon Basin level with Bordeaux are isolated seasonal holiday resorts of limited appeal, backed by lakes and forests on sand dunes. From Arcachon to the mouth of the Gironde seasonal holiday resorts rather than more permanent developments are also the norm.

Across the Gironde into the lower end of the Cognac region new and old property has increasingly found favour with some British buyers, drawn by the soft climate and traditions. The expansion of trade in old property from here to the south of Britanny has been spectacular during the late eighties, and specialist firms have blossomed offering anything from a cowshed to a château to British buyers unable to resist well-sited, picturesque bargains which the locals have been delighted to be rid of.

The French are not devoted to old buildings which need more than a coat of paint. Many outstanding properties were bought by eager British buyers in the Charente and Loire areas and some families retired early in order to live lives of almost ducal splendour in châteaux and *manoirs* surrounded by large estates. You will know that possessions can change personalities: old houses in classical French countryside can certainly do so and for some the purchase of such a home has been a truly liberating experience.

A few have been tempted to alter their whole lifestyle by the purchase of a home on the French Atlantic seaboard. The Chunnel with all its problems and opportunities concentrated minds, with companies from the South of England seriously considering relocating across the Channel, with encouragement and vigorous marketing applied by French Chambers of Commerce and local authorities. From Lille in the north of the area to Brittany attempts have been made to persuade British companies, property developers, tour operators and individuals to buy into a potential boom area. There have been successes and failures, depending finally on practicalities.

Some individuals able to work freelance have been tempted to relocate to Picardy and Normandy and commute to London or elsewhere in the south-east of England from their French homes. During the UK property boom of the late eighties this was an appealing option. Selling a British home at the height of the domestic market, before the collapse of 1989, and buying a bigger and better house in the French countryside four hours or so from the centre of London made romantic sense for some confident young businesslike self-employed high-flyers. But specialist agents report that this syndrome was more talked about than performed. The media readily accepted the growth of interest in northern France by British property buyers as newsworthy, particularly when some of the buyers were well-known media personalities. In practice – and this is finally the crucial aspect of commuting from and to your work or business – it makes sense for very few favoured individuals to buy a home in northern France when their income is derived from southern England. It is rare to find anyone who knows anyone who has actually done it.

Many more have, however, bought and enjoyed their rural homes in France as bolt-holes, to escape to without serious travel for long weekends and extended periods of rest and recuperation. The traditional English cottage hardly exists today except in easily accessible France.

The other market for French property which has enjoyed a boom is for the specialist ski apartments. Notoriously small, they have proved saleable to British skiers unwilling to put up with Swiss prices and limitations on foreign property ownership.

France is so large – almost two and a half times larger than the UK – that it is effectively divided into regions of totally different appeal: northern France is similar in physical respects to southern England; Les Landes with its long sandy beaches, forests and dunes, its chain of lakes and its somewhat wet climate; the Dordogne with its timeless and medieval villages; the rugged Midi; classical Provence; the very different mountainous areas of the Pyrenees and the Alps; its long Mediterranean coasts; the Vosges and the famous lakes; and vast areas without familiar names but equally strong identities. It is big enough and varied enough to provide any environment and specific property which you feel fits your personal needs – at prices which are still lower than those which prevail here. The investment potential is moderate but the return on pleasure is high.

16

GIBRALTAR

Just inside the mouth of the Mediterranean, 20km (12 miles) or so north of the African continent, the Rock of Gibraltar rises 427m (1,400ft) abruptly above sea level without geological logic. The Rock is on a thumb-like peninsula which partially encloses the Bay of Algeciras at almost the southernmost point of Europe. The peninsula is 6km (3⅗ miles) long and 5.5sq km (2.12sq miles) in area. Climatically it resembles the Costa del Sol with the additional feature of a cap of cloud which sometimes perches askew on top of the Rock, making the locals grumpy and the British visitors feel at home.

The Rock is honeycombed with natural and man-made tunnels and galleries. Some accommodate kilometres of roads which were once militarily useful. Others now enjoy new uses as museums and auditoria. There is great scope for future projects.

Given its location and dominating topography Gibraltar's place in history was understandable when sea-power was all-important. When the Moors were empire-building in the eighth century this was an entry point to the peninsula and a toll-gate between the Atlantic and the Mediterranean: the town of Tarifa just along the coast actually gave us the word 'tariff'. The first Moor to control the Rock gave us its name; he was Tarik-ibn-Zeyad and it became known as Jabal Tarik (the mountain of Tarik). Before the Moors were finally driven out of Spain altogether in the fifteenth century, Gibraltar withstood eight sieges between 1309 and 1462, leaving battlements on the Rock's western side and the knocked-about Tower of Homage as tourist attractions.

Admiral Rooke captured Gibraltar for the British in 1704 and it was formally ceded, with Menorca, in 1713 under the Treaty of Utrecht. The wording of this transfer of sovereignty has been in dispute since. The longest siege of Gibraltar lasted from 1779 to 1783 but two centuries later General Franco closed the frontier at La Linea until the democratic government reopened it almost ten years

after the dictator's death. Military needs determined the appearance
of Gibraltar – fortifications, dockyards, barracks etc – until tourism
and associated development received a boost from the removal of
the barriers at the frontier in 1985. Further pressure on the economy from announcements that British forces would be progressively
withdrawn from Gibraltar, and the election of a new administration
to supplant the forty-year dominance of Joshua Hassan were other
factors for change in the late eighties.

Four million tourists arrive on the Rock annually by plane,
car or ship. Those who cross the border from Spain are short-stay
visitors, attracted by duty-free bargains, and many are expatriates
who live on the Costa del Sol eager for the sight of Bobbies,
traditional red phone boxes, streaky bacon, Marmite and Marks
& Spencer's. Longer stay visitors can discover that Gibraltar has
many attractions over and above shopping: windsurfing from Eastern Beach; snorkelling and scuba diving off the rocks in clear water;
dolphin safaris, to view these playful and friendly creatures who act
as if trained to do so in the Straits; deep-sea fishing either in the
Atlantic or the Mediterranean, for bass or bream or even shark for
the intrepid; and sunbathing from any of the three sandy and four
rocky beaches although the towering Rock casts a long deep shadow
in the afternoons for much of the year. The famous apes on the upper
parts of the Rock are adept muggers, however.

There is an understandable but erroneous myth that the local
people are Spaniards who have preferred to live under British colonialism for centuries. This is not so: after the capture of Gibraltar
by Rooke in 1704 all but seventy of the Spaniards who lived there
decided to leave, to establish a 'new town' at San Roque a few
kilometres north of the Rock on a hilltop overlooking the Straits to
Africa. The embroidered Standard of Gibraltar is preserved here;
so are the records from 1500 until the time of the relocation of the
Rock's earlier inhabitants.

Today's 30,000 Gibraltarians are of mixed origins: Genoese who
arrived and settled in the eighteenth century; Catalans who came
with the British voluntarily, as refugees from turbulent northern
Spain at the same time; Jews escaping from persecution in Spain
and Portugal, via Morocco, who came to do business, supplying
the British forces, and who settled for stability and tolerance; some
Moroccan Muslims who came, stayed for a while and returned to
North Africa, to be replaced by substitutes who in turn remained for

no more than a decade or so; possible conscription into Napoleon's army provided a motive for more Genoese to settle in Gib, and this influx made them the majority of identifiable inhabitants until the middle of the last century; shipbuilders and repairers from Lisbon and Valletta in Malta were attracted to the permanent work offered by the British Fleet during the early and late years of last century; and some Scots, English, Welsh and Irish settlers came to evade punishment or prison back home. The result of this mixture is an identity and a commercial vigour which has an appeal out of all scale with the small size of the former military base.

Since the border restrictions with Spain were lifted many of Gibraltar's families have bought homes on the Costa del Sol and elsewhere within easy driving distance. Some actually live off the Rock and commute to their businesses daily. They may tell you that being confined to Gibraltar for a couple of decades had a claustrophobic effect upon them: they suffered from the condition known as being 'rock happy'. This should not necessarily deter you if the mouth of the Mediterranean appeals to you as a location for a holiday home or for more permanent living. No government is now likely to close its borders.

A solid case can be made for considering Gibraltar a resort with easy access to two continents. If your idea of the good life is to buy a resort home in which to stay put then this is not the spot for you: it is simply too small, too crowded and too popular with short-stay visitors. But if you have in mind a life of some mobility and excitement then the whole of Andalucia is on your doorstep; Portugal is just a few hours' hard drive away; and the whole of Africa is only a short ferry ride across the Straits.

It follows that the topography and size of Gibraltar are not conducive to low property values. Reclaimed land is seen as a viable means of providing future construction sites; major schemes are under way and more are planned. Low-density housing is not an option for Gibraltar, however. Reproducing the Georgian feel of the old townscape in new developments is not feasible either.

Leasehold tenure is the norm and ground rents reflect the shortage of building land. There are some freehold properties in Gibraltar: these derive from deeds drawn up on this basis during the last century. Solicitors' fees, stamp duty and all transfer costs are customarily paid by the purchaser. Holiday and other property offered for rental commands good returns. Non-nationals can, with the right professional advice, benefit from considerable income tax advantages as the government actively encourages offshore tax haven operations. There is no Capital Gains or Property Tax in Gibraltar.

The people who came to Gibraltar after the British conquest did so voluntarily and they remained voluntarily until some left via the reopened frontier with Spain. They have remained British voluntarily too, with only a derisory forty-four voters opting for a link with Spain in the referendum held in the eighties. Horse-trading and European Community policies and ambitions point to realistic solutions to the centuries-old problems of sovereignty of the Rock. However, some argue that one of today's major attractions of living on Gib is that you can now get off it easily.

Gibraltar is physically impressive rather than beautiful. The industrial area of the bay is patently ugly in spite of apologists who say that they don't notice it: certainly it mars the setting. But the prospect of new homes on reclaimed land around the Rock adds to the appeal of the place as a somewhat off-beat resort area. The romance of its history, including daring tales of U-boats and Italian midget submarines waiting across the Bay of Algeciras for the chance to strike at the Fleet, and its mixed nationalities, foods and customs, give Gib a unique identity. Best bitter, best butter, sherries and wines, tapas and teacakes and an almost comic conversational custom which involves the use of Spanglish – English and Spanish words freely mixed in the same sentence – ensures that it will continue to appeal to those who want to live abroad without having to make *all* the usual adjustments.

17

GREECE

A short list of words will serve to remind us how much we owe this difficult country: Achilles, Bacchus, Eros, Nemesis, Oedipus, Marathon, Olympic and Venus. As word and thought democracy began in Greece. A broad historical sense is a fundamental quality to be expected of anyone considering buying a resort home in Greece or on the islands.

For quite some while now Athens has not been the centre of the world as we know it. Nor is it high on the list of desirable city environments for foreigners. There are better places to live. But it has attracted Greeks from the outlying countryside, if not from the world at large: 2.5 million people – a quarter of the population – now live there. And it now physically joins the independent port city of Piraeus alongside. This port is more than a symbol of the country's past. Greece is a mountainous area at the very bottom of Europe but this is less important than the existence of a couple of thousand islands. The blue sea and the boats that sail on it between the islands are the simple factors which make for the Greek image.

Mythical and actual heroes, tumultuous international successes and failures, conquests and defeats, independent, democratic city states and autocracy, invasions and massacres, religious conversions and pagan attitudes: the past is peppered with these mixed and muddled affairs. The landscape is littered with the physical remains of this tumultuous history, to the delight of professional and amateur historians and archaeologists. There is a pride in the past but this pride also suffers from the memory of one of the painful defeats: this led to four centuries of Turkish rule which lasted until 1823; revolts and repression became routine; bandits became folk heroes; and the hatred of Greek for Turk, and vice versa, became permanent.

The Ottoman Turks were ousted with the help of Lord Byron: he convinced Western European opinion that the Greeks were fighting a clean and simple battle for independence. But the newly successful mercantile class, the clergy, the landowners and the bandits were not all fighting for the same ends. There was in-fighting for sectional advantage. But with some luck and international support independence was achieved. A number of political assassinations, revolts and a civil war followed. There was no agreement on who should rule. The crown was offered around; many declined to accept it until, for reasons incomprehensible today, an underaged Otto of Bavaria agreed to rule through a succession of regents. He ran the country from 1833 to 1863, unhappily, until he was ousted. More fighting in and out of the country followed. Territory was won from the old enemy, Turkey. Hundreds of thousands of Greeks emigrated to the USA. Greece entered World War I on the side of the Allies, against the Turks. Greece and Turkey continued fighting after everyone else had stopped until 1923, when half a million Muslims from Greece were removed to Turkey and a million Orthodox Greeks were removed to Greece from Turkey.

Greece was poor, overcrowded and badly governed. The king left. A more or less democratic republic was pronounced. The occasional military coup or dictatorship occurred. Monarchy returned, accompanied by a near-Fascist dictator Metaxas, in 1935. Mussolini's troops entered Greece from neighbouring Albania in the autumn of 1941; but the Greek history of fighting and banditry enabled them to rout the Italian crack troops and Hitler's more effective forces were obliged to take over the country a year later. Resistance continued in the rugged hills and mountains. The most effective resistance was undertaken by the Communist Party as the National Liberation Front. Churchill and the American administration undermined the power of this group after the war and manipulated the return of royalty with military support. Civil war followed. Democracy was thinly observed after the right won. Problems with Britain over the troubled island of Cyprus were resolved. A measure of material improvement benefitted the Greek people as the Western economies expanded. Young men went to West Germany for profitable work. A Liberal Government was elected at the end of 1963 against the wishes of the king and elements in the army. The colonels took power at the end of 1967.

The colonels were a throwback to thirties' thinking: they banned books, proclaimed the need for a return to what they called 'moral values' and tortured and killed those who disagreed with them. When the regime brutally broke up a peaceful demonstration by students the colonel's leader was replaced for being too soft. Clumsy adventurism at the time of the Turkish invasion of Cyprus caused the regime to collapse in 1974. Democracy, under the gaze of the military, returned and a Conservative Government was elected. This was replaced three years later by a Socialist Government whose bark was much worse than its pragmatic bite. This was in turn voted out in 1989 as a consequence of financial scandals and the conspicuous display by the old premier of his young mistress.

The past and recent events in Greece point up some aspects of the national character: these are added to the breathtaking beauty of the mountains, some of the countryside, most of the coast and most of the thousand populated islands by those who have fallen for this exasperating nation. Mountains and hills are the dominating topographical features, covering 70 per cent of the land. Mount Olympus is 2,900m (9,500ft) above sea level. The country is farmed where it's possible to farm. Elsewhere there are woodlands and typical Mediterranean vegetation. There are about a thousand uninhabited islands in the Ionian and Aegean Seas.

It is in character for Greeks to argue and to enjoy the process. Arguing with foreigners is unusual (unless their well-known pride has been bruised) but it can be prompted by the comical confusion brought about by language and gesture. When they say 'nay' and shake their heads they mean yes: the gesture for 'no' is a nod. A family lunch sounds as if blows will be the outcome; loud disagreements with plenty of head-shaking and nodding is normal. Pleasantly asked for, almost any kind of personal assistance will be freely given, but there is little likelihood of a Greek turning up for an appointment on time. In some communities the priest is more powerful than the mayor. Women are not yet considered equal with men except in the cities in enlightened circles.

Greek food is not special for the quantity of its fish or the quality of its meat. But the distinctive use of herbs and the high-grade olive oil give the dishes their Greek flavour. Mince in all its guises (except as 'doner') can be flavourful because of the liberal use of parsley, thyme, sage, bay leaves, rosemary and lemon juice and peel. Vegetables are full of flavour too and are cooked in a variety of dishes unlike our basic fodder. Cheeses, usually of goats' milk, and the reliable 'feta' are simple delights. Rough-textured bread is easy to overeat but the ubiquitous pitta is no more than a baker's joke, indigestible at best.

There are differing opinions about Greek drinks. But you will not consider buying a resort home in Greece unless you either do not drink or you actually like retsina and the rough reds and whites and are happy to take ouzo as an aperitif. You will in any event be aware that there is no great call for Greek wines in our supermarkets and wine merchants.

You will also be aware that in spite of the great beauty of Greece and her islands only around five million tourists a year make the journey. This compares with over ten million a year who visit Mallorca. You will argue that quality is generally better than quantity and that these tourists must be particularly discerning. Possibly. But the Greeks have no tradition of commercial hospitality – they are not the Swiss after all – and there is a relaxed 'take it or leave it' attitude to foreign visitors which is not unattractive. Tourist accommodation is unsophisticated in comparison with the norms in Spain and Portugal.

The business of selling resort homes to foreigners is also unsophisticated in the same way, although some British agents have taken the trouble – and the long view – and have made the necessary associations with reliable local businesses. There are strict rules which determine whether or not foreigners can legitimately buy property in specific areas of the country and there are plenty of places closed to you at this moment: these are generally designated the 'Border Areas' and there are many very attractive islands which fall under this prohibition. It strikes many civilised people as being paranoid but, given the permanent state of relations with the Turks, maybe the Greeks are understandably paranoid. This is not, of course, in tune with the Treaty of Rome. A less out-dated state of official mind is to be hoped for in future but in the mean time you would have to work within the rules if Greece was for you.

The only reason that the mainland and islands of Greece are not the resort area to end all resort areas is that Greeks either do not want this contribution to their economy, or that they do not understand the possible benefits. If they do not want you then their opinions must be respected. If they do not appreciate the possibilities then it is to be hoped that they will wake up and act positively by repealing absurd out-of-date laws before their mortal enemies take the business. In the mean time, there are increasingly successful attempts to sell resort homes in the Peloponnese to the British. This area is acceptably accessible by Greek standards. The coastline is in the idealised tradition. Porto Heli, opposite the islands of Spetses and Hydra, is becoming the centre of this commerce, with good infrastructure, ferries and hydrofoils, restaurants, tavernas and shops. Archaeologists have discovered enough actual treasure in the Peloponnese – gold and jewellery and gems – to make beachcombers watch where they are treading. And the area is the stuff of myths and heroes, temples and theatres of old, ancient cities and churches. Homes offered are new, designed and built for the international market.

Delphi, sited over 500m (1,640ft) up on Mount Parnassus, is yet another breathtaking location with homes available for foreign owners. Winter skiing adds something athletic to the cultural and contemplative life hereabouts. In complete contrast, the island of Mykonos, in the blue sea almost halfway between the Greek and Turkish mainlands, is about pleasure; so much so that the Greeks gave us the word – hedonistic – to describe it. Some claim that it is St Tropez and Ibiza rolled into one. This is another spot for homeowners to consider if ancient history is not priority number one. Greece and the islands are the resort areas of the future.

18

ITALY

Italy is 20 per cent larger than Britain with a population of a similar size and a higher standard of living. Outdated, comic-opera impressions of the average Italian persist in the minds of many British in their sixties: overweight and noisy men in vests conversing at full power in narrow streets; overgroomed young men with flashy good looks and a too-direct appeal to women from the colder and greyer north of Europe; aproned mammas with ten children and figures to match; girls who ripen early and families who violently protect their virtue; other 'families' who protect everything. . . at a price not to be refused.

Present-day reality is different. Some areas of Italy are grossly overcrowded by any civilised standards. But in the last decade of the twentieth century population statistics will show a further decline as deaths exceed births. By the early nineties the average Italian couple had less than 1.5 children with one-child families expected to become the norm. More pasta is eaten outside Italy than inside. When the UK press first reported in the mid-eighties that Italians enjoyed a higher standard of living than us leader writers expressed incredulity, rage, embarrassment and even suggested that, as in Italian soccer, the referees had been fixed.

The world's most successful shops for women's clothing are supplied by an Italian family business, stylish flair being supported by computerised efficiency in stock control and manufacturing according to sales demand. Compared with a Ferrari or a Lamborghini who would claim that a Rolls Royce represented the last word in practical and beautiful modern design? Flair and imagination created acceptable table wines, for export of course, from banana skins rather than boring grapes until spoilsports split on the gifted entrepreneurs involved in the late seventies. But Italian innovative skills are best demonstrated by the Naples-based manufacturer of pasta who wanted to increase sales worldwide; so he hired a successful car designer from Turin to create new shapes of pasta for the international market.

Contrasts are extreme. Lake Como and Catanzaro are in different countries for all except legal and political purposes. Overcrowding and depopulation, ostentatious wealth and obvious poverty, piety and near-paganism, Communism and Catholicism: these factors coexist without the complete breakdown of society. Political and financial scandals are commonplace. The Vatican, banks of all sizes, Christian Democrats in Rome, the joint Communist-Socialist administration in Florence, Social Democrat and Republican councillors in Naples: there is apparently no section of Italian commercial or political life which is scandal-free. And yet saints live amongst the sinners.

Somehow Italy works. The country was unified as recently as 1860 and regional interests continue to fight the dictates of central government. Democracy in Italy is, in any event, based openly upon the recognition of the power to deliver votes, money and benefits. The Mafia is a fact in Sicily: elsewhere in Italy it is called something different. It seems to be assumed generally that the state shall remain weak. Like others, the English language has one word for black and one for white: Latin has two for two different blacks and two for two different whites. Maybe the ancients were realistic.

Against this background your decision to buy a home in Italy is more likely to be emotional than rational. But clearly Italy has plenty to be emotional about. At any period in history, at any level, visual delight meets the eye. Man-made beauty complements nature in city and countryside. There is a gift bordering upon genius for making things look good, whether a barn or a baroque extravagence. Italy has so much art and treasure that Italians are regularly accused of indifference or vandalism by neglect by many international experts on such a heritage. But you are, of course, unlikely to be accused of neglect of any kind. You are most likely to be attracted by the possibilities of conservation and conversion, of the giving of new life to old buildings.

Tourism to Italy was culturally led from its beginning. Art and architecture was the draw and as a result the way our country looked was altered: the cool architecture of Andrea Palladio influenced all with the money to build spectacular and stylish homes in the English countryside in the sixteenth century. Round-topped Venetian windows dignified Regency and Georgian townhouses. Somewhat earlier, the way Britain looked was affected by four and a half centuries of Roman rule: roads, walls to keep the Scots in, terracotta tiles, and very civilised, centrally heated villas around cloistered gardens were examples of advanced thinking BC. On the other hand it is not possible to compile a list of British influences upon Italy or things Italian. Even the fellow who gave us radio was called Marconi.

Italian explorers from the city or nation states starting with Marco Polo in the thirteenth century discovered China, India, North and South America (if you believe Columbus to have been Italian) and the West Indies amongst other exotic spots. But, after the Romans, trade rather than conquest was the motivation with a concentration on finding things which looked, smelled and tasted good, until Mussolini's delusions of grandeur in the thirties.

Mass tourism to Italy now coexists with cultural tourism. Having been an exclusive resort for Italian nationals and a few foreigners from the 1850s Rimini began to develop into Europe's largest resort in the fifties. The numbers of visitors to Italy are now staggering: over fifty million a year to a country with a population of only a little more than that. Yet Italians no longer leave their own country in great numbers. Millions went to the USA in the early years of this century and hundreds of thousands went to Australia after World War II. EEC membership gave hungry and jobless Italians work in more advanced European countries: this outflow has also ceased. Now only 5 per cent of Italians travel abroad; most go no further than France or Yugoslavia. Italy bas become a better place to live.

However, Italy has not so far attracted the mainstream British buyer of resort homes. There is evidence to support the idea that the Romans were the first Europeans to enjoy second homes away from the midsummer heat and smell of the city. Villas were built in the mountains, on lakes and increasingly on the seashore for relaxed respite from strains of city life. It can be argued that the classical Roman villa still represents a viable plan for a resort home, give or take a possible adjustment for maximising views. But the purpose-built resort villa or apartment has not been the property which has attracted the British buyer except in the early days of the nineteenth century when romantics, poets and writers from the UK began to settle there. The British have been drawn to old houses or even farmbuildings made to house cattle in the countryside of Tuscany and Umbria.

A study completed in the mid-eighties revealed that Italy had *two million* homes built between six hundred and two hundred years ago – most of them suffering from neglect. Clearly, the great majority of these homes were in cities and some city administrations have embarked upon ambitious and successful campaigns of rehabilitation of whole areas of crumbling cityscape: the conservation programme carried out in Bologna by the Communist council was amongst the most impressive of its kind. But the rehabilitation and recycling of derelict rural property has been initiated by local agents and middlemen and mainly foreign buyers. A specialised trade evolved from the mid-seventies of the kind which arose in the Dordogne a decade or so earlier.

The area of Italy is a little over 300,000sq km (116,000sq miles) with a population of 56 million. It has over 500km (310 miles) of beaches on its Adriatic coast alone but the British buyer of Italian resort property has not so far shown interest in any Italian coastline. Given the accepted boot-shape of the country, the area behind the kneecap has been the limited zone in which specialist agents and British buyers have done business together. This odd territorial

restriction has puzzled many in the resort property business and it
has been seen by some as an opportunity to expand in all directions
Italian – so far with little success.

But in the medium and long term Italy is seen to be one of the
great potential areas for the ownership of resort homes, not only
for the British but also for those who live in the north of Europe
generally. The country's topography is varied, from alpine scenery,
and world-class ski resorts, and lakes and microclimates in the north
to the spectacular coastline of Calabria a thousand kilometres to the
south and the hills like slag-heaps which characterise Basilicata. By
definition property in ski resorts has not traditionally been created
for those limited by their jobs to a fortnight's annual holiday in
the summer months; the standards of development have therefore
mirrored the assumed needs of the clientele. Developments on the
magnificent Calabrian shores are however as disappointing as the
popular fifties' costas of Spain.

Between the extremes of north and south, given areas of industrial
sterilisation and pollution, Italy has almost 80 per cent of its land
contoured by hills and mountains. In the high table-land of much of
the south, winters are cold rather than Mediterranean. Geologically
young, Italy accepts earth tremors as everyday affairs; actual earthquakes occur every few years somewhere along the length of the
country; some volcanoes remain active, including Vesuvius.

Its overcrowded cities attract millions of visitors each year by
their timeless beauty; but Venice, Florence and Naples are hardly
growth areas for resort-property buyers from other countries. However, many of the small towns and villages in many parts of this long
country have true appeal for the kind of buyer attracted to Italy
generally. The buyer of a home in Italy is not at all the same kind
of person who is the buyer of a property in the resorts of Portugal,
Spain or France. A survey in the mid-eighties demonstrated that
British buyers of Italian property for fun were predominantly media
people drawn by the cultural delights, mostly visual, for which Italy
has always been famous. With a seemingly endless supply of old
property this kind of buyer is likely to continue to be on the books
of specialist agents. However, Tuscany and Umbria are not likely
to be the only areas to attract them as hitherto.

If the buyer of a home in Italy is currently drawn from a
narrow band of British citizens to a narrow range of Italian
property in romantic and idealised landscapes, and if demand and

supply continue as predicted, then what of the growing number of British and other Northern European nationals expected to acquire resort homes during the next decades? Can more of these mainstream buyers settle for newly developed complexes in the mountains, on the lakes and on the many coasts of Italy rather than in the usual destination countries of Spain, its islands and Portugal? The answer to this question depends only upon the desire of Italian authorities, developers and international estate agents to promote the products.

The legalities of buying real estate in Italy are covered elsewhere. Some local peculiarities are, however, worth noting which could affect you if Italy is to be considered as your chosen location. The Ancient Romans were avid tax gatherers; the Italian Government, like any government, is also diligent when it comes to collecting taxes; and taxpayers, particularly those who are self-employed, are never keen anywhere to pay more taxes than are absolutely necessary. Taxes levied on the transfer of ownership of real estate are higher generally in Europe than in Britain: traditionally these transactions have been considered easier to tax than income, simply because they are obliged to be formally registered. Italian practices have evolved on both sides to accord with human nature. You will want to listen carefully to the advice given by a specialist estate agent with a track record in the locality, preferably one who is a member of a body with a professional code of conduct if British, and certainly a registered agent if Italian. You will also want to listen to the opinions of the notary. But above all you will want to be guided by your specialist lawyer: if he is based in Britain or has a branch office here, so much the better. Yo will not, of course, want to pay more taxes than absolutely necessary but you will not want to build up a future tax liability, with possible penalties, for apparent short-term advantages.

A new law was introduced in March 1989 to concentrate minds. This required all owners of property to declare their ownership to the authorities immediately by completing Form 740 within two months. The exception was if the property had an 'official income' below Lire 360,000 per annum (this was not an actual letting income; it was akin to our old rateable value formula). Failure to declare ownership would result in the property becoming unsaleable in the future. Panic and lawyers working long hours resulted from this somewhat overdue measure.

Another new law was introduced a month earlier. This gave

legal effect to the need for estate agents to be registered. Hitherto the definition of estate agent had gone into soft-focus. Traders in property, who bought, resold *and* charged a commission in addition to making a profit on resale, could no longer act as estate agents. Agents were forbidden under this new Act to be anything other than estate agents whether full time or part time. An agent must now be registered at a Chamber of Commerce as such; so must every member of his staff. This clean-up was also overdue. The way is now clear for Italian resort property generally to be offered on the UK market to a wider spectrum of potential buyers.

19

PORTUGAL

We have stereotyped images of continentals, inherited from the colonial attitudes of our grandfathers, insensitive and offensive indifference of early aristocratic travellers from Britain, and the assumed superiority of things British in the days of our empire. But I challenge you to summon up from your mental computer a stereotype Portuguese.

Five hundred years ago Portuguese explorers rounded the Cape for the first time. They discovered the sea routes to India, Canton and the East Indies, and 'found' Japan, and named the Pacific Ocean. The names Vasco da Gama and Magellan mean something ancient and heroic to us; but what has happened in the mean time? Port. Cork. Out-dated colonialism in Africa. Salazar's almost forgotten dictatorship. The bloodless revolution of 1974, leading to increasingly stable democracy. And the Algarve. These factors would be mentioned instantly by any reasonably well-informed Briton if asked to tell all about Portugal. Lisbon as a centre for near-comic espionage in World War II, Leslie Howard's disappearance when his plane was shot down after leaving Lisbon airport, *vinho verde*, excellent shoes, Estoril for ex-kings: the very well informed may flip these factors out of the memory bank.

But what about the Portuguese themselves? How many do you know by name? Who is internationally recognised immediately for his or her nationality? You will know who runs France and Spain; you may be a week or two out when asked to name who runs Italy; but it is likely that the names of the Portuguese president and premier will escape you, temporarily, of course. However, the unknown qualities of the Portuguese and their varied, fascinating and unique country are beginning to pull inquisitive travellers from the increasingly crowded and cosmopolitan Algarve up and into the real Portugal.

British ignorance of things Portuguese is difficult to grasp given that the Anglo-Portuguese Alliance has held since 1386. Trade flourished, port wine being an outstanding product of Anglo-Portuguese co-operation more than three centuries ago. Wellington's legendary campaigns during the Peninsular War earned his dukedom and the love of the Portuguese in the early part of last century; freckles, introduced into the local genes by Wellington's Scottish troops, suggest general goodwill. Oppressive monarchies and Salazar's dictatorship had no ill-effects on the Alliance. Reid's Hotel in Madeira was known to 'society' as an elegant staging post or a holiday spot as soon as such people began to get about a bit. The Estoril area became outstandingly fashionable between the

wars, with what is arguably the largest casino in Europe as one of its attractions.

In 1943 some gentle arm twisting was needed to persuade the Salazar regime to provide facilities in the Azores for the British fleet's anti-submarine campaign. Throughout the war Lisbon served both sides with a centre for espionage and intrigue with the tacit co-operation of the authorities and a scenario appropriate to a Brian Rix farce. More recently approval was immediate to Britain's request for stopover facilities in the Azores during the Falklands War of 1982.

The first resort area of Portugal was the Costa do Estoril, a south-facing and favoured area at the mouth of the Tagus, just a few kilometres from the capital. Out of the direct blast of the onshore winds of the Atlantic coast, Estoril developed as a truly luxurious holiday and summer home area for Lisbon's upper class. After the war it attracted many kings or dictators who had no country left and other refugees with 'ex' as a prefix: Umberto of Italy, Admiral Horthy, the dictator of Hungary, the Queen of Bulgaria, Edward Prince of Wales, the parents of the present king of Spain, and so on. Its wide boulevards and spectacular, well-nurtured formal gardens remain today as a setting for nostalgic movies or good-quality developments aimed at the international or local middle class.

Half an hour's drive from Lisbon, the area hardly needs to be self-sufficient for everyday necessities. Bars, restaurants, cafés, some of real character in the one-time fishing village of Caiscais, others of old-time elegance in Estoril, provide a long-term challenge for those seriously devoted to sampling local food and drink. Kilometre after kilometre of tide-washed beaches and temperatures only a couple of degrees below those of the Algarve add to the attractions of the area in spring, summer and autumn. There are a half-dozen golf courses locally, which give important out-of-season advantages to those selling property here for the international market: more courses are planned.

Property in this acclaimed area varies in style, size and price almost to the point of absurdity, from an ex-king's palatial pad to an apartment in a multi-storey block. Quality is generally good not to be compared with Benidorm standards or those of the Algarve in the early days of its development.

Behind this corner of the Portuguese coast is a mountainous region around the town of Sintra, at most an hour's drive from Lisbon and its airport. Declared a National Park in the mid-eighties, new building is prohibited in much of the tranquil, heavily wooded countryside. The area is undergoing the kind of transition common elsewhere: depressed agriculture, loss of population to the work offered in the city, dereliction of empty country houses, discovery by romantic renovators, and an increase of prices as gentrification progresses.

Naturally, the intrepid and the bargain-hunters are now looking further away for today's snips. And they exist. But there is no organised market and without the help of international estate agents or high-powered property marketing firms to find the property for you it would be necessary to do your own hunting if the area and the old property appeal to you. But if a romantic ruin in the northern half of the country is what turns you on then you will find it. Given that the area does not have a Mediterranean climate it does not have mainstream appeal for resort-home buyers. However, the growth of British purchases of 'old stones' in France as far north as Picardy proves that the market is expanding in all directions to accommodate the needs of a wide spectrum of buyers not simply those who want 300 or more days of sun a year.

One of the major benefits of a home away from the tourist resorts of the Algarve and the Costa do Estoril is that the people are not yet internationalised. It follows that you would need to learn enough Portuguese to be able to make the most of this situation: conversation with naturally hospitable people qualifies as very satisfying fun. The Portuguese are enthusiastic celebrators of festivals from the religious to the pagan and some of these are robustly pagan, involving explicitly phallic worship and even the ritualised exchange of cakes and breads in the easily recognisable shapes of the human anatomy. A national passion for football and TV has not yet caused a decline in such earthy fun (most of the TV programmes are very professional products from Brazil, where the language is Portuguese). The energetic, almost balletic and non-lethal bullfighting also survives to thrill vociferous spectators. And like the neighbouring Spanish dining out with family and friends is taken seriously at all but the poorest rural levels of society.

Portugal is comparatively small in area – 92,000sq km (35,500sq miles) – and has a population of around 10 million. Incredibly, a further 5 million Portuguese live outside the country. The country is oblong in shape, traditionally isolated from the rest of Europe by its rivers and mountains. It has about 800km (500 miles) of coastline and an understandable nautical past. The capital Lisbon is two-thirds of the way down the coast and has more rainfall than London in January – and a higher temperature.

As elsewhere east of the Straits of Gibraltar, the Phoenicians settled as far up as the banks of the Tagus and gave the capital its name. The Romans followed and the Visigoths until the Moors arrived in 911 to influence the architecture and traditional decoration of the country until the present day: the narrow streets of the capital, the flat-roofed houses in the south and the absurd, inefficient, leaky but beautiful fretted chimneys, and the 'azulejos', the blue-and-white tiles used inside and out on old houses.

The long English connection began when our troops assisted in removing the Moors from Portugal, then helped see off the Spanish, resulting in the famous Treaty of Windsor signed in 1386 binding the two nations in friendship. Wellington's activities in the Peninsular War demonstrated the effect of this treaty by keeping Napoleon out of Portugal. Spain had ruled Portugal for sixty years from 1580, which explains the indifferent attitude of Portuguese waiters and others to the Spanish visitors to Lisbon. The Portuguese nautical skills and spirit of adventure led them to discover and colonise the choice parts of India, China, Africa and South America, and exotic spices flavour Portuguese cuisine as a result. It was the marriage of Charles II to Catherine of Braganza which brought Bombay to British rule as part of her dowry, the first toehold in the sub-continent which led to the Empire. Tea as well as curry spices in British supermarkets can be traced to this fortuitous marriage between our king and the Portuguese princess.

The world-famous drink which links Portugal to Britain was not originally port as we know it. It was a beefy red wine that was first offered to our Crusaders who stopped off in Oporto harbour on their way to fight the infidels. Much later it was fortified with grape brandy to enable it to travel to Britain in exchange for bartered goods when claret was not available due to one of the periodic squabbles of the eighteenth century with the French. It became the refined end-of-meal drink in the homes of the fashionable to the extent that a staggering 36 million bottles were being drunk in Britain annually by the beginning of the nineteenth century. It is not now such an important part of our intake, less than one-third of this amount being imported annually during the eighties.

But port is far from being the only wine worthy of deep

interest produced by Portugal. Over a hundred types of wine make for enjoyable investigation. Aggressive marketing has made Mateus Rosé a household name, belittled by wine-snobs (but a different, drier and welcomed drink served well chilled on a Portuguese terrace). The young *vinho verdes* whether green, white or red are the unique Portuguese contribution to drinking for pleasure apart from port itself. Served cold with robust regional dishes, or even sardines, the reds are a simple delight. The more serious reds are renowned and deserve dishes to complement them and time to enjoy them, especially the Daos from the granite ridges in the north – comparable in quality with burgundies or riojas. Some sparkling wines made by the champagne method are widely praised. Some brandies are also highly regarded; others are best avoided. To put wine production in this small country into perspective it is the fourth-largest producer in the world.

Portuguese cooking is little known and little appreciated outside its own country. French, Italian, Chinese, Indian, Turkish, Spanish and even Japanese restaurants can be found in Britain simply by looking for them. But there are no more than a handful of Portuguese restaurants in the whole of the United Kingdom. This is a pity, for the locals take their food seriously and so should anyone who appreciates good raw material well utilised. It follows that the long seaboard, and the long traditions of deep-sea fishing which prevail mean that fish figures large in local cooking. Except for 'bacalhau' (dried salt cod) which looks like grey cardboard but tastes worse, most fish dishes, if tried once will be tried again, whether simply grilled or fried or cooked with imagination in spices, herbs or sauces. Mackerel marinated in a sauce of onion, garlic, olive oil and white wine vinegar (*eschabeche*) is a delight: the same sauce adds something special to thinly sliced fresh tuna steaks. Casseroled in red wine, Falstaff's downfall, lampreys from the rivers of the north are as satisfying as those served in the same way in the gourmet restaurants in Bordeaux. Shellfish are well presented in most restaurants in season; so are sardines – grilled they are an experience.

Pork is much used in Portuguese kitchens. As ham it is the subject of imaginative treatment: simply smoked in the mountains of the north; smoked with spices; served with pickled vegetables; as *presunto* like Italian *prosciutto*; as loin meat smoked and spiced; and as belly of pork, like bacon, to flavour stews. A wide and rich variety of sausages is made from choice parts of the pig, some to be eaten sliced, some to be used in soups and stews for added flavour, and some served in terracotta dishes flamed in brandy as spectacular starters.

Free-range chickens roasted in port or brandy or casseroled with brandy, port, mustard, smoked ham and spices dignify this often mistreated meat. Rabbit paté with prunes is worth searching out. Kid roasted until brown and crackly is also worth the trouble to find on a displayed menu, but lamb is not considered highly for eating (wool is the main reason for the flocks seen in the countryside). Beef is becoming more highly rated as more attention is being paid to breeding stock – this is also an indication of the increasing standard of living.

Vegetables are not boiled and the resulting flavourful cooking liquid thrown away, as here, leaving the fibre to accompany a piece of overcooked meat in our national dish of 'meat and two veg'. Potatoes are often mashed into substantial soups, boiled in their skins, or chipped and fried, but they are not the flavourless, hygienic-looking varieties grown to look good in our supermarkets. Sweet potatoes are also grown in Portugal. Broad beans are cooked with chopped bacon, sliced sausage, coriander, onions and seasoning in a meat broth. Cabbage is finely shredded into the renowned soup, *caldo verde*, served with spiced sausage. Peas are cooked with smoked sausage, pork, slowly and surely, and the thick result topped with a poached egg. The spices brought to Portugal centuries ago from the Indies are extensively used.

Contrary to popular myth the Algarve was not invented by the ex-colonial British in 1964 appalled by the idea of returning from the remnants of our Empire to a grey Britain governed by a Labour Party led by Harold Wilson. Certainly there was an attraction for such people to the 'stability' of the quaint Fascist regime of Salazar, who took power in 1926 and ran the country like a ruthless and unimaginative civil servant. City, town and village bosses were loyally expected to ensure that nothing new happened. The policy was dedicated to keeping the country docile, with a rural economy, no contamination by democratic nonsense from outside its borders, secret police to control expressed thought, and the continuation of slavery in its African colonies. Against this background the appeal of the sun, fresh Atlantic breezes, cheap property prices, cheap booze and an apparently limitless supply of cheap servants grateful for the opportunity of work was obvious to many ex-colonials and others of a similar character.

The regime was in need of foreign exchange and was aware of the injection of tourist cash into the Spanish economy. The Algarve began to take off almost a decade later than the costas of Spain, with the government preference for somewhat isolated comprehensive developments for the foreigners, so that locals would not be unduly influenced by liberating contact. The first real estate developments were launched in 1964 in an area where fishermen and farm labourers still worked for a share in the catch or the crop rather than wages and where masons, electricians and plumbers were paid little more than 75p per day. By the end of 1964 there were three first-class hotels on the Algarve. A year later the airport at Faro was opened. Henry Cotton had designed the Penina golf course, the first on the coast, on rather boring land. More ambitious projects were planned with golf as the catalyst. Using Henry Cotton again for the course design, Sir Richard Costain began to create the Vale do Lobo estate. French planners began to design the Vilamoura estate on 1,600ha (4,000 acres) to accommodate 40,000 people.

Mass tourism was not considered the target for these new schemes: they were aimed at a more prosperous sector and villa development in large plots figured in most masterplans rather than high-rise apartments as on the Costa del Sol. The quality of some of the individual properties was more impressive than the quality of thinking which went into the projects at the concept stage. Vilamoura is an example of an imperfect concept: it was seen as a medium-sized town and planned as such. Twenty-five years or more later it is still incomplete; it is still a building site, with vast areas of serviced land undeveloped; sales stagnated; parts of the site were replanned, including the original golf facilities; and some development companies who had acquired tracts of land within the estate ran into difficulties. It is simply too big, too ambitious and too much like the urban landscape which holiday-makers and resort-home buyers want to escape from – it was not integrated into the local community.

Mass tourism followed the pioneers of more spacious schemes. But progess was halted by the Portuguese revolution of 1974. Salazar had died in a deck-chair in 1968. The next few years saw a decline in the economy, problems in the African colonies and disquiet in sections of the armed forces. Democracy was struggling for acceptance. There was a bloodless left-wing revolt; idealistic but inexperienced and unrealistic groups seized power locally, occupying workplaces, government offices, town halls and resort developments on the Algarve too. The foreign-owned complexes were seen in those heady days as the symbols of neo-colonial exploitation. Many foreign residents left, including the long-established Henry Cotton, who moved to Sotogrande on the Costa del Sol where Franco still ruled.

International confidence in the Algarve was shaken. The market for resort property was further depressed generally by the oil crisis of 1973/74 when the Arabs quadrupled the price of oil, jolting the economies of those countries which contained the potential buyers of resort property throughout the developing areas. Many bankruptcies of developers followed. Five poor trading years ended for resort developers when the Dollar Premium was phased out for British buyers of property outside the Sterling Area in 1979 in Anthony Barber's first budget. Meantime, Portuguese democrats were learning the hard way about how to run the country. There were sixteen governments in thirteen years. The constitution evolved from assumed socialism to pluralism until political stability was established in the mid-eighties under a moderate socialist president and a centre-right premier.

The Algarve boomed again under more settled conditions. The revival of confidence saw many new up-market golf developments being planned and built. Heavy investment in the stagnating Quinta do Lago estate near Faro was led by Bovis, resulting in further golf facilities being constructed on near-perfect golf terrain. Other troubled projects recovered. Many British groups put money into this coast rather than into the Costa del Sol for the fundamental reason that larger tracts of land on or near the coast were on offer. And for the first time the hitherto underdeveloped ocean front between Faro and the Spanish border to the east was seen to be an exploitable area; a half-dozen major projects including new golf facilities were under way by the late eighties. Seven courses had been in play, giving the Algarve its identity as the golf resort area of Europe, during its original development boom. Another twenty were on the stocks in the last few years of the last decade.

But in spite of the phenomenal growth of the Algarve it is clear that this is far from being the only area of appeal to resort-home buyers attracted to Portugal. Only Greece among the European Community members has lower wage rates than Portugal. Most of the country is within a couple of hours' hard drive from its international airports of Oporto, Lisbon and Faro. From the far north to the far south the country is generally attractive. The people are naturally welcoming and are enjoying their increased standard of living and freedoms. Traditional ways in some remote rural areas are still maintained alongside modern standards. Good value for money rather than bargains can be had when buying property on the Algarve or the Costa do Estoril. Bargains by our yardsticks can still be obtained elsewhere along the coast and in the countryside by mountains and rivers which are beautiful and generally unspoiled.

Portugal remains for the time being one of the comparatively undiscovered countries of Europe in spite of the understandable popularity of the Algarve.

20

SPAIN

It is accepted by historians that countries can suffer crises of identity. The way the British reacted at Suez and in the Falklands is considered by some to be an indirect consequence of our reduced role in world affairs following our loss of imperial status; our sometimes petulant attitude to the European Community during the eighties is also attributed in part to this syndrome. On this basis Spain's identity crisis as she lost her empire was severe. During the last century nothing went right. To begin with, Nelson trounced her fleet, for a second time, at Trafalgar. Then Napoleon had the audacity, and the muscle, to impose his brother Joseph as King of Spain. Because the Spanish were then too enfeebled to do it themselves the Duke of Wellington's army had to push the French back across the Pyrenees during the Peninsular War. Finally, Cuba and the Philippines were lost in a rather ambitious war against the USA.

With few other places to go Spain's military and ruling classes directed their colonial attitudes towards their own countrymen. The army and the para-military Guardia Civil acted like an occupation force. Generals with time on their hands, but no time for democracy, took turns in seizing power for themselves or for one or other of the contenders for the job of king. Like Italy, Spain had been stitched together like a patchwork quilt from separate nations; the stitches occasionally gave under sometimes violent strain until the army and the Guardia Civil yanked them tight again. Revolts, rising, riots and repression were everyday events, continuing into the twentieth century almost as part of a traditional pattern.

In the twenties and early thirties Spain had a king and a military dictator, a centre-left government and a republic, a right-wing elected government followed by another centre-left administration, with an army massacre of miners by the way, and a number of separatist regional governments created by popular vote. As a political movement rather than a loose term of abuse, anarchism was for some a serious alternative to parliamentary democracy. All of this transitional awkwardness was too much for the generals. The army rose against the elected government in 1936, assisted by the Fascist dictators of Italy and Germany. Three years of merciless civil war followed. Democracy lost. General Franco, who had taken command of the revolt when its original leader was killed in a plane crash early in the war, was installed as dictator of Spain in 1939. Many plazas and streets were named in his honour.

In payment of his debts to the Nazis Franco supplied Hitler with coal during the war in Europe which began just a few months after the Fascist victory in Spain. He also sent his Blue Division of volunteers to fight for Germany on the Russian Front. But Franco wisely avoided joining the other dictators in their war against the European democracies. He also, under a secret threat from Churchill, reneged on his agreement to cede the island of Menorca to Mussolini for his help in defeating the elected government of Spain.

Spain had not endeared herself to the victors of World War II. With no international friends, a ruined economy and a demoralised workforce a decade of aching poverty for millions was to follow. Any Spaniard old enough to know will be able to tell how tough it really was when simply feeding a family could not be taken for granted. Against this background packaged tourism, which began in Spain in the mid-fifties, was a welcomed gift. Pre-war tourism to Spain was limited. The courts, the government and the aristocracy traditionally relocated to the Atlantic coast to escape the summer heat of Madrid: Santander and San Sebastian developed in a style which we would recognise as Victorian and Edwardian to accommodate this exodus. Visits to ancestors from erstwhile Spanish colonies in Central and South America provided business for hotels in the ports on the Atlantic coast and in some major cities.

In the mid-twenties the publication of Hemingway's novel *Fiesta*, with much of its action set in Pamplona, made the author and the week-long July celebration of the feast of San Fermin famous, resulting in visits to that town, and elsewhere in Spain, by wealthy American and other intellectuals and playboys seeking local colour and adventure. The first of Spain's *paradores* was built, not on the coast but in the Gredos Mountains in the centre of the country, at about the same time, to encourage visits by hunters rather than sunbathers.

With few exceptions today's famous Mediterranean resorts were either for work not play or they were non-existent. In a despatch for his newspaper, Arthur Koestler, then writing for the *News Chronicle*, and spying for Stalin, mentioned in 1936 that he had passed a small fishing village called Torre Molinos. Denia was the centre for the export of raisins. Sitges, an easy journey south of Barcelona, was a simple resort, with the obligatory golf course for the British community. S'Agaro, an outstanding example of civilised resort planning until it was surrounded by less-sympathetic development in the seventies was created on the Costa Brava in the thirties and has hardly been bettered since. The Spanish islands are dealt with elsewhere.

The need for American Cold War bases in the Mediterranean and the birth of packaged tourism in the mid-fifties both provided jobs and foreign exchange for the dormant Spanish economy. Some would argue that the timing of these two factors prolonged the life of Franco's dictatorship. Tourism and the developments which accommodated it transformed the country's Mediterranean coastline. Nobody protested when this transformation sometimes became rape: undernourished and weak, who could resist?

Except in the traditional areas of international contact like Jerez where British customs were the norm, Spanish life in the deepest sense was not much changed by foreign influences until Franco died in 1975. The effects of tourism were only skin deep, to be seen only on the Mediterranean coasts and on the islands. Now rapid and radical change has removed Spain's isolation from the European mainstream. Franco's few remaining supporters have withered without much sign of regeneration; 'the Pyrenees have finally been abolished'. Spain now has a secure democracy, a popular monarchy and one of Europe's strongest economies: clearly it was not always so.

Spain remains different enough. Spanish businessmen will tell you that the siesta has been cancelled but you still cannot reach them for four hours in the middle of the day. Cities still suffer from four rush hours a day and Madrid still has traffic jams after midnight on Saturdays. Meals are still taken two or three hours later than elsewhere in Europe. Spanish children are still about when adults are asleep in other countries. And the *paseo* lives.

The resort property business as we know it began on Spain's Costa Blanca in the mid-sixties. Then property on the costas was built for the foreigner. Now the major market for homes on the coasts of Spain is Spain itself. The effect of this change is to put up

prices but the higher prices are underpinned by a larger market. Stability and affluence naturally increase the demand for the good life. Those who bought Spanish resort homes in the seventies have benefitted from increased values as buyers of homes in the UK also benefitted; and give or take a devaluation or two a purchase at that time should have proved a happy decision all round.

Not all areas of this country's long coastline have had similar increases in value or demand. Access and location are paramount, as has been repeated throughout this book; and it follows that they are as important for Spanish buyers as they are for those of other nationalities. You only have to study the values of resort areas within easy reach of the major cities and international airports for this obvious point to be proven. If you already own a property in an easily accessible location on Spain's Mediterranean coast then you will be reassured that there is an increasingly wide market available to you if and when you wish to sell it. If you are about to buy, the overall size of this growing market should give you comfort too even if you are not to enjoy the comparative bargains of earlier buyers.

Given that the most venerable builder of resort property on the Costa Blanca celebrated his twenty-fifth anniversary in the business in 1988 you may reasonably ask what happened before then. Before the mid-sixties builders were usually something else the way that waiters, barmen, chambermaids and cooks were something else. Overnight subsistance farmers, labourers and fishermen were able to put their usually unemployed children to work indoors in new hotels and restaurants or outdoors on construction sites, where the work was regular if seasonal. It is not necessary to be a highly experienced surveyor to know that many of the properties built in Spain for the foreign market in the early days are now showing signs of inexperienced workmanship. But many of these properties – and hotels built at that time – are in magnificent positions impossible to find in the brochures of today's highly professional builders and developers. If you own an elderly property on the Spanish coast, with uninterruptable sea views, pointing south, away from late noise, a walk away from basic shops, not much more than an hour from an international airport, with mature trees and flowering shrubs around it and a terrace big enough for eight people to feel comfortable seated at a dining-table then you have something of permanent value above mere money. If the roof leaks sometimes or there's a patch of damp on one of the walls or the electrical installation is not reliable these problems really can be fixed *mañana*.

Regional differences still exist after forty years of dictatorship during which it was intended they be abolished. These differences are constitutionally recognised now and autonomous governments are democratically elected to exercise real power in many important areas of activity. Streets and plazas quickly named after Franco in 1939 now usually have their earlier names in the regional language if one exists. Different histories, traditions, customs and languages make for different physical characteristics in cities, towns and villages in this large country, and the climatic variations added to the geographic and topographic variables create a wide choice of atmosphere and environment for foreigners who want to buy resort or retirement homes there.

With few exceptions those attracted to living in Spain permanently or semi-permanently or for holiday periods are drawn firstly by the understandable appeal of three hundred or so days of sun a year in the well-known resort areas. The dramatic but drizzly regions along the Bay of Biscay and the deeply indented coast of Galicia are therefore best thought of as magical areas to visit for carefully timed holidays rather than for places to buy property. Spain's other Atlantic coast, between the Portuguese border and Gibraltar, has a climate akin to that of the Algarve, sporadic rather than ribbon development along the coastline, attractive comparative property prices, and comparatively few foreigners, that is non-Spanish. A further attraction of this area is Seville, one of the world's great cities, but hot as a baker's oven in midsummer. But this south-western corner of Spain is not, at present, for those who need the usual facilities of international tourism in order to feel at home. Spanish ways prevail, even with the nearby commercial town of Jerez with its atmosphere a mix of British and Spanish traditions. But marinas and golf courses are being exploited to increase the area's international appeal, Porto Sherry being an example. High-rise construction is happily unobtrusive.

The other side of Gibraltar, the Costa del Sol, has some of Spain's best and worst resort development. Nobody would consider it well bred either before or after being developed as a resort area. It appeals to Arab princes, arms dealers, drug barons, East End 'company directors', professional comics who commute between the London Palladium and their fairway-fronting homes, and hundreds of thousands of 'ordinary' British, German, Scandinavian and other Europeans as an ideal spot for a retirement or holiday home. Now that more Spanish people are buying homes there it may eventually become more Spanish in ambience. There are properties for all these tastes: palaces on the boring beach, with armed guards for the security of sheiks; hideaways for varied villains, with very well-built staff; over-priced sub-standard apartments on the lethal coast road; high-rise horrors left over from earlier, less sophisticated times; some low-density, low-rise complexes which are the best of their kind; and many properties which are the very best of resort homes to be found anywhere. You can buy anything you want on the Costa del Sol, including peace and quiet, if you look hard enough and are prepared to pay the price.

But this famous area is likely to continue to suffer from its very success. More and more construction will take place as the

Costa del Sol, after only thirty years or so of development, begins increasingly to resemble the Riviera after two centuries of growth and change. As on the south coast of France, further change will come from redevelopment of some poorly conceived properties on prime sites as real estate values continue to rise. If this busy area is the place for you then you should ensure that your life is not lived to the sound of bulldozers, drills, piledrivers and cheerful craftsmen who begin work at eight in the morning.

The regional capital, Malaga, is a port, a commercial centre and the birthplace of Picasso. Behind the impressive new office blocks is Andalucian tradition: the bullring and the intricately tiled *paseo* which leads to it are renowned. The city effectively divides the coast and its developments in two.

Between Gibraltar and Malaga the Costa del Sol is associated with big developments, big properties and big money. *Latifundia*, the traditional ownership of large tracts of land by absentee proprietors, made the area either side of Marbella easy to develop with golf courses and comprehensive estates, where large areas in single ownership were essential for such projects to be feasible. *Minifundia*, the fragmented ownership of land as holdings were divided equally between surviving sons, was the norm east of Malaga. The assembly of development sites of suitable sizes was almost impossible as many plots of pocket-handkerchief dimensions were traditional in this area. Another problem was that the coast road here was notorious for its loose surface and hairpin bends: this road, now much improved, still winds around numerous rock outcrops. Sporadic and often low-quality urbanisations were built where land could be acquired in the early days of the development boom: some are eyesores. Newer projects on this stretch of the coast are better in overall design and quality of construction. Behind the coast some of the villages and small towns preserve their Andalucian atmosphere.

Almunecar, a very Spanish resort, with an attractive *paseo* which is unspoiled by cars, is on the coast near the major appeal of this mixed region: the road inland to the Sierra Nevada range of snow-capped peaks and Granada, possibly the most spectacular man-made environment in the Iberian Peninsula. Those attracted by the lower property prices and agreeable climate of this less fashionable sector of the Costa del Sol will have some compensations for the quantity of poor buildings of the sixties.

There are some golf courses on complexes which have had

unsuccessful commercial histories, marinas which have also produced less profits for their promotors than were forecast, and
other ambitious projects which have had a succession of optimistic
owners: in spite of their histories of losses such operations exist,
to be enjoyed by property owners who are within easy reach of
their facilities. Many newer developments on the coast between
Almunecar and Almeria are well conceived, well planned and
well built.

There is a stretch of coast some couple of hundred kilometres
long from Almeria to the naval base at Cartagena which is almost
unknown internationally. Access is difficult by the standards of
today's visitors – the airport at Almeria is seasonal and there is no fast
coast road – and development has not taken place as it has elsewhere
within an hour or so by road from airports on the Mediterranean.
This is an area for pioneers who do not want to be within shouting
distance of fellow-countrymen.

North of the Spanish equivalent of Portsmouth, where pock-
marked façades of government building offer reminders of the Civil
War, is the most unattractive sector of the coast. Around the mining
town of Portman, subsoil, shale and spoil provide a moonscape, and
the discharge of waterborne waste stains and sterilises the normally
clear Mediterranean.

The landlocked Mar Menor at La Manga is however clear,
warm and supposedly beneficial to health because of the high
mineral content of the water caused by millions of years of evap-
oration; there is a long beachfront on the sea too, giving this freak
of nature its odd identity. The isthmus separating the Mar Menor
from the Mediterranean is developed Miami-like, with a mixture of
tower blocks, slab blocks, low-rise apartment complexes and villas.
It is a unique holiday resort with a now-successful golf complex at
its southern end. The season here is long for those wanting plenty
of outdoor activities. There are limitations – to be expected in a
busy tourist resort built for the purpose – for anyone contemplating
permanent living or retirement.

Between La Manga and the city of Alicante is an area which has
been heavily developed in the eighties when land was comparatively
cheap and construction costs attractive to big developers. In units
sold into the British market during that decade the Torrevieja area
leads. The mass market for resort property has been demonstrated
to be successfully promoted here, with vast estates of small holiday

homes being offered at prices which are about those of luxury cara-
vans. Significantly, the largest developer of resort homes in Spain
has created his major project of many thousands of homes here. Like
the La Manga area the emphasis is on holiday property.

Alicante, the regional capital, is set to expand dramatically in
the nineties, an indication of the increasing prosperity in the area.
The city has all the necessities: an international airport, a motorway
link to the rest of Europe, a port, the regional administrative offices,
hospitals and high quality and varied shopping facilities. Up the
coast from the city is Playa de San Juan, now attracting the newly
created middle class from Alicante and Madrid as a place for smart
homes for permanent or holiday use. This civilised area deserves to
be considered as a retirement location by foreigners who prefer to
be near city comforts.

High above Alicante is the Castillo de Santa Barbara, the best
viewpoint for the spectacular 'Bonfires of Saint John' on 24 June
each year. Traditional fiestas are celebrated with great enthusiasm in
the still Spanish towns behind the cosmopolitan coastal strip. From
April through to September the annual fiesta of Moros y Cristianos
is staged in many towns and villages in varied forms, all enthusiastically. Many of these happenings are visually stunning, with a cast of
thousands, colourful costumes, lively music and fireworks displays.
The street parades are well drilled and in some cases are preceded
by carefully staged battles to commemorate the reconquest of Spain
from the Moors. Alcoy, an industrial town inland, is credited with the
most impressive display, involving a replica of a castle and set-piece
battles. Real castles abound behind the coast. Regular visitors to
the area, or those retired there, have the opportunity to explore the
cultural and physical attractions at their leisure and, unless putting
your mind into neutral is the reason for buying a home here, there
is enough of interest within a couple of hours' drive of the Mediterranean to give long-lasting pleasure.

Benidorm, less than an hour up the coast from the capital of the
region is, like Torremolinos on the Costa del Sol, an example of
Spain for the mass tourist from abroad. Both of these holiday towns
are better known outside Spain than their regional capitals which
are many times their size. There is, however, something truly odd
about this high-rise, barely Spanish phenomenon. In spite of the
jokes and changes of fashion and sentiment, it continues to grow,
upwards and sideways, with new tower blocks under construction

as if they had never become discredited, golf courses with the name of Ballesteros as designer and winter programmes of holidays for Spanish pensioners successfully sold in their thousands.

The Costa Blanca as understood by those planning to buy a home there is, however, very different. The well-named 'Sunrise Triangle' from Calpe to Denia, projecting towards the rising sun at Javea has attracted buyers of apartments, and more generally villas, since the mid-sixties. It continues to do so for the simplest of reasons: it is an attractive locality, with basic amenities, plenty of blue sky (the World Health Organisation declared that the area had the most beneficial climate in Europe) and local developers have a tradition of producing what the buyer wants.

From Calpe with its Gibraltar-like Ifach Rock just offshore and its quiet air, to Javea with its inland village and oceanside port and promenade over the headland, to Denia with its large marina and historical links with Britain from the days of the raisin trade, the triangle provides thousands of foreigners with what they expect from Spanish resort areas. Significantly, few hotel beds exist in this agreeable area: the development growth has been in villas and apartments since the early days of international attention. It follows that there is a wide selection of property available, from older, resale villas to new complexes of grouped housing around common pools and other facilities. There are few high-rise apartment buildings and the contrast between this part of the coast and Benidorm is extreme.

There are plenty of marina berths available, given temporary shortages as demand increases before more come on the market. The golfer has been poorly served until recently, however, with a few nine-hole courses unable to cope with local demand or attract the serious golfer to the region. As more courses are built the area is likely to attract a wider range of property buyers than hitherto. Water problems in the eighties have threatened to curb development, with ritualised political battles between local, regional and central government about funding.

Some professional providers of sheltered housing consider that this region still has great potential for the retired of Europe as facilities improve. Tighter planning controls should prevent the tendency towards sprawling villa estates which is beginning to pose a threat to the very character of this peaceful place. Camp sites on the beaches north of Denia are seasonally unattractive but only hard-bitten snobs would argue that they should be abolished in favour of expensive villas.

A mix of unappealing, raw and unobtrusive monolithic apartment blocks characterises the remaining coast before reaching Valencia, plus the occasional empty stretch of coastline, the rice-growing landscape behind the coast and finally the Ford Fiesta plant which helped to transform the economy of Valencia when it was most needed. Valencia itself is a no-nonsense, workaday city with little to appeal to the property buyer other than its facilities and services. These are what you would expect from Spain's third city. There is an opinion which says that in Franco's era the city was denied support because it was the seat of national government in the Civil War, when Franco's armies had Madrid almost surrounded. Certainly its international airport used the terminal building of the mid-thirties until it was replaced as recently as the mid-eighties.

Between Valencia and the Ebro Delta, however, are a number of resorts which, coming somewhat late on to the international scene, are worth considering as very different alternatives to the better-known areas. Primarily known for its ceramics, the area immediately above Valencia has little international appeal. Beyond Castellon the appeal widens. Marina developments, well-ordered villa complexes, a couple of golf courses, and sporadic resort areas of greater or lesser sophistication have been created along this comparatively quiet coast. The Law of the Coasts, enforced in the late eighties to ensure that desecration of the coastal land should cease, has had a beneficial effect upon some hitherto unsullied stretches of the coast here. Offshoots of petro-chemical industry, some offshore exploration for oil, and a notorious nuclear power station mark certain points which are best avoided. However, genuine, working fishing villages remain on the coast above the remarkable fortified town of Peniscola, a magical and mysterious place out of season. The development of apartments along this coast during the eighties was disappointingly boring; the grouped housing complexes in the area south of the town are, however, attractively planned.

The unique Ebro Delta is now mostly preserved from any development, designated as a nature reserve, farmed, with its waters fished, and its enormous expanses of beach left to be enjoyed by simple-lifers and informal campers. This freak of nature is the alluvial mouth of Spain's longest river which begins to flow into the Mediterranean from a lake behind the Atlantic coast city port of Santander the other side of the peninsula. This vast silt plain, cut by channels and holed by lakes, stretches 27km (17 miles) out into the sea from the rocky coastline. The strange atmosphere of this flat and very fertile area is tempered by the quality of produce, seafood, shellfish and frogs and the way in which they are cooked in the local restaurants. No concessions to foreign visitors should be expected here, although the *parador* at Tortosa a few kilometres inland from the coast road has a sound reputation for anyone attracted to converted castles.

Small coastal settlements occasionally appear with no real appeal for resort-property buyers – unless they want to escape from their own countrymen – until reaching the notorious resort of Salou, a few kilometres south of the ancient city of Tarragona and close to the thriving town of Reus inland. The notoriety of this holiday centre, much frequented by British tour operators at the bottom end of the market, concerns untreated sewage. It is best avoided.

The coast above the city port of Tarragona has little to attract the potential owner of a home on the Mediterranean until reaching Sitges. This small town with its old houses in narrow streets and modern apartments along its wide beachfront is a thriving resort for Barcelona just an hour away at busy times and half that out of season. It was a favourite spot for the British working in Barcelona in the twenties and thirties who built villas here and a small golf course of twelve holes. Sitges deserves to be better known by today's buyers of resort property. It has a number of very solid attractions. Firstly it is close to the most exciting of Spain's cities, Barcelona. It has in its hinterland the Penedes wine region, one of the most important in Spain, with progressively better whites, robust and sometimes outstanding reds and sparkling wine made by the champagne method. It attracts artists and intellectuals, weekenders, day-trippers, mostly Spanish and mostly well behaved. There is a lively tradition of music and singing, both well organised by societies, in the streets at various times of the year. The town itself is attractive, with many old houses restored for comfortable modern living.

Between Sitges and Barcelona are a number of low-grade short-term holiday developments and industrial plants from earlier, less environmentally aware decades. And the area in and around the southern half of the city is off-putting in every way: heavy industry mixed with housing, pollution of the atmosphere and every watercourse and incessant traffic noise.

Barcelona itself is still benefitting from its rebirth after forty years of Franco and the extra boost of its location as the venue of the 1992 Olympics. Public investment has encouraged private investment. Madrid has stated its aim to become the cultural capital of Europe, while Barcelona claims to have already taken this title from Paris. An evening stroll, the *paseo*, down the Ramblas from Plaza Cataluna to the statue of Columbus by the port, is still one of the great European experiences, not to be missed by any visitor or foreign resident of the Costa Brava. A turn off the Ramblas into the Gothic Quarter will be rewarded by the sight of truly grand old buildings lovingly restored; one of them houses the Picasso Museum containing the greatest collection of this Spanish master's works. Barcelona has all the department stores, fashionable boutiques, plazas, parks and parking problems to be expected in a progressive capital. A couple of bullrings, football stadia the like of which we simply do not have, four rush hours daily caused by the siesta habit, and the atmosphere surrounding a major port. These are some of the elements which give this centre of autonomous government its powerful identity.

Catalan culture now colours life on and behind the Costa Brava. The separate language is taught in schools after being banned under Franco. The unique local music and dance has a Pied Piper effect on Catalans of all ages. Catalans are in any event dynamic, pro-European and businesslike and the strength of their local economy testifies to their character. The local economy has also affected the resort property business from Barcelona to the French border. Demand from the increasingly affluent middle classes from Barcelona has underpinned the market throughout the eighties, and it is a factor which has improved standards, their expectations being somewhat higher than those of the average foreign buyer of resort homes on this coastline.

This region of Spain was where packaged tourism as we know it began in the fifties. Between Blanes and Barcelona the coast is spoiled by the road and the railway line running actually along the beach. But Blanes has bloomed as a town close to the capital which has retained much of its separate identity; plenty of new apartment buildings have been created in the last few years and the marina will transform the town further. New roads, easy access from the airport at Gerona and the railway, which cuts inland at the southern end of the town, would all ensure that this is a practical place for full retirement without being either exciting or as beautiful as some other areas on this spectacular coast.

The resorts of St Feliu, Tossa and Lloret are a throwback to the fifties. Redevelopment of their now-discredited egg-crate, high-rise, buildings may come as the potential of some truly outstanding sites becomes clear, but until then these are not locations to be recommended for the purchase of homes unless you have a nostalgia for resort architecture of the recent past.

S'Agaro, a few kilometres north of St Feliu, is however, a splendid example of resort planning of the past. Begun in the thirties, this oasis of attractive layout and high-quality individual homes now has lowest common denominator tourist development around some of its edges. But S'Agaro is an example of how civilised resort homes should be placed on a rugged coast and it is a pity that its standards were ignored in the understandable scramble for tourist income when much of the buildable Costa Brava was developed in the fifties and sixties. Families who are fortunate enough to own homes on the S'Agaro estate seldom place them on the market.

The cliffs, headlands and coves on the next stretch of coast between Palamos and Pals beach typify the Costa Brava in its popular image; many would argue that this is the most attractive part of this attractive coastline. It is also one of the most appealing parts on which to buy a resort property, either a new villa with outstanding sea and coast views from a clifftop, or an older home built to a lower specification but on a prime site, or one of the stone-terraced village houses with barrel-vaulted, ground-floor ceilings in narrow streets. The photogenic town of Pals a few kilometres inland from the Mediterranean is an object lesson in sympathetic or even inspired restoration, not to create a museum atmosphere but to provide homes for artists, writers, academics and business people with taste. Property here is expensive, valuable old homes part of the heritage of the area. This hill town is justifiably famous for the way in which the houses are loved.

The nearby golf course – British designed – has earned a high reputation with its tight, tree-lined fairways and lush grass. It lies behind Pals beach, ruined from the early days of the Cold War by the Eiffel Tower-like masts of Radio Free Europe which lined it as ugly reminders of ugly times. This is potentially a prime area for resort property of short- and long-term use. Estartit, an ex-fishing village at the north end of the beach thrives as a holiday resort of some character with some second home development on the south-facing ridge inland from the harbour.

At the French end of the Bay of Rosas are Ampuriabrava, a Venice-inspired resort of canal-side homes of mixed success, other waterside developments with marina facilities and the busy seasonal town of Rosas itself. Weekenders from the city are increasingly extending the season when the tramontana is not blowing. But on the extremity of the headland on which Rosas is placed is one of the true gems of the Mediterranean: the small town of Cadaques. Artists, architects and mere millionaires have transformed a beautiful village into a beautiful resort by creatively converting the terraced fishermen's cottages into homes which are individually and collectively simply stunning. Some, but not all, new building in and around the village is sympathetic too, with the external materials of stone, white-painted plaster, natural-coloured wood and terracotta tiles. Homes here come on to the market locally for short periods at ever-increasing prices.

Around the headland from Cadaques is Port Lligat where the home of Salvador Dali provides an example of inspired resort villa architecture, a modern but timeless expression of old shapes and materials. Further round the coast is Cabo Creus, featured in the background of many of Dali's paintings but much of this area is preserved from development by the lack of roads. The Dali Museum at Figueras inland is, for some, a cultural bonus while living or holidaying in this region.

From the perfection of Cadaques to the French border at Port Bou the attractions of the coast pall, with towns and villages of no real appeal. Inland is another matter. The traditional difficulties of access from the coast here into the Pyrenees are being improved, revealing magnificent scenery and dramatically sited villages and farmhouses.

There are clear indications that a newly developing taste for old village houses and farmhouses in rural Spain is being frustrated by the lack of agents willing or able to supply such property, with exceptions of course. There is no real market yet compared with that which evolved in the Dordogne in the seventies and in Tuscany and Umbria in the eighties. The reasons for this comparative lack of outlets are financial. The prices of romantic ruins in rural Spain are not yet high enough for real estate agents to consider them worth the effort of searching for buyers: commissions based upon percentages of value mean that below a certain price the earnings are small. Until this changes personal prospecting is called for if the old property is of interest to you.

There are exceptions in the hinterland of the Costa del Sol where romantics have bought in the White Towns of Andalucia, and in some areas in the foothills of the Pyrenees, where the stone villages like Rupit have been colonised by city-dwellers. Demographic changes in Spain followed by emptying of rural houses, followed in turn by the purchase of abandoned homes by comparatively wealthy incomers is expected to continue as elsewhere in Europe, with bargains for the early-bird buyers. There are still opportunities for the imaginative wanting to operate on a grand scale when it comes to the conversion and recycling of country property in Spain. In some areas there are whole villages which have been abandoned, usually the outcome of government supporters having left the scene after the Fascist rising in the thirties, or of death in battle. There are problems of title for anyone wanting to indulge their romanticism practically but the prospects – financial and visual – are difficult for some to resist. As the country is opened up by more and more expenditure on new roads there is every reason to expect that local and international interest in village and rural property in this vast country will grow.

The market for ski property in Spain will also grow with greater affluence locally and greater awareness internationally. The increased supply of homes in the ski resorts of the Pyrenees during the eighties resulted in steady sales of practical, and usually well designed and built apartments in styles and materials appropriate for the areas and free of the corny stylistic clichés common everywhere on the costas.

Property prices in the resort areas of Spain increased dramatically during the eighties as the Spanish economy drew closer to the norms of the European Community. New tough planning laws were passed to prevent building within 100m (110yd) of the coast. The consumer regulations introduced in the late eighties were designed to outlaw a number of sloppy or illegal practices in the real estate field which had brought disrepute to good and bad operators alike. The fag-end of the mass tourist market was slowly discarded. Some hitherto popular locations declined in perceived appeal. As predicted, Spain became more like the rest of Europe in respect of civilised amenities and standard of living while retaining those inexplicable elements which make it different from elsewhere.

In simple terms the way of life in Spain, along with the climate and scenery, is what attracts settlers from other countries. This attraction is likely to increase in spite of trends towards greater conformity with the standards and preconceptions which apply in the European Community generally. The paradox is that as Spain becomes more European in outlook the very Spanishness of life in the Iberian Peninsula becomes more attractive to northern Europeans who can afford to relocate.

There is still plenty of room if Spain appeals to you as the place to buy your second or retirement home. In area it is 510,000sq km (197,000sq miles). It has a population of 38 million or so. It is more than twice the size of Britain with a smaller population. Regional differences are great. It is after Switzerland the most mountainous country in Europe. Tourist food is basic: serious eaters will be rewarded with excellent dishes everywhere if prepared to search for them. The variety and quality of wines and spirits is such that a long and happy retirement could be spent devoted to detailed research of this subject. The sun continues to shine for more than 300 days annually in all of the usual resort areas.

21
SWITZERLAND

The list of associated images is long: secretive banks and even more secretive multinational companies; cities where international treaties are signed; the HQ of the United Nations in Europe; ski resorts, lakes and movie stars' retreats; well-ordered towns, stunning mountains and homes which look as if they are inspired by cuckoo clocks; compulsory nuclear shelters for every home (called 'storage areas' for reasons of diplomacy); neutrality (which sometimes rankles, as during World War II); chocolate, cheese with holes in it, watches and chemicals; a civilian army always on call; a shortage of comedians (who has ever heard a Swiss joke?); an architect and an artist (Le Corbusier and Paul Klee); no current internationally known personality; a national hero with as much credibility as Robin Hood (but worth much to the tourist industry); a reputation for commercial prudence, straight dealing and basic honesty; very professional hoteliers; efficiency; and a deeply entrenched democracy designed to allow real debate before the big decisions are taken (often by referenda).

The country is a little more than 41,000sq km (16,000sq miles) in area with a population of 6.5 million. It is a group of semi-autonomous cantons with different histories and languages (French, German, Italian, Romansch, Switzer-Deutch). Located between powerful neighbours historically, as reflected in its cantonal languages, its component parts have fought together or individually against every occupier with a ferocity seemingly out of character with present-day impressions. They have also fought bloodily against each other. Nowadays the Swiss coexist, with heated discussion taking the place of the warfare of the past, on the principle that the best argument finally wins and is democratically accepted by all. Abiding by the law is natural.

Some of the democratically debated, referenda-decided laws which you will have to abide by are specifically intended to keep people like you out of this beautiful country. You, as a tourist, are welcomed with the utmost professionalism. But if you want to buy a home in Switzerland your location and choice are limited. In some cantons you are not permitted to buy any property of any kind. A referendum held in the mid-eighties called for a ban on sales of building land or homes to foreigners. The proposal was narrowly defeated, but it did lead to a quota of little more than a couple of thousand applying for foreign ownership in any one year. And the decision was to reduce this amount annually by a hundred.

This is hardly 'red carpet treatment' and it gets worse . . . Some cantons, the German-speaking ones, don't want you at all; and it's impossible for foreigners to buy in the cities like Geneva, Berne or Basle. If you are granted a permit or find a property which has one as part of its appeal then you must be able to satisfy the authorities that you are going to use it personally for at least three weeks in any one year (so that you cannot buy a home simply for the income to be made from letting it on a long lease). But you will also be turned away if you want to live in your home yourself permanently unless you are over sixty years of age, have an income which is considered sufficient by the inquisitors, or, in some cases, you have children over the age of eighteen.

If you do pass all the difficult tests and buy your Swiss home you will be unable to sell it for five years and then only to a Swiss national. You can only offer your home for sale with a permit to allow a foreigner to buy it after you have owned it for ten years. The regulations have, of course, been put together like a Swiss watch: you may exercise your brain on possible methods of avoidance of these rules – company purchase by a Swiss or foreign company for example – but you would indeed be wasting your time if you thought that you could come up with an idea which had not been anticipated and blocked. There are some illegal methods which can work, but there is a real risk that your law-breaking would be revealed – because, as we have said, everyone can be assumed to be law-abiding in Switzerland unless proved otherwise – and you would then go to jail. This does not square with the philosophy that owning a home in another country is about fun.

This unwelcoming attitude is not xenophobia; there's nothing at all personal about it. Even the Swiss themselves are not permitted to sell their homes until they have owned them for five years. The objective is to eliminate property speculation; it

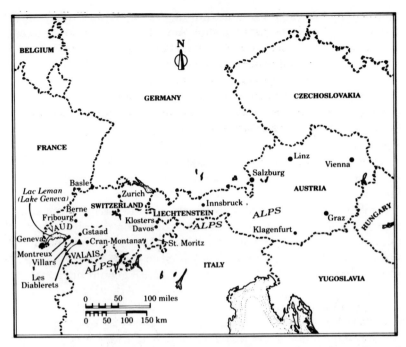

is actually considered immoral. Exceptions to the rules exist, of course, (because every eventuality has been considered in the tightly drawn laws): serious illness, bankruptcy and death are accepted as reasons to allow a sale inside the restricted period.

So where can you possibly buy a Swiss home, assuming that you are not put off by all this rigmarole? The tourist areas generally have available authorisations to buy, but just a few hundred each: Vaud, Valais, Crisons, Fribourg and Tessin. This means that from time to time, subject to change, and if you are lucky, you may be able to buy in Montreux, Crans-Montana, Les Diablerets, or Verbier for example. But if you have considered the alternatives and you know that Switzerland is the place for you in spite of the underwhelming welcome then you are going to find a home regardless of the obstacles.

One problem that you are unlikely to encounter is property which is poorly built. Neither the climate nor the regulations would permit less than high-quality materials properly used; and the Swiss expectations and characteristics lead to high-quality workmanship.

Climate and practical reactions to it logically determine the resort architecture. There are, naturally, no flat roofs. Generous roof overhangs are standard, to throw the sliding snow clear of the walls. The insulation needed thickens the walls. Upper floors are usually timber rather than masonry. Shutters sometimes augment the double or triple glazing. Windows are not oversized in spite of the spectacular views to be seen from them. Balconies are standard. In overall appearance apartment blocks look the same as villas but bigger, giving a visual unity which is not as monotonous as it would be without the backdrop of the peaks and pines. Some complexes, and individual buildings, incorporate swimming pools and saunas. Most are located in areas with winter and summer appeal.

It follows from the restrictions which apply to foreign ownership of property that retirement is less of a proposition than holiday use combined with lucrative holiday letting. With mortgages available at lower rates of interest than we are used to in the UK and longer repayment terms (as much as fifty years) there is genuine investment potential as well as pleasure to be obtained even with the red tape involved. Like everything else in Switzerland the terms on which mortgages are granted assume continued stability in social, political and economic matters and therefore no risk to the lender.

The investment potential is underpinned by past performance of the economy (although we should all be clear that the past is never a guarantee of the future). Since World War II the rise in property values has been steady, the Swiss Franc has become as solid a point of reference as the US$, and the local economy has prospered from the effects of efficiency, hard work and stability when these elementary commodities have been in short supply elsewhere. It can be argued that an investment in a holiday property in a well-managed complex or apartment block in an attractive resort in the Alps is an investment in the Swiss national character. A note of caution is necessary, however: borrowing in Swiss Francs and servicing the loan in Sterling is a risky business given the past strength of the Swiss Franc. Income in the local currency from letting, particularly at the peak of the seasons (Christmas, February and March, and for a month and a half during the summer) would eliminate this exchange-rate risk. With good local management this pattern of rentals should enable you to enjoy use of your property for most of the year happy in the knowledge that the finances are taking care of themselves comfortably.

Rentals are good for you but are considered bad for hotel operators. Strings have been pulled publicly, because the Swiss do such things openly, to ensure that some areas in some cantons do not take up their available quota for homes to be sold to foreigners because the foreigners would inevitably place accommodation on the local market for rental at the peak of season when the hoteliers would expect to make most of their profits. Self-interest here, as elsewhere, can be assumed to be the basic motivation in most things commercial.

In your own self-interest you would be well advised to choose a home in an area which has winter and summer appeal, both for your own benefit and for the benefit of your paying guests. Some resorts have golf courses, which ensures a twelve-month season. Exploitation of nearby lakes during the summer is also an important factor for easy rental. International events, regularly staged, like the hot-air ballooning which takes place at Château d'Oex close to Gstaad, also add something to the potential. So does the increasing use of the nearby Sarine River for all forms of practical water sports.

Location, location and location are the three most vital factors in Switzerland as everywhere else when it comes to selecting prime property. Given that spectacular views are the norm here, this translates as access, access and access. Back in the last century, when the tourist possibilities of this mountainous country were originally being exploited, it was the train which provided the means of access. The Swiss hotel as we know it was created at that time. Impressive civil engineering opened up the locations to locomotives and travellers and the almost impossible inclines were scaled by funiculars and rack-and-pinion railways.

The natural attractions are so spectacular that it is too easy to overlook man-made reminders of the much more turbulent past. There are the remains of fortifications, Roman settlements (Julius Caesar was here in person), and fairy-tale castles at dominating points in the landscape. There are villages of the kind designed by Walt Disney for his most corny cartoons and lively cities. Geneva is arguably the most cosmopolitan city in Europe, with every language heard at the tables of its many restaurants and conference suites. The other major cities are either exciting or a little vulgar according to taste, dedicated to making money out of money or money out of tourists.

Some of the fashionable resorts attract similar emotions. St Moritz is a place of huge, somewhat flashy, hotels with people to match. It was not always thus. Originally a spa town, our own Arnold Lunn, son of Sir Henry of tourist agency fame, made St Moritz famous as a ski centre at the turn of the century. Today it has the Cresta Run and a hundred or so ski runs and an air of coarse vulgarity during the season. Davos, however, retains much of its earlier charm; so does Klosters nearby, with its continuing appeal for celebrities who want to be more or less alone. Last century Mark Twain lived here for a while; so did Robert Louis Stevenson. The regular long-stay visitors included Yeats, Conan Doyle and Augustus John. Homeowners recently here were writer Irwin Shaw and actress Deborah Kerr. Greta Garbo was frequently alone in Klosters.

Resorts which had permits and publicity during the last few years are Verbier (some say it has the best skiing and food in the country), Crans-Montana (Crans has the highest golf course in Europe), and Villars just 25km (15½ miles) from the festival city of Montreux on Lake Geneva – or Lac Leman as the locals fiercely prefer. So keen have been the local estate agents in these developing areas that they have set near records in completing the necessary legalities of buying. Forty-eight hours is usual; half that time is possible. There is an element of sharp marketing involved in this ploy which is quite understandable, based upon the ancient premise that if something is in short supply then you had better hurry up and buy.

Each of Switzerland's twenty-five cantons has the right to make its own laws on some subjects and real estate matters are within these powers. There are, therefore, differences in detail and sometimes in substance between one area and another. Do not assume that you can 'do it yourself' when it comes to the legalities of buying a home anywhere in this diverse and complex country. Broadly these legalities are similar to those in other continental European countries – the legally obsessed Napoleon Bonaparte was here too, imposing his code wherever he conquered – so binding preliminary contracts are the norm.

One of the unspoken attractions of owning a home in this magical landscape is that Switzerland is still a tax haven, with all the potential financial romanticism that implies. Some of this mystery evaporates when you receive the simple and straightforward response to your whispered request over a Zurich bank counter for your very own numbered account.

22

TURKEY

In the late eighties packaged tourism to Spain underwent a period of crisis. Holiday bookings stagnated. Major tour operators failed to renew contracts with hundreds of one- and two-star hotels. Economic problems in Britain accounted for part of this decline. Standards and expectations drifted apart. Turkey's burgeoning tourist industry benefitted. At the same time, and for similar underlying reasons, there was a decline in interest in mainstream Spanish resort property. Agents who had learned their trade in Spain began looking elsewhere for a saleable product. Some chose Turkey as the boom area of the future.

Both the adventurous tour operators and the real estate agents began enthusiastically to promote their wares. Turkey had undeniably a fabulously beautiful and relatively unspoiled coastline, a very agreeable climate and an exotic atmosphere. It also had low wage rates. While prices of almost everything Spanish rose as a result of increased living standards those in Turkey seemed to be on a level with those of earlier times. Prices of resort homes particularly were very competitive.

New airports were built to give easy access to the Aegean and Mediterranean coasts. Infrastructure, hotels and holiday complexes were supported by government grants and publicity. Some areas were selected for particular attention. Laws were updated. Foreigners were allowed to buy property on a freehold basis in municipalities (2,000 inhabitants being the yardstick); tenure on a 999-year lease applied outside these communities.

There were other attractions. Rental income obtained by foreigners from the letting of their holiday property was not subject to tax in Turkey. Sales proceeds were freely exportable provided that the original importation of purchase funds was formally made through an approved bank. Annual property taxes (rates) were low. Capital Gains Tax did not apply to profits on the sale of foreign-owned homes

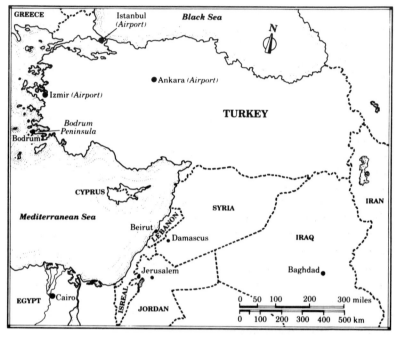

provided they were not sold within one year of purchase.

While the publicity built up in favour of Turkey as the resort area of the future the press began to carry stories of less appeal. Democracy in this beautiful but frustrating country was imperfect. The army was in part a law unto itself. The police routinely beat peaceful demonstrators in the streets and torture was normal but would, said the authorities, be phased out. . . Toilets were often disgustingly filthy even in the tourist complexes. The social and cultural gaps were, for many visitors, unbridgeable. Worst of all, given that buyers of resort homes are almost invariably couples, women do not count in Turkey even if they are potential buyers on property inspection visits. It is to be hoped that during the nineties attitudes will change. Turkey is actively lobbying for entry into the European Community. Serious attempts are being made to attract foreign investment into most areas of the economy. Nobody should underestimate the difficult adjustments to be made; and the Turkish social and commercial customs must change if real success is to be made to happen.

It is said that the Turkish male has a sense of personal honour which is even more up-front than its Spanish equivalent. Certainly the open friendliness is legendary but remember that women are traditionally excluded from everyday society. The penalty, which is the reverse side of this coin, is that there is an apparent inability to accept even well-meaning and commercially progressive advice. Comments on poor standards of construction and finishing of resort homes, often sited superbly, intended to be commercially helpful and diplomatically expressed have generally been met with indifference at best and deeply offended reactions at worst. Spanish builders and developers stayed in business for decades by responding to the same kinds of advice positively, in other words, by producing what the customers needed.

The direct result of the favourable publicity, climate, property prices and picturesque coastline has been a steady supply of potential buyers of resort homes. Conversion of these prospects into actual buyers has, however, been disappointing and most agents who were enthusiastically offering property in Turkey removed it from their inventories. But there is no doubt about the attractions of Turkey and no doubt that, given basic attitude changes, its time will come as a major resort destination. The food is considered comparable in quality with that of France and China; and this is one important aspect of Turkish life which hopefully will not change in favour of 'international standards'. The wines vary from the undrinkable to the outstanding. Spectator sports include the famous wrestling with competitors covered from head to toe in lashings of oil. No other country has more recognised archaeological sites. The Izmir Hilton Golf and Country Club will be one amongst many golf facilities to be enjoyed as plans mature. Marinas are being created. The islands and bays off the main routes are there to be explored by your own or a hired boat. Snorkelling, scuba-diving, fishing and all other watersports best undertaken in clear, warm waters are provided for in idyllic surroundings. The country has ski resorts in its mountains. Bazaar shopping is fascinating or irritating according to your response to relentless opportuning.

The formalities of real estate purchase are fundamentally similar to those of Spain. Under no circumstances should you sign anything you do not understand completely; nor should you proceed to the point of any kind of legal commitment without the advice of a competent lawyer.

Much attention from the authorities and potential buyers of resort property on the coast has been focused upon the Bodrum peninsula. If progress is to be made it is likely to show here first because of the area's touristic importance. The location is spectacular, with the well-preserved fifteenth-century castle of St Peter, the boat-filled bay, and the blue sky and sea divided by the backdrop of blue hills. Bodrum has been described as an Oriental St Tropez. Plenty of property has been built in this favoured area and, like the wines, some is outstanding.

CONCLUSION

The pace of change in the last decade of the twentieth century continues to accelerate, '1992 and all that' symbolises the removal of yet more barriers between European Community members. East and West are no longer rigidly defined mental and physical states. Frontiers are no longer 'fire-zones'. The newly free can wander for business, pleasure or simple curiosity. After forty years of restrictions caused by out-dated ideology and fear the word 'European' is being continually redefined.

We have seen that freedom and ease of travel created the demand to live in somebody else's country. It is now normal to want to live part of our lives – or the rest of our lives – outside the familiar surroundings in which we grew and matured. Mostly the motive is a form of practical escapism, but for increasing numbers the attractions are work and business in a different, changing and challenging commercial environment.

Many solid, responsible and rational arguments can be produced to justify buying a home in another country. I have heard them all over almost two and a half decades of involvement with many thousands of people who have become owners of a piece of land abroad. I don't believe a word of these sensible, reasonable and easily accepted reasons for what is, in the final analysis, an impulsive act. The word, I believe, which describes the underlying motive for buying a home in another country is *pleasure*. The dictionary says it all. *Pleasure*: to please; the gratification of the mind and senses; enjoyment, delight, wish, choice, desire. This is motive enough.

Now that you have reached the last page of this handbook I hope that your pleasure will be preceded by thoughtful planning and informed anticipation. You should now know enough to let your instincts be your guide to where you want to be.

Useful Addresses

Air Travel Advisory Bureau, 320 Regent Street,
London W1R 5AB   *Tel*: 071 636 5000

British Association of Removers, 3 Churchill Court
58 Station Road, North Harrow, Middlesex HA2 7SA
Tel: 081 861 3331

Department of Social Security (Overseas Branch), Central Office,
Benton Park Road, Newcastle-upon-Tyne NE98 1YX
Tel: 091 285 7111

Federation of Overseas Property Developers, Agents and
Consultants, PO Box 981, Brighton, Sussex BN2 2FT
Tel: 0273 777647

Inland Revenue, West Wing, Somerset House, Strand,
London WC2R 1LB   *Tel*: 071 438 6420

Medical Advisory Services for Travellers Abroad,
London School of Hygiene and Tropical Medicine, Keppel Street,
London WC1E 7HT   *Tel*: 071 631 4408

Royal Institute of British Architects, 66 Portland Place,
London W1N 4AD

Austria
Embassy and Consular Section, 18 Belgrave Mews West,
London SW1X 8HU   *Tel*: 071 235 3731

Tourist Office, 30 St George Street, London W1R 0AL
Tel: 071 629 0461

Cyprus
High Commission, 93 Park Street, London W1Y 4ET
Tel: 071 499 8272

Tourist Office, 213 Regent Street, London W1R 8DA
Tel: 071 734 9822

France
Consulate General, 21 Cromwell Road, London SW7 2DQ
Tel: 071 823 9555

Tourist Office, 178 Piccadilly, London   *Tel*: 071 491 7622

Greece
Consulate General, 1a Holland Park, London W11 3TP
Tel: 071 727 8040

Italy
Consulate General, 38 Eaton Place, London SW1X 8AN
Tel: 071 235 9371

Malta
High Commission, 16 Kensington Square, London W8 5HH
Tel: 071 938 1712

Portugal
Consulate General, 62 Brompton Road, London SW3 1BJ
Tel: 071 581 3598

Spain
Consulate, 20 Draycott Place, London SW3 2RZ
Tel: 071 581 5921

Switzerland
Embassy, 16 Montagu Place, London W1A 2BQ
Tel: 071 723 0701

FURTHER READING

Allied Dunbar's Expatriate Tax and Investment Guide (Longman, 1989)

Dawood, Dr R. *How to Stay Healthy Abroad* (Oxford University Press, 1989)

Department of Social Security, SA 29 *Your Social Security, Health Care and Pension Rights in the European Community.*

SA 40 *Before You Go*

SA 41 *While You're Away*

NI38 *Social Security Abroad*

These leaflets are available from your local DSS Office.

Employment Conditions Abroad: Outlines for Expatriates Available from Anchor House, 15 Britten Street, London SW3 3TY

Resident Abroad, The Financial Times magazine for expatriates available from Subscription Dept, Central House, 27 Park Street, Croydon CR0 1YD

Retiring Abroad Available from *Financial Times* Business Information, 50/64 Broadway, London SW1H 0DB

Furnell, M. *Living and Retiring Abroad, The Daily Telegraph Guide* (Kogan Page, 1989)

Inland Revenue IR20 *Residents' and Non-Residents' Liability to Tax in the UK* Available from Inland Revenue, Somerset House, Strand, London WC2R 1LB

ACKNOWLEDGEMENTS

I should like to record my thanks to the many members and Committee members of the Federation of Overseas Property Developers, Agents and Consultants who have assisted me in the research for this book. I am particularly grateful to Steve Emmett of Brian French & Co, Keith Baker of John Venn & Sons, Gerard Henry of Gerard Henry & Co, David Bishop of R.M. Brooker Ltd, Bill Rayner of Arts International Movers, Ann Morgan and Pauline Goring of Cometa, Arlette Adler of Villas Abroad Golf Consultants, Charles Brownlee of Healthsearch Ltd, Jorge Zanoletty of Inter Spain SA, Andrew Davy of Villamed Properties and Enrique Llopis Garcia, Presidente of The Colegio Oficial de Agentes de la Propiedad Inmobiliaria de Alicante y su Provincia. My special thanks are due to the thousands of owners and would-be owners of homes overseas to whom I have talked, usually convivially, about their hopes and expectations and how best to achieve them.

INDEX